City-States in
the Global Economy

Transitions: Asia and Asian America
Series Editor, *Mark Selden*

City-States in
the Global Economy

Industrial Restructuring
in Hong Kong and Singapore

Stephen W.K. Chiu
K. C. Ho
Tai-lok Lui

WestviewPress

A Division of HarperCollins*Publishers*

Transitions: Asia and Asian America

Copyright © 1997 by Westview Press, A Division of HarperCollins Publishers, Inc.

Published in 1997 in the United States of America by Westview Press, 5500 Central Avenue, Boulder, Colorado 80301-2877, and in the United Kingdom by Westview Press, 12 Hid's Copse Road, Cumnor Hill, Oxford OX2 9JJ

Library of Congress Cataloging-in-Publication Data
Chiu, Stephen Wing-Kai
    City-states in the global economy : industrial restructuring in
Hong Kong and Singapore / Stephen W.K. Chiu, K. C. Ho and Tai-lok
Lui.
        p.   cm.—(Transitions—Asia and Asian America)
    Includes bibliographical references and index.
    ISBN 0-8133-8863-5 (hardcover)
    1. Hong Kong—Economic conditions.   2. Singapore—Economic
conditions.   3. Structural adjustment (Economic policy)—Hong Kong.
4. Structural adjustment (Economic policy)—Singapore.   I. Ho, Kong
Chong, 1955–   . II. Lui, Tai-lok, 1958–   . III. Title.   IV. Series.
HC497.H6C495   1997
338.95125—dc20
                                                                        96-34931
                                                                            CIP

The paper used in this publication meets the requirements of the American National Standard for Permanence of Paper for Printed Library Materials Z39.48-1984.

10   9   8   7   6   5   4   3   2   1

Contents

Tables and Figures

Tables

Figures

Preface

Despite being small city-states, Hong Kong and Singapore's positions in the global industrial economy are more important than those of many larger countries. This book presents a systematic comparative analysis of how these two economies, sharing fairly similar histories, have come to develop very different paths to industrialization.

Research on East Asian economies has now settled into clear disciplinary and conceptual boundaries: statist, free market, neo-modernist, and international political economy approaches. Our argument, instead, is to suggest that history and institutions matter, and that more systematic insights can be derived by analysing the development paths countries take. The institutional approach we adopt requires us to part company with a substantial portion of the East Asian development literature which has tended to treat Singapore, Hong Kong, Taiwan and South Korea as a single, undifferentiated case — the "dragons of Asia."

By moving away from the East Asian Development Model and focusing on Hong Kong and Singapore, we build our analysis around the interrelationships of three institutional spheres: the state, the financial system, and the institutions of industrial relations. We look at the institutional configuration of industrial development in the two city-states and analyse how they have followed different "logics" and paths in industrial restructuring. At the level of firms, we focus on the electronics and garment industries and demonstrate how corporate strategy in the two city-states are influenced not only by the nature of markets and characteristics of the particular industries, but also by the different institutional environments in Hong Kong and Singapore. We show in the last chapter how this comparative analysis allows us to address issues central to the development literature as well as specific problems, issues and consequences of economic restructuring for Hong Kong and Singapore.

This book grew out of a research collaboration initiated and funded by the East-West Center (Hawaii, United States). We are grateful to Won-Bae Kim and Gordon Clark for their leadership and encouragement. To the members of the "Industrial Restructuring and Regional Adjustment in the Asian NIEs" project team — Gordon Clark, Won-Bae Kim, Jung-Duk Lim, Sam-Ock Park, Ching-Lung Tsay — thanks for five years of collaboration.

We enjoyed the discussions and the mutual learning process that went with it.

K.C. Ho acknowledges the National University of Singapore for financing the enterprise survey of Singapore firms, and for the timely sabbatical leave and financial support. He also thanks Professor Jin-Hui Ong of the Center of Advanced Studies for believing in the project enough to support a workshop at a crucial phase when researchers from the various countries needed to meet to discuss research methodology. He is grateful for the facilities provided by the Population Program of the East-West Center and the Monash Asia Institute during the initial writing phases of the book.

Stephen W.K. Chiu and Tai-lok Lui thank The Chinese University of Hong Kong for the internal grants which supported the project on economic restructuring. They also thank Terence Poon for his assistance in organizing the survey on enterprise strategy. Tai-lok Lui was a visiting scholar at Robinson College, Cambridge University on the CUHK-Robinson College Exchange Programme when this book project started. He would like to thank Robinson College for its hospitality and The Chinese University of Hong Kong for its support of his sabbatical leave.

We acknowledge Elsevier Science Limited for its kind permission for reproducing Figures 3.1 and 4.1 from *Political Geography*, Vol. 15, Nos. 7/8.

We thank the following individuals with whom we had the wonderful opportunity to discuss our project and enjoyed the benefit of their views: Chieh-hsuan Chen, Beng-Huat Chua, Michael Douglass, Kuniko Fujita, Cheng-shu Kao, Hagen Koo, Reginald Kwok, David Levin, John McKay, Yoshio Okunishi, Tony Tam, Ern-Ser Tan, Alvin So, Michael Webber. We are particularly grateful to Mark Selden for his most valuable comments on our drafts and encouragement throughout this project.

Excellent editorial assistance was provided by Sharon Teo and Teck-Meng Wee. Special thanks are due to Shirley Po-san Wan, for her generosity and much needed support. She read every page of the manuscript and helped us with the final revisions.

Finally, we could not have completed this work without the quiet encouragement of our families.

Stephen W.K. Chiu
K. C. Ho
Tai-lok Lui

1

Hong Kong and Singapore in the World Economy

[T]here would clearly be much less interest in the four Asian Newly Industrializing Countries (NICs) if they had not been so remarkably successful in achieving rapid economic growth.... The natural question to ask is "Can the miracle continue?"
—Krause, 1985:3

[T]he East Asian countries range in population size from city states to middle-sized countries and have widely divergent resource endowments and economic histories, but they have faced the same international environment as other countries. Why is their economic performance so successful?
—Hughes, 1988:xv

An art collector will naturally be drawn to Florence, a mountain climber to the Himalayas. In very much the same way a social scientist interested in modernization will have his attention fixed on East Asia, to the point where he may reasonably conclude that this is the most interesting region in the world today... it is not just a question of understanding East Asia, but rather a question of understanding what happens elsewhere (including the West) in the light of this Asian experience.
—Berger, 1988:3-4

City-States in the World Economy

There is little doubt that rapidly growing economies attract the research attention of development scholars the same way flowers attract bees. Within Asia, it was Japan in the 1960s and 1970s, while the "blooms" of the 1980s are the Newly Industrialized Economies (NIEs) of Korea, Taiwan, Hong Kong and Singapore. By the late 1980s, the questions of how and why, transferability, and continuity resulted in a huge East Asia development literature. However, while the phenomenal growth of the East Asian economies has drawn much attention, and research on this topic has become a growing industry, there are signs indicating that the newly industrialized economies in the region are undergoing a restructuring process. Indeed, in different ways, the Asian NIEs (Korea, Taiwan, Hong Kong and Singapore) are restructuring their industries in response to changes in their comparative advantages and to the changing environment of the global economy.

The growth of the East Asian economies was a product of a turbulent and competitive world economy. The last thirty to forty years saw a rapid internationalization of production. This was an outcome of two factors: the breakdown of international regulatory arrangements (such as the Bretton Woods Agreement of 1944) which had underpinned the growth of world production and trade since the Second World War (Linge and Rich 1991); and the exodus of capital from the industrial areas of the first world, pushed by rising costs and pulled by the attractions of cheap third world labor pools topped up by incentives offered by newly independent governments anxious to embark on economic programs (Fröbel et al. 1980).

By the 1970s, it appeared that the growth of advanced capitalist economies had slowed down and moved into a gradual and protracted phase of stagnation with periods of decline. These economic shifts contain geo-political consequences. In particular, the hegemonic status of the United States in the world is weakening; and a multi-polar world order is steadily in the making. Japan, and the European Community under the unified Germany, began to challenge the United States' hitherto undisputed (at least among the "Free World") leadership in international affairs. Apart from the slackening pace of growth, the transformation of the world economy also led to a string of other changes. One example is the rise of protectionism and unilateralism in the management of international trade. The United States relied increasingly on unilateral actions to extract concessions on trade from its trading partners. Most important of all, the United States forced Japan to appreciate its currency in an attempt to reduce its own trade deficit. However, the "strong yen" in turn increased Japan's costs for domestic production and reduced the comparative cost of producing overseas. The result is a progressive build-up of Japanese investment in the world. In Asia, a Japan-centered production network has emerged, leading to rapid industrialization among Southeast Asian countries.

As Japanese, American and European investments moved into Asia, Asian governments (with a fair bit of learning from each other) had been responsive in embarking on domestic reforms which removed the barriers to exports and foreign investment. The result is entry of multinational corporations (MNCs), which capitalizing on cheap labor supplies, have spearheaded the growth of the export-oriented manufacturing sector. Figure 1.1, which shows the value of manufacturing exports, shows two sets of countries classified by the size of their export-oriented manufacturing sectors. Between 1975 and 1985, the Asian NIEs were the chief beneficiaries of foreign direct investment and experienced five- to six-fold increases in the value of manufacturing exports.

From the 1980s to the 1990s, while Japan and the Asian NIEs (with the exception of Hong Kong) continued to register significant growth in manufacturing exports, a second set of countries entered the scene. In Southeast Asia, Malaysia and Thailand, experienced remarkable manufacturing export growth in the 1980s, are now competitors to the Asian NIEs in labor-intensive productions. The 1980s also saw market reform in China and its entry into the world market. As Figure 1.1 indicates, China has emerged as a significant player with its abundant supply of low cost labor for labor-intensive export-oriented industrialization. The bustling South China region has become a new powerhouse of export production.

The entry of new players in the market for export-oriented manufacturing indicates the rapidly changing regional division of labor in Asia, and challenges faced by the Asian NIEs. The central theme for this book, therefore, is to illustrate how Hong Kong and Singapore can respond to these global and regional changes and restructure their industries accordingly. As production becomes globalized and relative international competitiveness becomes keener, Hong Kong and Singapore's industries must adjust and transform in order to survive.

This process of industrial restructuring poses new questions to current research on East Asian capitalism. Firstly, what were once the competitive edges of these NIEs, particularly the low-cost labor and attractive terms for foreign investments, have been gradually eroded over time. Secondly, growing protectionism puts further constraints on the industries in the NIEs. Thirdly, concomitant with changes in their comparative advantages, the NIEs have to restructure their industries in changing domestic political and economic conditions. Those structural conditions and state policies, which were conducive to rapid growth and development in the past two decades, are not necessarily sufficient for tackling the new problems arising in the process of industrial restructuring. Accounts of the "success stories" of the Asian NIEs are many. Yet, most of the existing studies fail to observe that early success is no guarantee of continuous industrial growth and development. The industrial structures of these NIEs, which were conducive to rapid development in the earlier period, may restrict how

FIGURE 1.1   Value of Manufacturing Exports among Newly
Industrialized Economies in Asia, 1975-1990

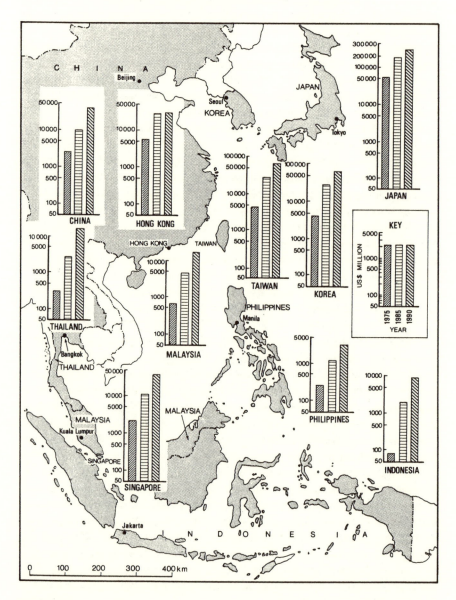

Source: United Nations Conference on Trade and Development. 1994. *Handbook of International Trade and Development Statistics 1993.* New York: United Nations.

they can now respond to the changing business environment of the global economy. In short, a new research agenda is required to explain the performance of the Asian NIEs in the changing global economic environment.

Our observation is that, while the Asian NIEs are under tremendous pressure from rising production costs, growing protectionism, and the emergence of new competitors from other developing economies, they remain competitive. Our studies of Hong Kong and Singapore confirm that economic development is definitely not an "either-or" question. Our story is not only about how they have succeeded in restructuring their industries and economies and adjusting to challenges and stimuli from the world economy, but is also concerned with how they succeeded to do so differently: why, despite experiencing broadly similar external challenges, we see very different responses from Hong Kong and Singapore. We hope that as the story unfolds, crucial aspects of the divergent restructuring process will become clear to the reader. Furthermore, we hope to develop and apply an institutional approach and unravel the "puzzle" of why the outcomes of industrial change in these two countries differ, despite similar conditions like resource-endowment, colonial history and the level of economic development. The answer, we contend, lies in the historical constitution of divergent development paths in the postwar era as well as the presence of diametrically different configurations of domestic institutions.

The Asian NIEs and Research Interest

We have noted earlier that research on Asian development is now a growing industry. At some risk of simplifying this complex literature, four conceptual strands can be discerned, each with its specific focus and explanation of the development of Asian countries.

The Neo-Modernist version of the Asian phenomenon focuses on people and values (Hsiao 1988:13). The emphasis is on facets of a common cultural stock which influenced economic development: work ethic, propensity to save, value of education, family entrepreneurialism, tendency towards collectivism and paternalistic authority (Pye 1988; Wong 1988; Tai 1989; Harrison 1992). More recent efforts on culture and economic development focus on Chinese *guanxi* (social relationships) between East Asian countries as a basis for cross-border investment efforts (Kotkin 1992), as well as the ideological use of the East Asian success to challenge Western hegemony in the Asia-Pacific region (Mahbubani 1994).

Free-market advocates have suggested that market liberalization is the driving force behind economic development in East Asia. Such an explanation is premised on the view that the role of government is to clear various obstacles so that markets (price signals) can work to allocate resources efficiently and effectively. Development is a result of a combination of right policies and incentives (e.g., export promotion). The government's role is essentially supportive: to create a modern infrastructure and regulatory framework, and to provide a stable incentive system (Balassa 1988; Riedel 1988:28-38; Friedman and Friedman 1980:54-55).

As the name implies, the statist version has focused on the role of the state in guiding the development of East Asian countries. This perspective, much inspired by Johnson's notion of the capitalist developmental state in his study of Japan (1982), and the growing interest in developing a state-centered approach to sociological analysis (Evans, Rueschemeyer, and Skocpol 1985), draws upon the argument that successful "late development" takes a route very different from earlier industrializing countries (Gerschenkron 1966). The development process of the "late industrializer" is less "spontaneous," with the state acting as the major agent of socio-economic transformations. In many ways, governments are found shaping the market in a manner that neoclassical economics assumes the bureaucrats cannot get right. Thus by highlighting the role of the state in economic development, the statist literature is engaged in a debate with an older market/liberal tradition (Onis 1991; Wade 1990). Statists provide accounts of the rise of the developmental state, the determinants of its effectiveness, and the mechanisms of control available to the developmental state (e.g., Johnson 1982; Amsden 1989; Castells 1992).

The economic growth enjoyed by the Asian NIEs also attracted another group of scholars who see the increasing interconnectedness of the world as part of an older world system which has been transforming itself. For this group, the Asian NIEs are interesting from two angles: as a structural category within a world hierarchy differentiated in terms of economic and political power, and as a phase and a place within which the process of capitalist development works itself out (Frank 1982; Martin 1990). Development in East Asia is accounted for by an expansion of the global economy in the postwar decades (Dicken 1992), the interventionist role of the United States and Japan, the entry of multinational corporations (Hamilton 1983; Cumings 1987), and the nature of firm linkages into the global economy (Gereffi 1992). There is also a technological variant to this literature where the movement of manufacturing capital between countries is accounted for in terms of the stages of the product cycle. Thus the resultant division between countries in the global economy can be explained in terms of the domestic capacity of various countries for hosting the manufacture of products at different stages of technological sophistication. In this depiction of Asian development, a "flying geese" pattern is proposed to explain the takeoff and the interconnectedness of concerned economies.

Research on East Asian development continues to proceed into the 1990s. However, if one were to take a step backwards and gaze at this mountain of research, one cannot help but feel overwhelmed by the breadth and burdened by the weight of this literature: the nectar of the hardworking scholar "bees." What new insights can East Asia offer? Will new directions in this field become an intensification of debates between rival explanations, as in the polarization between market-based (Balassa 1988) and state-based explanations (Wade 1990; Henderson and Appelbaum 1992)? Will research attention encompass broader comparisons between regions along the paths paved by Gereffi (1990) and Haggard (1990)? Or will focus move to emerging growth areas like Malaysia, Thailand, and China, the new "blooms" of the Pacific economy?

Extracting Hong Kong and Singapore from the East Asian Development Model

We cannot answer all these questions here. But a significant departure of our study from most current studies is that ours tends to "divide" rather than "unify" the two city-states. Our view is that the Asian NIEs or East Asian literature consists of insights derived from an implicit comparative strategy of treating the Asian NIEs as a group. Most of the works cited in the earlier section take this grouping as a given. The criteria for membership for the East Asian Development Model rests on their phenomenal growth rates and the fact that this rapid development happened at around the same period — the late 1960s through the next two decades, and/or a presumed cultural similarity.[1]

There is no doubt that a variety of insights has been drawn from such comparative strategies, but the decision to classify the Asian NIEs as a group means that important features of individual country distinctiveness have been sacrificed in favor of a more abstract level of comparative analysis. The need to recognize this trade-off stems from a more general point: particular insights emerge and are, at the same time, limited by the number and the type of countries chosen for the analysis, a necessary methodological constraint that is often not made clear in comparative research.

Our suggestion and the rationale for this study are that an important contribution can be made by extracting Hong Kong and Singapore from the East Asian Development Model. This strategy of disaggregation serves two purposes. Firstly, it highlights the complexity of the development experience of Asian NIEs. Our main argument is that there are diverse paths to industrialism. To subsume such diversity under a single, homogeneous model of development will not only generate spurious explanations, but will also fail to explain how these NIEs come to the current state of economic development through very different courses of industrialization. Secondly, by highlighting the complexity and diversity within East Asian capitalism, we argue for an approach to the question which conceives economic development as an instituted process (Polanyi 1957). Both Hong Kong and Singapore develop their economies in specific historical contexts shaped by the interactions between domestic institutional factors and the world economy. Indeed, any rigorous research on the topic must start from a recognition of the historical structuration of the opportunity of rapid economic growth through export-oriented industrialization and the local response to such an opening of opportunity in the global economy. To talk about the world economic system, the role of the state, and the relationship between capital and labor in abstract and ahistorical terms is simply missing the point (cf. Fields 1995). A comparative study of industrial restructuring in Hong Kong and Singapore creates the opportunity to understand the instituted processes involved. On the one hand, such a comparative study of Hong Kong and Singapore illustrates the similarities and diversities of the path of economic development in the two city-states. On the other, through a deepening of our understanding of the peculiarities of the two city-states, we come to have a better grasp of the comparability among the four Little Dragons themselves.

Industrialization as an Instituted Process

By extracting Hong Kong and Singapore from the East Asian Development Model, we move to a more focused comparative analysis of the relationship between the institutional structure and development outcomes of the two city-states. The emphasis on the institutional configuration of industrialization shows our dissatisfaction with current explanations of East Asian development. The Neo-Modernist or culturalist thesis, in addition to various problems associated with the often loosely defined notions of culture (for a review, see DiMaggio 1994), "[concentrates] on secondary causes, primordial constants that undergird everything,... works poorly when one attempts to examine a changing organizational environment or to analyze differences among organizations in the same cultural area" (Hamilton and Biggart 1988:70). The culturalist thesis is often based upon *post hoc* deductions (Balassa 1988) and neglects the important fact that key institutions responsible for economic transformations in the East Asian region are of recent origins (Balassa 1988; Onis 1991). As for the free-market advocates, they assume, often rather simplistically, that the market system itself will clear the way for economic growth. What they have failed to recognize is the centrality of non-market forces in shaping the course of industrialization, the mediation between market signals and the response of the firms to the changing economy. The market does not operate in a vacuum.

An emphasis on the role of the developmental state in the process of economic development is the main argument of the statists. While the statist argument alerts us to the peculiarity of late-industrialization and the central role of the state in some NIEs, more effort is still needed to work on the substance of its explanation. First of all, late-industrialization does not, in a functionalist manner, automatically create a developmental state to catch up with economic development (Lui and Chiu 1996). Furthermore, though some researchers have come to recognize the role of the state, they have however brought the free-market thesis back in through the back door by conceiving the state as market-conforming (see, for example, World Bank 1993). Also important is the fact that state policies and state capacity are historically structured. A complete answer to the statist question must therefore include an analysis of the historical formation of the state. Last but not least, by emphasizing the developmental function of the state, statists have been criticized for giving too much emphasis on domestic capacity in bringing about economic transformations.

While the world economy thesis highlights the significance of the international political economy in opening opportunities for the NIEs, it carries a strong dose of economic determinism, and especially core-determinism (Gilpin 1987). As a result, this perspective largely ignores the process through which the local economies are able to capitalize on such openings for their economic growth and development. Our proposed institutional approach is intended for explaining the historical structuration and cross-national variations in the paths to industrialism (cf. Hall 1986). It alerts us to the significance of the interplay of global economic forces and domestic institutional factors in shaping the industrialization and industrial restructuring in Hong Kong and Singapore.

In other words, the processes of industrial restructuring are both socially instituted and historically embedded. As we shall show in subsequent discussions, the outcomes of the diverse patterns of industrial restructuring in Hong Kong and Singapore are essentially shaped by two processes: the interactions of historically constituted societal, institutional forces (including the state), and the responses of corporations. For Hong Kong and Singapore, the question of how two colonial port cities with similar legacies eventually parted ways and traveled on different developmental paths will be one of the main themes of this book. The attention to history and institutions will allow us to answer why this parting of ways was inevitable and analyze the different roles legacies and discontinuities played in shaping the development paths of the two city-states. The important analytical position of this study, therefore, is the path-dependent nature of economic change (North 1990; David 1986, 1994). But for the purpose of analyzing specifically industrial changes, path-dependence can be conceptually distinguished into two parallel processes: the corporate level and the societal level. At the corporate level, firm behaviors and strategic choices are shaped by their own organizational histories (cf. Arrow 1974:55-56). At the societal level, the persistence of critical institutional spheres impinging on the corporate strategies similarly moved economies to evolve along a definite trajectory. First of all, as Hong Kong and Singapore bifurcated from their common colonial and entrepôt histories, different organizational "logics" evolved in their respective industrial systems. Chapter 2 will delineate how the manufacturing industries in the two economies differed in ownership, size, product mix and technological frontier. While Hong Kong and Singapore initially industrialized in similar market niches (low-end, labor-intensive mass consumption product markets in the West), important differences quickly emerged with respect to their target market niches and production methods. Without a sufficient recognition of these organizational differences that emerged from their early industrial histories, it will be impossible to acquire an adequate comprehension of their restructuring processes. In a sense, in both economies, firms continued to do what they were good at doing all along. Organizations, like human beings, have their own learning curves and learning processes. Once firms acquire certain types of knowledge and competence at certain tasks, such expertise are inscribed in operational routines and organizational structures. The fact that organizational practices persist over time should not be construed simply as organizational inertia or resistance to change, but as organizational histories endowed with a specific set of capacities and constraints for future action.

How Hong Kong and Singapore are connected with the global economy is a relevant question here. Current research on the world economy underlines the growing tendency for nations in the developing world to be integrated into the manufacturing system of the industrialized West. Within an increasingly interconnected global economy, the competitiveness of particular economies can no longer be explained by the strengths of their domestic factors, but also where a location sits in the organization of production chains, commerce, and finance. This involves, among other things, an awareness of the economic geographies of particular industries and the roles played by Hong Kong and Singaporean firms within the networks of such industries.

We reject, however, the notion that such linkages to the global production system should be conceived as somehow "external"; such linkages are instead "internalized" in the domestic industrial system and embedded in the organizational structures and practices of the corporations. Indeed, being largely shaped by domestic institutional factors, Hong Kong and Singapore are linked up with the global economy and "internalized" differently — while the former plays the role of OEM (original equipment manufacturing) manufacturer within the international commercial subcontracting network, foreign direct investments assume a dominant position in the latter. The divergent paths of economic restructuring in Hong Kong and Singapore are both constituted and constitutive of the long-term transformation of the two economies. As we shall see in subsequent discussion, one of the development strategies of the two city-states is to strengthen their connections with the system of world cities (Friedmann and Wolff 1982; Friedmann 1986, 1995). The emergence of Hong Kong and Singapore as two world cities in the East Asian region reflects the double restructuring process the two city-states have been undergoing. Firstly, they experience restructuring in their manufacturing sectors in an environment of changing domestic conditions and broader changes in the global economy. Secondly, the restructuring of their manufacturing industries is embedded in the sectoral shift of the two economies towards commerce, finance, and services. In other words, industrial restructuring is part of the structural transformation of the economies of the city-states. Both Hong Kong and Singapore have joined the league of world cities because of their economic functions within the region. But they are world cities performing different roles. While Hong Kong is a financial center actively articulated with the world financial and commercial system, Singapore works more as a regional headquarters for coordinating production activities of multinational corporations in Southeast Asia. Such difference in their experience in climbing up the urban hierarchy of the global economy again highlights the path-dependent nature of economic development. Whatever their origins, the divergent paths of industrial development and organizational configurations then presented a guiding thread to our subsequent analyses.

This brings us to the second level of analysis in this study: the impact of the wider socio-economic and political context on the course of industrial development in the two city-states. To avoid the pitfalls of using such "contexts" as a set of amorphous, unspecified variables and *deus ex machina* that explains everything, we have conceptualized these variables as a set of institutional structures that is linked to and also impinges on the industrial system. For this study, the wider institutional backdrop to industrial development incorporates at least three key spheres: the state, the financial system, and industrial relations, which exert the greatest impact and have most interactions with industrial firms. As Hall (1986) points out, they are intrinsic to the socioeconomic structure of a nation, because they determine the organization of politics, capital, and labor. The first refers to the internal organization of the state apparatus, understood as the agencies that perform the legislative, executive, and judicial functions of the nation; the second refers principally to the organizational relationship between financial and industrial capital; while the third refers primarily to the organization of the working class in the labor market (Hall 1986:232). Hall separates the broader organization of the political system such as the electoral and party system from the organization of the state, but here we think it is unnecessary to adopt such a restrictive conception of the state. The institutional sphere of state as used here therefore includes not only the state organization itself, but also its political interfaces with the society and the economy.

As mentioned above, the role of the state has received prominent attention in the East Asian development literature in the market versus state debate. This debate has been useful in sharpening the role of the state in relation to the market. Following directions suggested in the debate, this book will highlight the role of state leadership in industrial development and analyze the nature of industrial policies and their impact on the economy. In other words, we shall examine how the state as an institutional sphere shapes the course of economic change in the two city-states. In the statist literature, a strong state is said to be internally cohesive and capable, politically insulated from societal pressures, and influential in shaping corporate investment and production decisions. A weak state, on the other hand, is regarded as institutionally fragmented and weak, often captured by societal interests, and leaving resource allocation to the market mechanism. At first sight, Hong Kong and Singapore seems to fall neatly into this polar distinction: the Singaporean state was pivotal in engineering the process of industrial takeoff, while the colonial state in Hong Kong has often been regarded as a *laissez-faire* one.

We shall argue, however, that crude distinctions between strong and weak, and developmental and *laissez-faire* state really do not square with the complex reality. As we proceed, a more nuanced picture of the impact of state actions (and inactions) on industrial restructuring will emerge. The strong state that exists in Singapore does not necessarily mean that it is omnipotent. At the same time, the *laissez-faire* state of Hong Kong is not necessarily inconsequential in every aspect of the economy. Furthermore, presenting an institutional analysis means that while the state is a key factor, it is not the only factor affecting economic change. It requires that we have an open view of state intervention and analyze how this is carried out in the process of adjustment and accommodation. Such a view also requires us to look at how state intervention is conditioned by other institutional spheres, particularly with regard to the organization of capital and industrial relations.

The role of capital, or rather the institutional organization of capital, in the financial system has received much attention in the literature (see, for example, Zysman 1983; Patrick and Park 1994; Haggard, Lee and Maxfield 1993). In economic terms, a financial system is the collection of institutions (banks, stock exchanges, bills and bonds markets, insurance companies, etc.) performing the function of financial intermediation, the process "by which savings are transformed into investments and then allocated among competing users" (Zysman 1983:55).[2] In the economic literature, it is generally believed that as the range or scope of financial institutions increases, economic growth will be boosted, though we should also be aware of the debate among economists concerning the exact relationship between financial and economic development (Kitchen 1986).[3] We do not think the so-called "depth" of financial development alone determines the course of development. More important is the specific institutional organization of the financial system that determines how capital is allocated between different sectors and usages.

At least two features of the organization of the financial system are important for understanding the process of industrial change. First, the institutional linkage between the financial and industrial sectors is significant in shaping corporate decisions regarding restructuring. As Zysman (1983) points out, business firms in different places often have very different sources of capital. In Japan, South Korea, and Germany, corporate financing is very much done by the banks. In the United States and United Kingdom, industrial financing is basically either endogenous to the firm or conducted through the capital market (stock or bonds market). And then there is what Ingham (1984) called an "institutional separation between industry and finance." The different institutional linkages between industry and finance, and different sources of industrial financing will certainly generate different outcomes in industrial restructuring.

The other factor is the ownership structure of the financial sector (Haggard, Lee and Maxfield 1993). In a system where the important financial institutions belong to the public sector or are heavily influenced by the public sector, such as in South Korea and Japan respectively, the state invariably has an important leverage in directing the pace or direction of industrial restructuring. Where financial institutions are privately owned and autonomous from discretionary state intervention, as in the United States and Britain, the state often lacks the capacity to engineer desired outcomes in the marketplace.

In a sense, both Hong Kong and Singapore's financial systems are well-developed by developing countries' standard. A long history of entrepôt development had endowed them with a wide range of financial institutions capable of mobilizing savings for investment and mediating economic transactions. Yet the linkages of the financial system with other institutions, especially the state and the industrial sector, showed remarkable differences and contributed to their divergent experiences of restructuring. The discussion of Hong Kong and Singapore's experience of industrialization in Chapter 2 will show that historically different relations between the financial sector and the industrial sector developed in the postwar era. Commercial banks had played a more prominent role in mobilizing capital for investment in Singapore. In Hong Kong, by contrast, we found the phenomenon of "institutional separation" between finance and industry (cf. Ingham 1984). Moreover, the state also established different linkages to the financial systems in the two economies. In Singapore, as we shall see, the state plays a much more direct role in the financial system through the state-owned financial institutions, while in Hong Kong, the state's leverages over an entirely privately owned financial system have been minimal. This difference eventually bifurcated their patterns of industrial restructuring in the 1980s.

The third area of our institutional analysis is the industrial relations system. The development of the labor movement and state regulations of labor relations are pertinent to the formation of business strategy and the organization of production (cf. Berger and Piore 1980). Labor unions can play a critical role in shaping the direction of employers' strategy in response to the changing environment. Experiences of advanced countries suggest that they can impose restrictions on the adoption of flexible labor strategies and exert pressures on capital to move towards a particular path of industrial development. Unions can also affect the ways training and skills formation are conducted at the shopfloor or community level. The state's capacity for macroeconomic management is also a function of the cooperation or resistance of the organized labor.

The timing and nature of industrial restructuring suggest that we have to adopt a more flexible and broader institutional framework that will allow us to describe and interpret the contemporary development experiences of Hong Kong and Singapore. The actions of state and firms are key elements in this framework, but their actions are necessarily constrained by the labor market as well as other country-specific institutional relations. Such actions are also path-dependent in the sense that they occur within an institutional context that is shaped by historical legacies as well as geo-political constraints and opportunities. The awareness that industrial change is a path-dependent process requires a historical awareness of such legacies.

We want to make clear from the outset, however, that we do not intend to write a comprehensive developmental history of the two city-states and that we will not and cannot offer a full explanation of the origin of the institutional matrix governing the growth process. In particular, it is likely that readers with a keen eye on global and regional contexts of East Asia's development will find our account myopic and too restricted. While we plead guilty to this charge, we want to highlight that there are advantages to our approach. Our approach is intended to bring out the institutional nuances of the restructuring process. In other words, we seek to bring out the proximate determinants of the process of economic and industrial transformation in the 1980s. If our study loses in scope, it gains in depth: we benefit by unearthing the textures and details of the process.

Furthermore, while we treat global and regional events and structures as background to our study, they are not completely alienated from our analyses. We take the view that the institutional and organizational framework is an intermediate variable linking the broader global and regional context and the concrete firms' responses. Institutions are, to a certain extent, the "internalization" of regional dynamics if we probe deeper into their genesis. Regional and global factors of a previous phase would invariably leave their mark in the institutional structure of a society and become internalized in the current phase of development (So and Chiu 1995a:278). For instance, colonialism undoubtedly has a significant impact on state strength in both economies (cf. Chiu 1992). American hegemony in the postwar international system also left an imprint on the early industrial development of the two city-states. The effects of these external factors were then "internalized" in the institutional framework which in turn shaped the restructuring process.

Industrial Restructuring and Firms' Response

Industrial restructuring therefore has to be understood as a process which is constrained by an institutional configuration that in turn is historically constituted. However, unpacking this institutional configuration requires considering the key economic agents in the process. Our interest is to examine how manufacturers in the two city-states, given the aforementioned institutional constraints, respond to the changing business environment. At the same time, we shall see how particular paths of

industrial development and restructuring are a product of such organizational responses. Thus, by looking at industrial restructuring at the societal
and corporate levels, our analysis serves to bridge the micro-macro
linkage in our understanding of the socio-economic organization of
economic activities.

In the 1990s, with three decades of rapid economic growth, the Asian
NIEs are faced with an increasingly costly domestic environment coupled
with a growing turbulent external environment marked by an increasingly
protectionist first world and a competitive third world. Caught within this
squeeze are the manufacturers. The East Asian development literature has
focused almost exclusively on the problem of adjustment by using
countries as cases. We argue that because the pressure points for change
are first felt by manufacturers, the pattern of industrial restructuring has to
be understood in terms of the strategies adopted by firms producing in the
Asian NIEs.

Thus, the questions ought to be rephrased with firms in mind: as the
favorable conditions of low cost and abundant labor are steadily eroded,
how are firms adjusting? Will more firms choose the option of moving
production operations overseas or will they move closer to the first world
strategy of maintaining competitiveness through product and design
innovations?

It is also important to note that the strategies available to local
enterprises in the Asian NIEs (perhaps with the exception of Korea) are
not as diverse (either because of firm size or product specialization) as
MNCs from the industrialized countries, which can dictate the terms of
production and the pace of research and product development from the
corporate headquarters and research facilities at home.

To understand firms' response to industrial restructuring, we will rely
on a matching pair of sample surveys conducted in Hong Kong and
Singapore in 1992. As one of the key problems facing the Asian NIEs has
been the shortage and rising cost of labor (Bauer 1992), we have
deliberately chosen two labor-intensive industries (electronics and tex-
tiles/garments) in an effort to show how firms in industries under the
greatest threat of restructuring are responding.

The survey questionnaire solicited detailed information on the current
and future strategies of manufacturing firms in such areas as human
resource management, technology, marketing, and overseas investment
(see Appendix). The resultant dataset will allow us to understand a firm's
response from three levels:

1. Labor strategy — In a labor scarce and fluctuating production output environment, what mix of labor strategies prevail: overtime

work, using alternative sources of labor, labor rotation in shifts, incentive structures?

2. Technology strategy — Is technology a key tool in restructuring? Is technology driven by costs (e.g., reduce labor dependence) or output (increase volume, quality, new products)?

3. Locational strategy — Are firms headed overseas? Where are the new targets of foreign direct investment? Are firms driven by cost factors or emergent market opportunities?

As a country's economic destiny is closely tied to the production and investment decisions of firms, studying firms' response will provide vital clues in gauging where Hong Kong and Singapore are headed as Asian NIEs. For Singapore particularly, to understand how national strategies to attract foreign direct investment (FDI) are holding up, it is necessary to study MNCs and see their perception of the host environment, *vis-à-vis* other overseas and regional opportunities.

Summary

This book is about industrial change in the light of the contemporary industrial restructuring experiences of Hong Kong and Singapore. The domestic capacities of these two city-states have to be understood within an institutional framework which includes the following key elements: the state, the financial system, labor, and firms. This institutional structure is path-dependent: it is a result of the legacies shaped by history, geo-politics, and the imperatives of size and the absence of countryside. Chapter 2 traces the development of Hong Kong and Singapore as colonial port cities. As entrepôts, both Hong Kong and Singapore experienced similar development paths under British colonial rule. The emphasis is on describing the colonial strategy of development for the two city-states, for example, the stress on the development of entrepôt trade, communications, and transportation infrastructure. The implications of this pattern of development will also be discussed (for example, the growth of a trading class and the emphasis on economic development at the expense of social development).

As British power weakened in the 1950s, both Hong Kong and Singapore faced a common fate — the disappearance of an economic hinterland which was vital for entrepôt trade. The developmental paths taken by the two city-states after the 1950s were quite different. The second half of Chapter 2 traces the adjustment process in the 1960s. Of particular interest is the role of the trading class which was a major force in developing and expanding the entrepôt economy. As the prospects for entrepôt trade diminished, were the roles of this class transformed? A question which is pertinent to the Singapore experience is the emergence of the independent state and the reshaping of institutional arrangements.

Where Chapter 2 ends with a description of the divergent paths taken by the two city-states, Chapters 3 and 4 provide an in-depth account of the developmental experiences of Hong Kong and Singapore respectively.

Chapter 3 looks at some of the major forces facing Hong Kong businesses in the 1980s and 1990s, and analyzes the strategies adopted by firms in adjusting to these forces. The data presented in this chapter include both secondary statistical industry data as well as the results of an enterprise survey conducted in 1992. The chapter will focus on how firms tailor their technology, labor and relocation strategies according to international and domestic pressures.

Like the Hong Kong chapter, the Singapore chapter will provide an in-depth examination of some of the major forces facing Singapore businesses in the 1990s and accompanying firms' strategies. The data presented in this chapter will be comparable to the Hong Kong data. A different element in the Singapore story is the role played by foreign capital in the form of multinational enterprises. Central to the Singapore story will be the different strategies adopted by local and foreign capital.

Chapter 5 contains a statistical comparative analysis of firms' restructuring strategies in the two city-states with the aim of determining the strength of the institutional context on firms' decision-making. Chapter 6 proceeds to highlight the institutional differences between the two industrial economies. This chapter, which focuses on the development of the three institutional elements of state, finance and labor from the 1980s onward, will complete the story of divergent development paths which began in Chapter 2.

The concluding chapter will pick up the main comparative and conceptual threads from earlier discussion by posing these as questions. It will also discuss the economic prospects of Hong Kong and Singapore in the light of our analysis of their industrial development paths.

Walton (1992:122) points out that "in the logic of research, we endeavor to find fertile cases, measure their fundamental aspects, demonstrate causal connections among those elements, and suggest something about the potential generality of the results." Hong Kong and Singapore, in our opinion, offer two fertile cases for comparative analysis. The extraction of Hong Kong and Singapore from the East Asian Development Model is an attempt to move beyond the constraints of the model. Our book will show why events unfold in one way and not another, how legacies and institutional structure respond in contemporary situations, and what these responses are for the state, the financial system, corporations, and labor.

Notes

1. Berger (1986:141) is driven to remark that Singapore, "because of its ethnic composition, is a sort of East Asian outpost in Southeast Asia."

2. For an introduction to economic theories of the financial system, see Fry (1988).

3. The debate is between the structuralists and neoclassical economists.

2

Historical Trajectories: Common Legacies, Different Outcomes

The comparative strategy we sketched in Chapter 1 highlighted the institutionalized nature of economic development. From this perspective, the respective developmental histories of the two city-states, we argue, are fundamental in explicating the restructuring processes because industrial change must be conceived as path-dependent. Choices that the two city-states made in the past tend to preclude certain options in the current scenario, but they also facilitate the adoption of certain restructuring strategies. The road of industrial development then can be seen as a road of no return. Once we began our journey, whether out of our own will or compelled by environmental exigencies, things can never be the same again.

In this chapter, therefore, we would like to delineate the historical trajectories of development for Hong Kong and Singapore. For an observer in the late 1940s, Hong Kong and Singapore looked almost identical. Both were British colonies, both specialized in the enterpôt trade between the Far East and Western industrial countries, and both were small city-states populated largely by ethnic Chinese. Their affinities did not stop here. In the 1950s, the two city-states faced a similar challenge: how to sustain an increasing population with the economy experiencing dwindling trade. Both eventually chose to solve their employment problem with rapid industrialization.

Nevertheless, by the late 1970s when signs of industrial restructuring began to be seen in both places, visitors found them to be so different that they could never imagine the striking similarities in the 1940s. Even the most superficial observation would set them apart. In Singapore, everything seemed so clean and tidy. In Hong Kong, chaos seemed to be the rule of the day. Here we shall highlight more important differences: the pattern of industrial development and the institutional configurations that sustained industrial development. In particular, we are going to single out the relationship between the state and industry, the industrial relations system, and the structure of the financial system. A major source of differentiation between Hong Kong and Singapore, we shall argue, was the divergent political development after the Second World War: Singapore became independent, while Hong Kong remained a colony. We shall not attempt here to write a comprehensive economic history for Hong Kong and Singapore nor to offer an explanation of the historical development of the two city-states; we are interested in those facets of their histories which are most relevant for industrial restructuring. Hence, our account is highly selective, but hopefully this chapter will set the stage for our subsequent discussion.

Common History

In many respects, Hong Kong and Singapore can be seen as sharing a common history. Both were "created" by British colonial adventures in the Far East, and both were built by the British as trading posts for their commercial penetration into the Far East. The common entrepôt development also left behind similar starting points for industrial development, namely, a well-developed infrastructure and an extensive commercial network with the world economy. Before the incorporation into the capitalist world economy, both Hong Kong and Singapore were little-known fishing villages with a small population, but both were adjacent to a large hinterland and involved in an active intra-regional trade. For example, as Hamashita (1991) contends, from the seventeenth century onward, there emerged an extensive exchange network involving China, Japan, and Southeast Asia. By the nineteenth century, trade with Europe also contributed to the commercial boom in coastal China and parts of Southeast Asia. Nevertheless, before the British military and territorial intrusion, both Hong Kong and Singapore were not a central component of the network. In South China, Canton was the gateway to the West, while Malacca in the Malaya Peninsula was the commercial center in Southeast Asia. Their strategic location along established trade routes, however, greatly facilitated the entrepôt development of both city-states after their colonization. The development of the Straits Chinese community, for example, constituted the backbone of the early Singapore population. Hong Kong also benefited from the experience of the Cantonese merchant community.

"Modern" Singapore began life when Sir Stamford Raffles established a trading and military post on the island's southern shore in 1819. Under the auspices of the East India Company, he searched for a new base of trade at the center of the Archipelago (Sumatra and Java, present day Indonesia). He eventually picked Singapore. Raffles's vision for Singapore was to develop a base to protect the China trade in times of war and to outflank the Dutch at Malacca. Furthermore, "[i]n his imperial vision of British greatness in the East, he saw the new port as the springboard to clothe the teeming millions of Southeast Asians and Chinese in British cotton dress. He also envisioned Singapore developing into the opium market of the Archipelago, and even of the northern Chinese ports, via the Chinese junks." (Wong 1978:52). In short, Singapore would become the "new Alexandra" in the Far East. To this end, one of the most important decisions was made by the British authority in Singapore, namely, the establishment of Singapore as a free port. It was hoped that a free trade policy would lure traders to Singapore.

Despite some skepticism in official circles in London about the future of Singapore, it quickly developed into a trading center for Southeast Asia. Between 1824 and 1872, the total value of the colony's trade increased eight times (Buchanan 1972:28). Singapore became the distribution center of local produce from the Archipelago, Malaya, and Indochina for shipment to Europe, North America, and China. With the development of tin mining, gambier, and pepper cultivation in western Malaya, Singapore's volume of trade with the Malaya Peninsula gradually caught up with that of her other trading partners by the middle of the nineteenth century. Subsequently, Singapore was used by the British as a base to penetrate into the Malaya Peninsula. Finally, in the 1870s, Malaya was formally brought under British colonial control in place of the previous indirect rule through the local Sultans. Later, Malaya's economic connections to Singapore's were further increased by the boom in tin mining and the development of rubber plantations. Laborers, mainly coolies from southern China, were also shipped to Malayan mines and plantations via Singapore.

Between the two World Wars, entrepôt trade boomed after the conclusion of the First World War. After the mid-1920s, the volume of trade passing through Singapore began to slide, from the peak of S$1,886.7 million in 1926 to S$251.8 million in 1935 (Wong 1991). The principal cause of Singapore's changing fortune was the recession in the Western world. The other reason was the growth of direct trade between other Southeast Asian countries and the industrial economies. Trade with Britain declined, but Singapore's significance to the United States and Japan increased.

Similarly, trade was also the *raison d'être* for the British acquisition of Hong Kong. Britain was looking for a place from which to conduct trade with China, protected by British naval power (Mills 1942:373). Despite a sluggish start due to China's limited purchasing power for foreign goods and the competition from Shanghai, trade in nineteenth century Hong Kong increased steadily.[1] In particular, more and more people, Chinese and foreign, came to Hong Kong from 1860 onward (as a result of political upheavals in China), and trade flourished to provide supplies to the fast-increasing population in Hong Kong. Furthermore, the notorious "coolie" trade also utilized Hong Kong as a transit center for the southern areas. But it was entrepôt trade that emerged as the main form of economic activity in nineteenth century Hong Kong. Opium was to remain, for some years after 1841, the principal commodity traded through Hong Kong, with salt and sugar as other important articles of trade.

Hong Kong's fortunes improved even more towards the end of the nineteenth century. The gradual build-up and completion of infrastructure and logistic services like shipping, banking, and insurance not only contributed to further growth in trade, but also led to Hong Kong's development as the service center for the China coast. According to the Chinese Imperial Maritime Custom Service, Hong Kong alone handled 21% of China's total exports and 37% of its imports in 1880. As the demand for foreign commodities in China increased, Hong Kong also became the center for the supply of British and European goods to China. The increase in trade then led to a need for banks to handle foreign exchange. British banks monopolized the banking system until 1864, when a group of leading British merchants in Hong Kong established the Hongkong and Shanghai Banking Corporation.

There are no precise statistics on Hong Kong's trade in the nineteenth century, but the volume of trade can be calculated approximately by the number and tonnage of vessels visiting the harbor.[2] In 1850, there were 1,082 vessels with a total tonnage of 377,084 entering Hong Kong. The number of vessels increased to 4,791 in 1870, and the tonnage increased tremendously to more than 2.6 million tons. In 1900, the number and tonnage of vessels entering Hong Kong had reached 10,940 and 14 million respectively (Government Printer 1932). Commerce continued to grow in Hong Kong after the turn of the century despite the demise of the opium trade. The First World War had disrupted this process, but soon after the war, Hong Kong emerged as one of the world's principal ports. In the early 1920s, the total tonnage of vessels entering Hong Kong exceeded New York and London (Chiu 1987:88). Similar to Singapore, Hong Kong experienced a slump in the late 1920s and early 1930s, but the Japanese invasion of China after the mid-1930s, and especially of Shanghai, increased the volume of trade going through Hong Kong.

The period of colonial development as entrepôt cities strongly influenced Hong Kong and Singapore's industrial development after the Second World War. Compared to other colonial powers, the British were relatively more tolerant of indigenous business endeavors. The contrast is indeed stark when we look at Japanese colonies like Taiwan and Korea where Japanese *zaibatsu* almost monopolized the economy. In Singapore and Hong Kong, local business grew alongside British ones, developing a kind of symbiotic relationship between the two. Chinese merchants performed an intermediary role between the Europeans and the local societies. For example, the Malacca-born Chinese, with their ability to speak English, and their knowledge of the habits and practices of the Western merchants, played a major role as middlemen in Singapore. By the early twentieth century in both places, a complementary structure of control and ownership had developed between the Chinese and the European merchants. European businessmen had the overall control of the economy, especially in primary production (e.g., rubber in Malaya) and the international trade associated with it. The Chinese merchants, on the other hand, controlled "the intricate network of domestic commerce, of small scale collection, distribution, and retailing" (Buchanan 1972:43). It was not a symmetrical structure, to be sure, and Europeans had more control of the direction and operation of Singapore and Malaya's economy. Nevertheless, some Chinese merchants had risen above small shopkeepers and traders. With hard work and luck, there was a number of Chinese capitalists who became large export-importers, plantation owners, tin-mine proprietors, contractors, property owners, and financiers (Smith 1971; Yen 1986:142).[3] Furthermore, a multitude of small trading firms also sprang into existence. The presence of these merchants and their extensive business networks then constituted a solid foundation for later industrial development.

Second, development as entrepôts in Hong Kong and Singapore also bequeathed them with transport and communication facilities, as well as a relatively efficient and stable administrative machinery. Both Hong Kong and Singapore are natural deep-water harbors, but they have to be equipped with various logistics in order to be able to handle the large volume of entrepôt trade coming through the harbors. The port development of Singapore showed a sustained effort at investing in the port's technological base, as can be seen from developments in facilities for unloading, storage, and transportation. One indicator is the development of cargo handling facilities, notably in the length of wharves. In Singapore, the first line of wharves was built in 1866 stretching for 750 feet. Successive renovation and extension eventually extended the line of wharves to 12,224 feet by the late 1930s (Ho 1988:3). The two cities also saw the development of various support services to entrepôt trade such as insurance, shipping, and financing unparalleled in most cities in Asia. A Hong Kong business handbook published in the 1950s captured this commercial infrastructure succinctly:

> First there are the great agency houses which have been typical of the China trade since private English first broke into the trading monopoly of the East India Company in Canton. Jardine and Matheson, with worldwide interests which vary from shipping to engineering, from trade to textiles.... Second, there are the great Exchange Banks — Hong Kong's own Hong Kong and Shanghai Banking Corporation, the Chartered Bank of India, Australia, and China, and the Mercantile Bank of India. These, together with the other 91 licensed banks in the colony, including a total of 26 authorized to deal in foreign exchange, are one measure of the Colony's ability to finance the Far East's trade and at the same time find funds for new industries. But if these firms stand out in the mind of an economic historian, there are others that are just as important today — the insurance companies, an essential part of the shipping industry; the transportation and private utility companies without which the Colony could never expand; and hundreds of trading companies which at one time handled the bulk of the China import trade. (The Hong Kong Junior Chamber of Commerce 1955:1)

The existence of such an extensive institutional network for handling commercial transactions not only contributed to the dynamic entrepôt development before the Second World War, but also served the needs of manufacturing industries that emerged later. In particular, the export-oriented nature of manufacturing firms capitalized on the strength of the local business organizations' commercial links with the world market.

The infrastructural development in Hong Kong and Singapore, however, also revealed a significant differentiation in the system of governance in the two colonies. In Hong Kong, the development of port facilities was primarily the responsibility of the private sector. Docks, piers, wharves, and godowns during the pre-Second World War period were mostly privately-built and owned. As a scholar of the port development in Hong Kong observes: "In the history of the administration of the port is to be found one of the most convincing expressions of the community's preference for the *laissez-faire* attitude of the Government" (Chiu 1973:48). The administration of the port was run in a decentralized fashion, and no overarching plan was devised for the development of port facilities. The idea of establishing a Harbour Board (the model of port authorities at major Commonwealth ports like Liverpool and Calcutta) with executive power to coordinate the port administration was voiced several times at no avail (Davies 1949).

By contrast, in Singapore, the twentieth century saw the gradual expansion of the role of the public sector in port development. Although *laissez-faire* was still the dominant principle of governance in Singapore under British rule, port development was a notable exception (Lee 1989). In 1905, the colonial government expropriated the inefficient Tanjong Pagar Dock Company, a monopoly in building and operating wharves and dockyards.[4] In 1913, the Singapore Harbour Board (SHB) was established to operate the wharves and further develop port facilities. The SHB also had the exclusive right to supply labor through its link to three private labor contractors. Under the SHB, the infrastructure of the port continued to expand in anticipation of new demands right into the post-Second World War period (Huff 1994:139-42). This "pocket" of state activism in economic development adumbrated the extensive state intervention in industrialization during the postcolonial era.

Crossroads Ahead

The first two and a half decades after the Second World War could be characterized as a period of American hegemony in the capitalist world economy and the geo-political rivalry between the United States and the Soviet Union in the Cold War (So and Chiu 1995a; Selden n.d.). This had led to significant changes in the regional political economy of East Asia. The confluence of this regional context with the domestic events in Hong Kong paved the way for the rapid industrial takeoff after the war. Meanwhile, political turmoil in Singapore due to the decolonization process delayed industrialization in Singapore until the late 1960s.

After the Second World War, the basic structure of the Singapore economy remained fairly similar to that before the war. It was still very much dependent on entrepôt trade as in the prewar era. Malaya remained the most important trading partner. In 1949, Singapore handled 71% and 67% of Malaya's imports and exports respectively, which amounted to one-third of its total trade (Rodan 1989:43-44). Trade with Malaya was boosted by the rehabilitation of tin mines and rubber plantations after the war, and the subsequent boom in primary products during the Korean War. The newly independent Indonesia (the Dutch Archipelago colonies) also continued to trade with the rest of the world through Singapore, despite a considerable upsurge of economic nationalism there (Ho and So forthcoming).

A glimpse of the structure of the labor force in 1957 testifies to the importance of trade to Singapore on the eve of self governance (Table 2.1).

TABLE 2.1   Employment by Industry in Singapore, 1947 and 1957 Censuses

Industry	1947		1957		% change
	Persons	%	Persons	%	
Agriculture and fishing	29,086	8.1	32,424	6.9	11.5
Mining and quarrying	1,247	0.3	1,598	0.3	28.2
Manufacturing	58,922	16.5	76,837	16.3	30.4
Construction	9,375	2.6	22,028	4.7	135.0
Electricity, gas and water	750	0.2	4,038	0.9	438.4
Commerce	83,049	23.2	135,157	28.6	62.7
Transport, storage and communication	52,976	14.8	49,434	10.5	-6.7
Services	110,374	30.9	148,306	31.4	34.4
Others	11,756	3.3	2,096	0.4	-82.2
Total employment	357,535		471,918		32.0

Source: Adapted from Rodan (1989:46).

The tertiary sector, which mainly served the entrepôt economy (commerce, transport, storage and communication, and services), accounted for 70.5% of the entire working population. In contrast, only 16.3% of the labor force were engaged in manufacturing, and 21.9% in the entire secondary sector (manufacturing, utilities, and construction).[5]

In Hong Kong, on the other hand, manufacturing industries had considerable development during the interwar period. Some forms of import-substitution for the commodities previously traded had also occurred. For example, sugar was previously imported from Southeast Asia (principally Java) and then re-exported to China. After Jardine and Swire decided to import raw sugar directly and refine it into white sugar, sugar manufactured in Hong Kong dominated the Guangdong market at the turn of the century, even competing successfully against Japanese sugar produced in Taiwan. By 1931, it was estimated that some 23.6% of the 470,794 economically active population engaged in manufacturing, although most of them were employed in the handicraft industries (Butters 1939).[6] Manufacturing then received a further boost from the Ottawa Conference and the resultant Imperial Preference Scheme in the early 1930s.[7] With the inflow of refugee capital from China after the Japanese invasion and the increase in Chinese demand for manufactured goods from Hong Kong, many new Chinese manufacturing firms were established. By 1941, there were an estimated 7,500 factories and workshops with over 100,000 workers (Leeming 1975).

But what really drove the two city-states into different developmental paths was their divergent political fate. In Singapore, the process of decolonization began in the 1950s.[8] The State of Singapore Act in 1958, passed by both the British Parliament and the Singapore Legislative Council, declared the internal self governance of Singapore in 1959.[9] Anticipating the decolonization, the People's Action Party (PAP) was established in 1954. Eventually, the Party was divided into two groups, the radicals and the moderates, or the English-educated, middle class members of the colonial society, and the radicals from the lower classes. The internal struggles of the PAP merely reflected the wider social schism characterizing Singapore's decolonization process. Under the leadership of the radical Chinese-speaking unionists, organized labor began to acquire more influence over industrial relations and the political scene. These Chinese-speaking unionists also allied with other Chinese intellectuals, teachers, and students of the Chinese schools in Singapore which were discriminated against under British rule. Their objective was to establish an independent republic with a socialist bent. There were also communal conflicts between the Chinese and the Malays.

By the early 1960s, however, the domestic political scene was more stabilized. The split of the PAP and the subsequent purge of radicals weakened opposition to the now moderate PAP leadership. Various social programs in public housing, health, and education provided the PAP with popular support. The PAP also espoused the principle of a multi-ethnic and multi-cultural Singapore, seeking to minimize the possibilities of ethnic conflicts. As a result, the PAP won overwhelming victories in the general elections of the late 1960s and 1970s.

While Singapore was becoming an independent nation, Hong Kong remained a British colony after the Second World War. The *Guomindang* had begun to recover sovereignty over a number of treaty ports and foreign settlements before the war. After the surrender of Japan in the Pacific War, Taiwan, a former Japanese colony, was also returned to China. Yet there were no plans for the decolonization of Hong Kong. Under the strained relationship between China and the capitalist world amidst the Cold War atmosphere, Britain was in no hurry to return Hong Kong to China. After all, the British leases for Kowloon and the New Territories would not expire until 1997, and Hong Kong was ceded permanently.

The British government had planned to gradually liberalize Hong Kong's colonial constitutional structure by the end of the war (Tsang 1988). But with the coming to power of the Chinese Communist Party, the plan was quickly scrapped. The colonial bureaucracy headed by the Crown-appointed Governor wielded absolute power in Hong Kong, while the only "popular" element in the central government was the appointed unofficial members of the Legislative Council and the Executive Council, the two consultative bodies to the Governor. The political structure stayed this way until the 1980s.

The stalling of political change in Hong Kong coincided with other social and economic problems. Due to the political upheaval in mainland China, Hong Kong's population increased from 1,600,000 in 1941 to some 2,360,000 in 1950. It was estimated that in 1954 there were about 667,000 refugees who came mainly from the mainland for political and economic reasons (Hambro 1955:162). An official report gave a portrait of the problems caused by the entrance of these refugees:

> They had to find housing; they had to find food and clothing; they needed medical treatment when sick; and their children needed schooling. The Colony was already short of these facilities for its existing population. The pressure on buildings and on the small area of developable land became intense. (Government Information Service 1958:6)

A sample survey conducted in 1954 by the United Nations High Commission for Refugees in Hong Kong also revealed an alarming level of unemployment, especially among the postwar immigrants. The unemployment rate was 8% for all Hong Kong-born adults, 11.5% for prewar immigrants, and a staggering 15.1% for postwar immigrants. This gave a total of about 160,000 persons looking for jobs (Hambro 1955:47). Thus the integration of this large number of refugees into the labor market posed serious social and economic problems for Hong Kong.

The early phase of the Korean War caused a short-lived boom in local commerce. But the war quickly prompted the United Nations to impose an embargo on trade with China in June 1951. The embargo dealt a crippling blow to Hong Kong's trade, since China was the Colony's largest trading partner. The value index of trade plummeted from 254 to 182 in 1952, and dropped further in 1953 and 1954. In 1954, the total value of trade was a meager 60% of the 1948 level. The trade depression generated a huge deficit in the balance of trade, raising the 1954 deficit to twice the level of 1948 (Szczepanik 1958:45). Exports to China, which represented 18% of Hong Kong's total exports in 1948, dropped to 4% of the total by 1956 (Government Information Service 1958:8). Apart from the embargo, entrepôt trade with China also declined in the 1950s because of the

People's Republic of China's (PRC) rigid control of foreign trade. The Chinese government preferred to deal directly with foreign governments, effectively by-passing most traders in Hong Kong.

The immediate effects of the embargo and the decline in entrepôt trade were disastrous.[10] According to one estimate, the value of export earnings from entrepôt trade fell by more than one-third between 1951 and 1952, from HK$644 million to HK$421 million (Szczepanik 1958). But this was only part of the loss due to the embargo, for indirect earnings from entrepôt trade of warehouses, transport, banking, and insurance were also adversely affected. The combined effect of the decrease in the direct and indirect earnings from entrepôt trade can perhaps be gauged by the changes in Gross Domestic Product (GDP). In real terms, the GDP growth rate was 19.3% in 1950, but dropped to -5.5% in 1951 and 6.1% in 1952 (Ho 1979).

Singapore faced similar economic malaise by the early 1960s. As Cheng (1991:184) remarks:

> The 1940s closed with periodically recurrent but nevertheless quite often well-founded expressions of anxiety regarding the prospects for the future development of entrepôt trade. The bugbears this time were growing economic nationalism and the desire to regulate and conserve foreign exchange on the part of neighboring territories, besides the usual commercial rivalry. These considerations reinforced fears in Singapore that the entrepôt trade could no longer be depended upon to provide for increased employment and economic growth.

In the early postwar decades, both natural increase and inward migration contributed to a faster population increase than in the prewar era. Between 1931 and 1957, the Singaporean population increased from 557,745 to 1,445,929. Before the Second World War, the annual population rate hovered around 3%, but during 1947-1957, the figure jumped to a 4.5%. Among the net growth of 507,785 between 1947 and 1957, over one-third was due to natural increase, while the rest was attributable to net immigration (Saw 1991). The decline in the death rate contributed to the steep rise in natural population. While immigration from China and other overseas countries dropped due to stricter regulation, those from Malaya Peninsula continued unabated. Burdened with a fast expanding labor force, a government report in 1959 estimated that about 5% of the working population was unemployed and the unemployment rate was expected to rise even further in the next few years (Cheng 1991:188). This prediction turned out to be correct when the unemployment rate increased to 9.1% in 1966. Youth unemployment was particularly high, with some 23% of men and over 35% of women under 20 years old unemployed (Clark 1971:311).

Nonetheless, the fear of the imminent economic collapse did not materialize in the 1950s, when trade still contributed to the bulk of economic activities in Singapore, accounting for one-third of the GDP in 1959. Trade with the Malaya Peninsula and Indonesia continued. While the Korean War almost crippled Hong Kong's entrepôt trade, it created a boom in prices of primary commodities such as rubber and petroleum, the staples of Singapore's entrepôt trade.

Perhaps because of the continual importance of trade, and more importantly because of the political instability caused by the decolonization process, the secondary industries did not make any significant progress during the 1950s. Industrial conflicts and agitations by militant unions dampened investors' confidence. Traders were, in general, reluctant to take the risk and invest in manufacturing industries which they were not familiar with and which had a long payoff period. Consequently, the share of manufacturing in employment was 16.3% in 1957, more or less the same as in 1947 (see Table 2.1). In 1960, manufacturing still accounted for no more than 12% of GDP at current prices, and export-oriented industries barely existed. Most manufacturing firms in Singapore were oriented towards the domestic market or the processing of commodities traded through Singapore.

Even though this level of industrial development was quite impressive by Asian standards, it still lagged behind Hong Kong. Refugee was a burden to Hong Kong. However, the refugees also brought considerable capital and, more importantly, experiences and expertise in industrial undertakings. For example, the communist victory in Shanghai led many Shanghainese textile firms to divert their production to Hong Kong, greatly accelerating the growth of industrial production in the Colony. A number of large scale textile mills were set up with capital and machinery relocated from Shanghai, giving local industry a head start over those in other Asian cities. In the long run, the large number of refugees from China also constituted a large pool of potential entrepreneurs whose only channel of escaping wage labor was through petty entrepreneurship (Lui and Wong 1994). Refugees with industrial experience set up the first batch of small scale manufacturing industries in the early postwar years. At that time, the scarcity of consumer goods in Southeast Asia created a ready market for Hong Kong products, which were cheaper than other imports. Therefore, while Hong Kong and Singapore faced similar challenges to industrialization, developments in the 1950s propelled Hong Kong ahead of Singapore.

The contrasting political development of the two city-states in the aftermath of the Second World War also had important repercussions on their subsequent industrialization. Industrial development in Singapore was then overseen by a newly formed government with considerable popular support. Hong Kong, on the other hand, industrialized under the same colonial state which had been in place for over a century. Economically, Singapore in the 1960s was in approximately the same situation as Hong Kong in the early 1950s. Both faced considerable economic stress in the early postwar years, Hong Kong by the Korean War-induced trade embargo on China which devastated its entrepôt trade, Singapore by the surging nationalism in Malaysia and Indonesia which threatened Singapore's status as the middleman between the latter and the West. Both had enormous problems of unemployment. While Hong Kong was burdened with a massive influx of refugees from China, Singapore's young population created pressures for finding new employment opportunities.

Parting Ways

The year 1970 marked a major transition in the regional political economy of East Asia: the end of US dollar convertibility into gold, the proclamation of the Nixon Doctrine, and the end of China's cultural revolution (Selden n.d.). Japan also began its first wave of foreign direct manufacturing investment in Asia, marking the decline of American hegemony and the rise of Japan in the regional political economy. The "new international division of labor" also spread to Asia, as European and American MNCs began to build significant production capacities in East Asia (Fröbel et al. 1980). While these international developments gave Hong Kong a second boost in its industrial development, their impact on Singapore was even more phenomenal (So and Chiu 1995a, 1995b; Arrighi 1994). By 1970, Singapore had already established a regime friendly to business, especially foreign business. It therefore rode on this wave of foreign direct investments in manufacturing by Japan and other Western countries and embarked on a phase of rapid industrial growth.

From the late 1960s, manufacturing industries began to grow rapidly in Singapore, following the path of Hong Kong in the previous decade. This was only achieved after several regional and domestic political tensions were resolved. For a brief period from 1963 to 1965, Singapore became a part of Malaysia, but retained the right to local self-government. The PAP favored a merger with Malaysia, partly because a custom union with the much larger Malaysian market would give Singapore's fledgling manufacturing industries a great boost. The Malaysian political elite, however, perceived the predominantly Chinese Singapore as a threat to Malay political leadership (Yeo and Lau 1991). In August 1965, Singapore was expelled from the Malaysian Federation, and it duly declared its independence, assuming full sovereignty over its territory.[11]

In the early 1960s Singapore also had trouble with Indonesia. As Lau (1991:372) notes:

> Singapore was viewed by Indonesian leaders as a refuge for and source of fifth columnists among the Overseas Chinese. It was feared that Singapore could eventually come under the sway of Peking. A further obstacle to friendly relations between Indonesia and Singapore was the fact that Singapore provided a sanctuary for rebel leaders from Indonesia, including those who had led a rebellion in Sumatra in the mid-1950s.

When Singapore joined the Federation, Indonesia enforced a policy of "confrontation" against Singapore and Malaysia due to its suspicion of Britain using the Federation as an agent for its neocolonial aggression. An embargo was thus imposed against the Federation. While Singapore had previously conducted barter trade with Indonesia in the form of smuggling along the borders, Kuala Lumper put a ban on it, claiming that such smuggling was a security risk (Richter 1966). Such setbacks in Singapore's economic and political relations with its neighbors, therefore, significantly closed off options for regional economic cooperation and pushed the city-state towards an industrial strategy which relied on multinational capital producing for Western markets.

Domestic instabilities caused by the struggle for power among local political parties were also resolved. After the mid-1960s, the PAP had successfully controlled its main adversaries: the left-wing student groups and unions. It also put in place various social programs (notably a public housing scheme) which provided the PAP with the popular support needed to launch other developmental programs.

While real manufacturing value-added increased by 5.9% in 1961, and 8.6% in 1962, the growth rate shot up to 16.8% in 1963. For the 1961-1965 period, real annual growth of manufacturing value-added averaged at 9.7%. Manufacturing growth accelerated in the 1966-1970 period, with the same growth rate averaged at close to 20%. Even though the oil crisis in 1973 dented the growth process, the manufacturing sector still scored an average growth of 10.8% from 1971 to 1975 (Department of Statistics 1983). Measured at current prices, manufacturing's share of GDP jumped from 11.9% in 1960 to 19.7% in 1970, and further to 23.8% in 1975 (Table 2.2).

On the other hand, by the 1960s, Hong Kong's transformation from an entrepôt to an industrial economy was more or less completed. Though manufacturing only accounted for about a quarter of the GDP in the financial year of 1960-61, it had become the largest sector in terms of employment (Chang 1969:66). In the 1961 census, it was found that some

TABLE 2.2   Sectoral Percentage Distribution of GDP in Hong Kong and
             Singapore (at current factor cost)

Sector	Hong Kong			Singapore		
	1961	*1970*	*1975*	*1960*	*1970*	*1975*
Primary sectors	3.6	2.2	1.5	4.1	2.9	2.4
Manufacturing	24.7	30.9	26.9	11.9	19.7	23.8
Utilities	2.4	2.0	1.8	2.5	2.8	2.0
Construction	5.3	4.2	5.7	3.6	7.3	8.5
Trade	20.4	19.6	20.7	35.9	30.2	28.2
Transport and communication	9.4	7.6	7.2	14.2	11.2	11.6
Financial and business services	9.7	14.9	17.0	11.3	14.2	15.9
Other services	18.0	18.0	18.7	18.2	13.8	11.9
Others (statistical adjustment)	6.5	0.6	0.5	- 1.7	- 2.1	- 4.3

Sources: Chang (1969:66); Census and Statistics Department (1992); Department of
Statistics (1983).

42% of the economically active population were engaged in the manufacturing sector. In 1961, the value of domestic exports (locally manufactured
articles) reached the record level of HK$2,939 million. Domestic exports
amounted to 75% of the export total, indicating that Hong Kong's
manufacturing industries had exceeded the entrepôt trade as the source of
foreign earnings (Government Information Service 1961:74).

The growth of Hong Kong's manufacturing industries after 1960 was
equally phenomenal. Manufacturing accounted for 24.7% of GDP in 1961,
and 30.9% in 1970 (Table 2.2; Census and Statistics Department 1992:73).
Between 1961 and 1971, the number of manufacturing establishments
more than tripled from 5,980 to 17,865, and manufacturing workers
increased from 229,857 to 593,494 (Commissioner for Labour 1962, 1972).

Manufacturing industries in Hong Kong and Singapore were
remarkably similar in their export orientation. Merchandise exports grew
exceedingly fast during the period of industrial takeoff, achieving an
annual average of 20.5% in Hong Kong and 17.9% in Singapore from 1965

to 1973 (Krause 1988:47). In both economies, the ratio of exports to GDP was very high, suggesting a high dependence on exports.[12]

This characteristic of Hong Kong and Singapore's manufacturing was largely a result of a fundamental transformation in the structure of the world economy after the Second World War. In the 1930s, the upsurge in protectionism contributed to the severe economic depression which destabilized the world economy and fueled the development of fascism. After the Allied victory, the United States strove to liberalize the world economy in order to prevent the spread of communism and enhance the interdependence of the capitalist "free" world (see Chiu 1994; Gilpin 1987). It took the lead by opening its domestic market to foreign imports, and was instrumental to the construction of the global economic infrastructure. The General Agreement on Tariffs and Trade (GATT) created a liberal international trade system, the International Monetary Fund (IMF) stabilized international monetary matters, and the World Bank offered capital to underdeveloped Third World economies. Under American leadership, the postwar international economic order became much more liberal, multilateral and interdependent. Whatever the limitations of the Bretton Woods and the GATT systems in creating a genuine multilateral and liberal international economic order, the new world order did lead to an expansion in world trade. From 1950 to the mid-1980s, the volume of world merchandise exports increased nine-fold. The average propensity for nations to export also increased (this is indicated by the volume of world commodity output, which increased about five-fold). World trade, therefore, grew nearly twice as fast as world output (Grimwade 1989:51-53).

In addition, as domestic costs rose in the advanced industrial countries in the 1960s, firms there began to search for low cost production sites. The revolution in communication and transport technology also facilitated the flow of information between firms in advanced countries and those in industrializing countries (Fröbel et al. 1980). The two city-states were already economically well endowed and took advantage of this movement. Specifically, their extensive international commercial network, excellent infrastructural framework, and external transportation and communication facilities helped integrate industrial firms in an international production network.

Nevertheless, the similarities between manufacturing industries in Hong Kong and Singapore stopped here. While both of their manufacturing industries were oriented to the world market, they stood in different relations to the global economy. Though both city-states were integral members of the new international division of labor, their forms of integration were diametrically different. In Singapore's industrialization process, FDI was the most important source of investment capital and entrepreneurship, especially in the manufacturing sector. It was foreign capital that transformed Singapore from a trading entrepôt port to an industrial city. The most complete data series on the magnitude of foreign investment in Singapore's manufacturing industry is measured in terms of the growth of foreign-owned gross fixed assets collected by the Economic Development Board (EDB) (See Figure 2.1).[13] It shows that foreign investment increased rapidly after the late 1960s, though the oil crisis slackened investment inflow after 1973. While Hong Kong's manufacturing industry developed before the inflow of FDI from advanced economies, Singapore's industrial sector was largely a consequence of the transfer and expansion of production capacity from Japan and other Western countries.

The increasing weight of foreign investment can be gauged by looking at several cross-sections of Singapore's ownership structure in the manufacturing industries (Table 2.3). In 1959, foreign-controlled firms owned some 22% of the total paid-up capital.[14] In 1963, the share of wholly-owned foreign firms in the total manufacturing capital-expenditure (i.e., investment in fixed assets) alone increased to 38.9%, while jointly-owned firms accounted for another 5.6%. By 1966, investment by foreign-controlled firms had come to exceed that of domestic firms, accounting for 64% of the total capital expenditure.

After 1968, the inflow of FDI accelerated as a result of additional incentives from the Singaporean state and the intensification of the global activities of multinationals. Consequently, foreign-controlled firms further increased their dominance in Singapore's industrialization process. From 1966 to 1972, for example, foreign firms' percentage share in employment increased from 25 to 44; output from 42 to 60; value-added from 44 to 55; and capital expenditure from 64 to 71. Between 1972 and 1977, local firms invested more than foreign ones such that the latter's share in investment dropped slightly from 71% to 67.4%. But in terms of employment, output, and value-added, foreign firms' dominance in 1977 was further accentuated with percentage shares of 54.4, 73.4, and 65.2 respectively. It is thus evident that penetration by MNCs into the economy went hand in hand with Singapore's industrialization. Consequently, foreign-invested firms accounted for an overwhelming share of total exports, some 83.5% in 1970, and 91.8% in 1978 (Haggard 1990:218).

In Hong Kong, on the other hand, exports were generated by a largely locally-owned industrial sector. Export sales of foreign firms were estimated to account for only 10% in 1974 (Haggard 1990:218). While foreign manufacturing firms were not insignificant in Hong Kong, being larger and technologically more advanced than most local firms, their

38

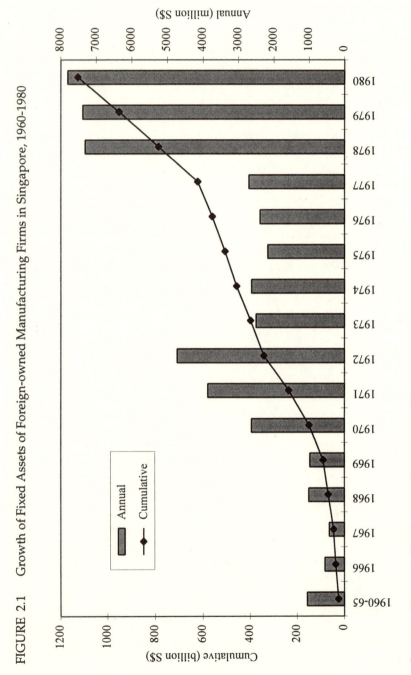

FIGURE 2.1   Growth of Fixed Assets of Foreign-owned Manufacturing Firms in Singapore, 1960-1980

Source: Economic Development Board, Annual Report, various years.

Table 2.3   Ownership Structure in Singapore's Manufacturing
             Industries, 1963-1977 (in percentage)

Ownership Structure	Establish- ments	Employ- ment	Output	Value- added	Paid-up capital
1963					
Wholly foreign	5	12	31	29	39
Joint venture	7	20	23	29	22
Wholly local	88	67	46	42	39
1966					
Foreign controlled	10	25	42	44	64
Locally controlled	90	75	58	56	36
1972					
Foreign controlled	17	44	60	55	71
Locally controlled	83	56	40	45	29
1977					
Foreign controlled	23	55	73	65	67
Locally controlled	77	45	27	35	33

Sources: 1963 and 1977 figures from Chia (1981:453); 1966 and 1972 figures from Yoshihara (1976:180). Original source is from the Department of Statistics, Singapore.

aggregate weight in the economy was no match to their counterparts in Singapore. The multitude of local firms was the spearhead of Hong Kong's export drive. Their strategy was to enter into subcontracting and OEM arrangements with foreign buyers or local trading firms. As a result, in 1973, foreign firms only accounted for some 11% of the total number of workers employed, 12.9% of total output, and 13.9% of fixed assets in manufacturing (Lin and Mok 1985:249).

Another consequence of the different modes of Hong Kong and Singapore's integration with the world economy was the size distribution of the industrial sector. Singapore's industrialization was accompanied by an increasing average scale of production. The average size of industrial establishments was 43 workers in 1963, which rose to 59 in 1969, and reached 80 in 1975. The presence of a large number of MNCs in Singapore contributed to the pervasiveness of large scale production there, exemplified by the mammoth oil refinery and shipbuilding ventures established in the 1960s. In contrast, Hong Kong witnessed a long-term decline in the average scale of production, with its average factory size shrinking from 45 in 1960 to 22 in 1975 (Deyo 1989:39). Save for a few large scale spinning mills, most of Hong Kong's local firms were family businesses hiring a few workers. Over 65% of Hong Kong's manufacturing establishments, therefore, employed less than 10 workers in 1978 (Commissioner for Labour 1979).

A third difference in the two city-states' industrial structure is in the sectoral mix within the manufacturing sector. In the 1960s, with a heavy dose of foreign investment, an oil refining industry emerged in Singapore.[15] Other heavy industries, such as shipbuilding and repairing, also enjoyed spectacular growth in the same period. The result is a more "balanced" industrial structure by the mid-1970s. In 1976, the capital-intensive heavy industries (chemical and petroleum products, and transport equipment) accounted for some 49.5% of all manufacturing output, and 38.2% of total value-added, though they were much less important in terms of contribution to employment (Cheng 1991:207). In Hong Kong, on the other hand, shipbuilding and repairing declined during the export-oriented industrial takeoff of the 1950s, and the oil-refining industry was non-existent. Therefore, Hong Kong's industrial structure can be characterized by a lopsidedness skewed towards labor-intensive, light industries.

Contrasting Institutional Framework of Export-led Growth

Apart from divergences in industrial structure, Hong Kong and Singapore's export-led industrialization was also supported by contrasting institutional frameworks. In Singapore, we saw a state which participated actively in the various aspects of industrial development, while in Hong Kong the state was renowned for its *laissez-faire* approach to economic management. Other institutional bifurcations seem to follow from this basic difference. Industrial relations in Singapore were a lot more "organized" than in Hong Kong, with a heavier emphasis on tripartite coordination between the state, unions, and employers. Finally, the financial system in Singapore was also more closely tied to the industrial sector, as the state played a more active role in industrial financing, while commercial banks in Hong Kong were more "detached" from industrial investment.

State-Industry Relations

The first, and perhaps the most remarkable, institutional difference between Hong Kong and Singapore was the role of the state in industrial development. While the Singapore government played an active *guiding* role in industrialization, the colonial state in Hong Kong was contented with a more indirect and passive *facilitating* role. First of all, the EDB was established in 1961 in Singapore to coordinate the state's promotion efforts. The EDB was entrusted with the implementation of the first and only development plan in Singapore's history. The plan, which covered the period 1961-1964, spelt out the problems of Singapore's economy and the necessity for industrialization. Under the EDB, the principal measures to encourage new industries involved the provision of infrastructure, tariff protection, and fiscal incentives (Goh 1977:8).

As for infrastructure, Singapore already had an excellent port and port facilities. The EDB then built a large industrial estate in Jurong, equipped with all the necessities of industrial production, including power and water supplies, road and rail connections with other parts of Singapore, and its own port for handling cargo. Subsequently, the Jurong Town Corporation took over the function of industrial land development in 1968, and other industrial estates (13 in total) were also developed.

Singapore briefly attempted to employ the strategy of import-substitution to develop local industries. It imposed import tariffs on a number of selected items, such as steel bars, chocolates, flour, electric bulbs, and soap. The rate of protection for local production, however, was considered mild, and its impact on industrial investment was minimal. The Singapore government attempted to develop a common market with Malaysia by joining the Federation of Malaysia in 1963. But the plan never materialized due to the expulsion of Singapore from the Federation in 1965. After 1965, the focus was on sponsoring the development of export industries rather than import-substituting ones.

The most direct incentive for industrial investment came from the various tax incentives for industries. A legislation granting pioneer status to industrial firms had been passed in 1959 before the PAP took power. The PAP kept this policy and continued to offer income tax holidays to pioneer firms for periods up to five years. Other concessions included accelerated depreciation allowances, tax deduction on interest paid to foreign loans, and tax exemptions on royalty payments. After 1968, export industries were given special encouragement by granting export earnings concessionary tax rates. In addition, the EDB also provided other financial assistance to private firms in the form of loans and equity participation. Armed with an array of incentives for industrial development, the Singapore government (through the EDB and other statutory bodies) was thus able to play an active role in steering the economy towards export-led industrial growth. It is important to note that such incentives are selective rather than universal. The EDB conducted feasibility studies of various industries to determine their viability and potential. Upon receiving an application, the EDB would also examine the condition of the firm and tax concessions would only be granted on a discretionary merit-based criteria.

Compared with Singapore, the role of the colonial state in Hong Kong's industrial development was more facilitating rather than guiding, and more indirect rather than direct.[16] Indeed, a low level of state intervention in the economy had been the dominant style of economic management in the early period of industrialization, i.e., the 1950s and 1960s. State assistance in industrial development was limited to promotion and regulation of manufactured goods. Most of the promotion efforts were connected to the marketing of products overseas. The first one was the establishment of a system of certification of origin of Hong Kong manufactured exports. Despite Hong Kong's early start in export manufacturing, selling Hong Kong manufactured products overseas, especially to Western markets, was not a straightforward matter in the 1950s. For example, there had been allegations from Commonwealth countries that some exports from Hong Kong were merely re-exports of Japanese products falsely declared and labeled in order to enjoy the advantages of Imperial Preference. This necessitated the establishment of a system of certifying the origin and local contents of Hong Kong exports. Furthermore, under the Korean War embargo, the United States government enacted a Foreign Assets Control Regulation in 1952, banning the import of goods originated from China and North Korea. Since Hong Kong produced a lot of traditional commodities that were also supplied by China, the colonial state had to set up a system of inspection and certification of such goods manufactured in Hong Kong.

The other important aspect of industrial promotion by the Hong Kong government was an extensive publicity campaign with regard to Hong Kong's manufacturing industries. The first such venture was Hong Kong's participation in the 1948 British Industries Fair. Subsequently, Hong Kong had an exhibit at the annual Fair for the next seven years. From 1954 onward, the colonial state arranged displays of local manufactured products in Seattle, Toronto, Frankfurt, and New York. Apart from participation in trade fairs, the colonial state published various guides to foreign buyers, furnishing them with commercial information concerning Hong Kong. From 1953, the state also published the *Commerce, Industry and Finance Directory*, an irregular publication containing useful information about Hong Kong's economy to foreign buyers. Then in 1954, the

Commerce and Industry Department began to publish a monthly *Trade Bulletin*, which was circulated among overseas businessmen.

Certification of origin, participation in trade fairs, and trade publications more or less exhausted what the colonial state did to *selectively* promote industrial growth. Still, we do not agree with the portrayal of Hong Kong as a totally *laissez-faire* economy, in which the state had no significant impact on the economy. While the Hong Kong state was a far cry from the developmental states in East Asia, it did play a major facilitating role with respect to economic growth in general. First of all, it offered an attractive regulatory framework in which businessmen could operate. Laws and statutes in Hong Kong, following the British system, carry clear commitment to and definition of private property. The merits of this legal system are that it allows private transactions to be relatively free of administrative encumbrance, and offers protection against fraud by the legal enforcement of contracts. The statutes regulating the economy are also clear and simple, which facilitate business calculations. The formation of companies, public or private, limited or unlimited, was easy and straightforward. Secondly, the colonial state supplied the basic infrastructure for economic activities. It built and managed roads, railways, harbors, an airport, and other transport facilities. Thirdly, the colonial state was responsible for the maintenance of law and order, as well as the protection of private property. Fourth, and perhaps most importantly, it provided low-cost housing to the majority of the working class households, contributing significantly to the socialization of collective consumption and to the prevention of wage spiral in the course of rapid industrialization. The public health system provided cheap medical services to citizens, and the state-subvented education system was the most important agent of human resource development.

What is more conspicuous from a comparative perspective, however, is not what the colonial state had done, but what it had not done. In contrast to the Singaporean state, the colonial state was especially reluctant to offer selective assistance to the development of manufacturing industries. It offered services which were available universally to all sectors and firms, but had not practiced the kind of industrial targeting implicit in Singapore's industrial policies. Hence, there was a long list of industrial policies that were common to Singapore but had never been practiced in Hong Kong. In the words of an economist:

> In Hong Kong, one finds no five-year plans, no Government-sponsored steel mill or any attempt to promote large-scale operations or to protect cottage industries. Market forces are allowed to shape the economy — selecting the industries to be developed and sizes of the firms composing them. When these forces spell the ruin of many enterprises, or even entire industries such

as cement and steel, the Government does not exercise a boxing referee's discretionary function of stopping the fight. No attempt is ever made to distort factor prices in favor of any particular type of development: investment allowances, tax-holidays, loans to small firms, rent controls on industrial premises and minimum wage legislation find no place in a scheme of things in which industries pay the economic value of all factors they exploit. (Owen 1971:155)

Industrial Relations

The divergent role of the state can also be seen in another institutional sphere, namely, industrial relations. During the industrial takeoff, the Singaporean state engineered a more organized tripartite framework of industrial relations. In contrast, the industrial relations system in Hong Kong had been much more decentralized, and the state played a minimal role in influencing the relationship between workers and employers.

Before the mid-1960s, unions were militant, challenging both management and the new government.[17] The newly independent state thus acted to replace them. Firstly, the state nurtured the National Trade Union Congress (NTUC) and its affiliates to rival the established unions. The PAP exercised tight control of the NTUC. Radical unions were suppressed and union leaders were jailed. In 1966, the Trade Union (Amendment) Bill declared strikes and other industrial action illegal unless they were carried out with the approval of union members through a secret ballot. Sympathy strikes and strikes in essential services were also banned. Finally in 1968, the state introduced two new laws regulating industrial relations, the Employment Act and the Industrial Relations (Amendment) Act. The Employment Act "rationalized the pay structure by doing away with certain abuses on overtime practice and also protected young industries against excessive retrenchment benefits" (Goh 1977:9). In other words, it reduced the employers' burden of labor cost. The Industrial Relations (Amendment) Act buttressed certain managerial prerogatives against unions' challenges. Issues such as promotion, transfer, recruitment, retrenchment, and task assignment were placed beyond the range of collective bargaining and were left to the management's unilateral decision.

In the early 1970s, Singapore was approaching full employment and pressures for wage increase intensified as shortage for labor became apparent. The NTUC could no longer contain workers' discontentment. A higher rate of wage increase was demanded and industrial disputes broke out frequently (Rodan 1989:106). In order to regulate the process of wage adjustment, the state established the National Wages Council (NWC) in 1972. It was a tripartite body with representatives from the state, employer organizations, and the NTUC. Each year it issued guidelines for wage increases, which though not mandatory, had considerable influence on the conduct of collective bargaining.

In Hong Kong, on the other hand, a collective bargaining relationship was virtually non-existent in manufacturing, save in a few traditional craft-based occupations. Union organizations were autonomous, but they were numerically weak. Throughout the industrial takeoff, less than a quarter of the entire labor force were union members, and unions had no shopfloor organizations capable of representing workers *vis-à-vis* their employers. Furthermore, the union movement was politically divided by their different allegiances to the Chinese Communist Party (CCP) and the *Guomindang* (see Levin and Chiu 1993; England 1989; Turner et al. 1980).

The colonial state had maintained a "voluntarist" approach to industrial relations, preferring to let employers and workers settle their employment relations between themselves (Ng 1982). The state set the basic conditions of employment by statutory measures; regulating such issues as industrial safety, and women and children's employment. It had never attempted to set minimum wage and stayed away from interfering with managerial prerogatives at the shopfloor. Though it had taken occasional actions against the left-wing unions (loyal to the CCP) in the early 1950s, it had never attempted to exert direct control over the union movement as in Singapore.

The differences in industrial relations institutions in the two places were not simply a result of state actions. The disparate industrial structures also mattered. The mass of small- and medium-sized manufacturing firms in Hong Kong had been inimical to the labor organization. The industrial structure had instead fostered an atomized strategy on the part of the workers to pursue their interests. The "exit" option had been more appealing to the workers than "voice." Rather than waging collective action to improve their lot, workers resorted to job mobility to seek better employment conditions (Levin and Chiu 1993). In contrast, with the larger number of big firms in Singapore, the relationship between employers and workers tended to be more stable and hence more conducive for collective action. Being more likely to be subsidiaries of multinationals, Singaporean manufacturing firms were also more susceptible to a more institutionalized and formal approach to industrial relations, especially when they were facing a state and union movement largely sympathetic to their interests.

Financial System

Another contrasting institutional framework for industrial development in Hong Kong and Singapore is the financial system. The financial system played a very different role in both economies with respect to industrialization. In Singapore, it was more active in mobilizing capital for industrial enterprises, whereas in Hong Kong, a more detached relationship existed. Due to the entrepôt history of the two city-states, their banking system looked remarkably similar. Both composed mainly of commercial banks deriving their income from the financing of foreign trade. British-origin banks had a major presence in the financial system, but local banks had come to assume an increasing share of the business. On the whole, both Hong Kong and Singapore enjoyed a well-developed financial system compared to the rest of the Third World by the early postwar years. This contributed significantly to their export-led industrial growth.[18]

While the financial system in both cities had an undisputed positive influence on industrial development, the degree of integration between the financial sector and manufacturing was quite divergent. This can be gauged by the sectoral distribution of loans and advances by banks. In Singapore, the manufacturing sector obtained a rising share of the credit from the banking sector as industrialization proceeded. Bank credit to the manufacturing sector accounted for only 12.7% of total loans and advances to non-bank customers in 1962, when industrialization had just begun. This increased to 17.2% in 1966, continued to rise to 30% in 1972, and then dropped slightly to 28.9% in 1975 (Department of Statistics 1983:176). In contrast, during the same period, loans and advances granted to manufacturing in Hong Kong accounted for a relative stable share of around 20% for most of the 1960s, but had begun to slide by the early 1970s, reaching 11.9% in 1975 (*Annual Digest of Statistics* various years). It is evident that "commercial banks in Singapore have become more aggressively involved in industrial financing" (Jao 1974:119). Perhaps as an indicator of the aggressiveness in financing industrialization, the ratio of loans to deposits of Singaporean banks also rose markedly during the 1960s and early 1970s, from 69.9% in 1960 to 82.8% in mid-1972. The growth of bank credit in Singapore was considerably higher than that of bank deposits during this period of high-speed industrial growth. In Hong Kong, on the other hand, the loan-deposit ratio did not exhibit a long-term trend of increase during the same period of time (Jao 1974:118).

During the entrepôt port period, commercial banks in Hong Kong, especially the large British banks, had followed the British-originated "real-bills doctrine," in which a bank "is supposed to make only short-term 'self-liquidating' loans to traders and to finance the holding of inventories during the period required for their sale" (Jao 1974:43). While the progress of industrialization had led to a departure from this principle when banks allocated a considerable portion of their credit to the industrial sector, it appeared that Hong Kong banks had modified rather than replaced the real-bills doctrine (Jao 1974). For example, although loans were granted to industrial firms, many of these were short-term loans actually used for financing the export of manufactured goods and the import of raw materials used in export production. So in the end, industrial financing was still trade-related.

Consequently, many industrial firms, especially the smaller ones, complained about the scarcity of finance and the inadequacy of support from the banks. Only larger firms with substantial collateral managed to solicit help from the banks; smaller firms were often denied financial assistance. As a study conducted in the early 1960s observed, "the degree of self-financing in Hong Kong industry is indeed abnormally high; a substantial number of firms rely exclusively on their own resources" (Economist Intelligence Unit 1962:16). The same study also pointed out that even for the larger firms, long-term capital investments were likely to be self-financed and most bank loans were directed to the financing of short-term working capital. Later studies also reveal the same pattern of the "institutional separation" of small scale manufacturing from the financial sector (for example, Sit et al. 1979).

In Singapore, on the other hand, we saw an increasing commitment of the banking sector to industrial growth. As in Hong Kong, many loans to the industrial sector were trade-related, but the much higher share of industrial loans suggest that some of them must have been of longer term and for the financing of plant and machinery. One reason for the difference can be traced to the divergent industrial structures in Hong Kong and Singapore. Singapore's manufacturing industries, as mentioned earlier, had more large scale enterprises and subsidiaries of MNCs. In the eyes of bankers, these firms must be more "credit-worthy" than the multitude of family-run, small cottage industries in Hong Kong (cf. Lau 1994).

The state also made a difference here. The state's more positive approach to industrial development certainly had a "demonstration effect" on the banking sector. In 1968, the government established the Development Bank of Singapore (DBS) as an industrial bank to provide long-term financing for the nascent industrial sector. As an official research report observes:

> However, some banks are now beginning to grant term loan of say up to five years to industries. This step may have been taken as a result of the establishment of the Development Bank of Singapore. The provision of term loans may lead to opportunities for the more lucrative short-term financing. Unless banks want to lose business to Development Bank of Singapore, which

also provides short-term loans, it may be to their interest to consider giving term loans to manufacturers. (Tan 1969:13)

During the early stage of Hong Kong's industrialization, manufacturers had also voiced their demands for the establishment of an industrial bank to alleviate the shortage of long-term financing. Throughout the 1950s, they pressed the government again and again, leading to the formation of the Industrial Bank Committee, composed of leading bankers and a colonial official, to deliberate on the issue of the financing need of the industrial sector and the need for an industrial bank. In the end, the committee recommended against the establishment of an industrial bank, concluding that "the need for an industrial bank for the finance of industry in Hong Kong is not proven" (Industrial Bank Committee 1960:15). In the 1960s, the industrialists tried again, and their efforts resulted in the establishment of a small-industry loan scheme. The scheme, however, suffered from a small capital base and the state imposed strict rules of eligibility to screen applicants. Consequently, very few small industrialists applied and the scheme was allowed to peter out gradually (Sutu et al. 1973).

Conclusion

A decade of rapid export-led growth affected both Singapore and Hong Kong tremendously. Given their high level of dependence on the Western markets, the recession there unavoidably reverberated in the two city-states. Exports plummeted, output levels fell, factories closed, and workers were retrenched. For the first time since their industrial takeoff, Singapore and Hong Kong faced a sharp decline in the growth of GDP. Nevertheless, by 1975, the pace of economic growth had begun to pick up again. The manufacturing sector in both economies experienced another phase of brisk expansion. Hence, there was no impetus for a major reorientation in the pattern of industrial development, at least not until the 1980s.

But when the 1970s came to a close, two distinctive systems of industrial production and their institutional concomitants were evident in Hong Kong and Singapore. Not only was the structure of industrial production in Singapore relatively more large-scale and balanced (with both heavy and light industries), the principal agent of industrialization was foreign, and not local capital. Hong Kong, on the other hand, built its industrial strength around thousands of locally-owned, small-scale enterprises producing low-end consumer products. While the Singaporean state played a major role in steering manufacturing industries towards a desirable form and direction, the Hong Kong state preferred to play a more indirect role in industrial development by letting the market determine the allocation of resources. While Singapore's unionized workers had their wages regulated by a tripartite body, the Hong Kong workers could only resort to individual actions in the quest for better conditions of employment, as the unions were numerically weak and organizationally fragmented. While the banks (state- and privately-owned) in Singapore played a more active role in financing industrial growth and investment, Hong Kong's small- and medium-sized industrial firms constantly complained against the inadequacy of support from the financial system.

Notes

1. For an overview of the development of Hong Kong's economy in the nineteenth century, see Endacott and Hinton (1968).

2. The collection of trade statistics had not begun until 1918.

3. It is important to remember that the majority of Singapore's Chinese population were laborers, not merchants.

4. The reasons behind this expropriation await further historical research. One motivation was perhaps the desire to correct for a genuine market failure. The military significance of the port of Singapore may be another factor.

5. But this is an impressive figure for a developing country. As a matter of fact, secondary sector employment in Singapore was almost half of that in Malaya — 66,800 compared with 135,700, despite the fact that the latter's total working population was 4.4 times that of Singapore's (Wheelwright 1965:210). There was considerable development in manufacturing both before and after the war, especially for those serving the domestic and the Malayan markets, such as foodstuffs and building materials. Between 1947 and 1957, employment in manufacturing actually increased in absolute terms by 30.4%.

6. Only 16% of Singapore's labor force was engaged in the manufacturing sector by 1957.

7. An Imperial Economic Conference was held in Ottawa in 1932, attended by the majority of the Commonwealth countries. It was decided in the conference that all manufactured goods using at least 50% of raw materials or labor from the Commonwealth were eligible for preferential tariff treatment within the United Kingdom and its overseas dominion (see Breen 1935).

8. See Turnbull (1969) for a review of the constitutional development of Singapore. Unless otherwise stated, the discussion in this paragraph is based upon the work of Turnbull.

9. The Act installed a ceremonial Head of State who formally appointed the Prime Minister, commanding the confidence of the majority of members in the new Singapore Parliament. The Prime Minister, in turn, formed a Cabinet consisting of ministers chosen from the Parliament. The Cabinet was modeled on the British system, in which it was responsible collectively to the Parliament. Under the new

constitution, all adult Singapore citizens were eligible to vote, and voting was later made compulsory.

10. The most helpful analysis of the embargo and its effects is still Szczepanik (1958).

11. The constitution for the newly independent Republic of Singapore, promulgated in 1967, followed closely the previous one. Legislative power was still kept in a 51-member Parliament. Members of Parliament were to be elected by compulsory voting by all adult citizens, and for a tenure of five years. Executive power was in the hands of a Prime Minister and the Cabinet.

12. In 1975, exports of goods and services (domestic exports plus re-exports) accounted for 63.4% of GDP in Hong Kong, and 146.8% in Singapore (Census and Statistics Department 1992; Department of Statistics 1983).

13. In the late 1960s, the exchange rate between US dollar and Singapore dollar was fixed at US$1=S$3.1.

14. Foreign-controlled firms refer to companies with more than half of their shares being owned by foreign investors.

15. While the foreign origin of Singapore's oil industry is unmistakable, the initial growth of the industry was more a result of fortuitous circumstances rather than a conscious product of government policies.

16. The following section on Hong Kong's "industrial policy" is adapted from Chiu (1992).

17. The following discussion of industrial relations in Singapore is based on Chew (1991).

18. By 1971, there were 73 banks with 431 offices in Hong Kong, as against 42 banks with 192 offices in Singapore.

3

Hong Kong:
Locked into Labor-intensive
Manufacturing

In Chapter 2 we discussed the common colonial and trading port legacies of Hong Kong and Singapore and how the two city-states have taken different paths of development since the 1960s. In this and the following chapters, we shall examine how the changing environment and the domestic institutional factors continued to shape the divergent paths of industrial development in Hong Kong and Singapore respectively. The case of Hong Kong is a continuation of labor-intensive production in the context of fierce competition from other NIEs in the region, rising production costs, and intensified protectionism from its export markets. Using the garment and electronics industries as illustrative cases, we shall illustrate how Hong Kong's industries cope with the pressures for industrial restructuring. The process of industrial restructuring in Hong Kong can hardly be described as a success. Being left on their own, small local capitals either show limited interest or are incapable of enhancing the technological sophistication of their production. By the late 1980s, it is quite clear that the major strategy is that of industrial relocation, particularly to the Pearl River Delta of southern China. Labor-intensive production survives, but is largely dependent on the opportunity of moving the production processes across the border.

Patterns of Industrial Development

The sectoral shift from entrepôt trade to manufacturing after the Korean War embargo was largely smooth and successful. From modest beginnings in the late 1940s, Hong Kong's manufacturing sector grew rapidly and, by 1961, it accounted for 24.7% of GDP and 43% of total employment (see Table 2.2; Census and Statistics Department 1982:138). In 1971, manufacturing employed 47.0% of all economically active persons and contributed to 28.2% of GDP. In this process of industrial growth, garment-making developed rapidly in the 1950s and since the early 1960s has overtaken the textile industry as the leading industry. Table 3.1 gives a summary of the development of Hong Kong's manufacturing industries in the postwar decades (1961-1991) in terms of their contributions to employment. The garment-making industry reached its height in the mid-1970s, employing about 38% of the manufacturing workforce (Lui and Chiu 1994:54). It continued to grow until 1986, when there was a drop in its employment.

The second largest manufacturing industry in Hong Kong is electronics. Compared with garment-making and textiles, the electronics industry is a late starter — it began in the late 1950s, and it was only in the 1970s that it experienced rapid growth. Between 1975 and 1985, it grew rapidly, with an average annual growth of 10.3% in the number of establishments (Industry Department 1990:48). Once started, the electronics industry developed rapidly, and by the late 1970s it had secured a dominant place in the manufacturing sector next to garment-making. However, like garment-making, its employment began to fall in the late 1980s, declining from 109,677 persons in 1988 to 99,455 persons in 1989. Reflecting the general trend of deindustrialization in Hong Kong, the electronics industry also experienced a halt in growth.

The rapid growth of the manufacturing sector in the 1960s and 1970s was facilitated by heavy government involvement in infrastructural construction. In particular, the active role of the government in urban development and mass public housing was of great significance in supporting the manufacturing strategy of labor-intensive, low-wage production (Castells, Goh and Kwok 1990). Concomitant with the process of industrial development, new towns were rapidly developed (Wigglesworth 1971; Leung 1986; Bristow 1984). The early satellite towns such as Tsuen Wan and Kwun Tong were the primary locations of manufacturing in the 1960s. The subsequent development of Tuen Mun, Shatin, and Tai Po had also served the purpose of finding new space for local industries. It should be noted that the mass public housing program is an important component of the government's new town development strategy. New town residents are an important source of labor for industry moving to the new towns. Furthermore, public housing functions as a form of subsidy to the working class families facilitating the reproduction of labor power

TABLE 3.1   Employment Share of Dominant Industries in Hong Kong,
1960-1990

Dominant Industry	1960	1970	1980	1990
Textiles	54,759	77,057	88,812	68,638
(%)	(24.4)	(14.0)	(10.0)	(9.4)
Clothing	51,918	158,025	275,818	251,746
(%)	(23.8)	(28.8)	(30.9)	(34.5)
Electronics [a]	183	38,454	93,005	85,169
(%)	(0.1)	(7.0)	(10.4)	(11.7)
Plastics [b]	18,131	70,958	86,314	53,137
(%)	(8.3)	(12.9)	(9.7)	(7.3)
Metal products	18,515	35,565	62,751	41,780
(%)	(8.5)	(6.5)	(7.0)	(5.7)
Printing	8,784	18,397	26,449	37,487
(%)	(4.0)	(3.3)	(3.0)	(5.1)
Toy [bc]	7,430	39,473	55,644	24,734
(%)	(3.3)	(7.2)	(6.2)	(3.4)
Watches and clocks	2,433	9,773	49,454	27,154
(%)	(1.1)	(1.8)	(5.5)	(3.7)

[a]   Figures for the electronics industry before 1986 do not include "Electronic watches and clocks" which were then grouped under the watches and clocks industry and could not be separately classified. "Electronic watches and clocks" are included under both industries from 1986 onward.

[b]   Figures for the plastics and the toy industries both include "Plastic toys and dolls."

[c]   Figures for the toy industry before 1986 do not include "Electronic toys" which were then grouped under the electronics industry and could not be separately classified. "Electronic toys" are included under both industries from 1986 onward.

Source: Industry Department (1994:31).

(Castells, Goh and Kwok 1990; Schiffer 1991), the development of new towns also makes labor-intensive production viable.

However, Hong Kong's manufacturers began to feel the pressures from the competition of other NIEs and protectionism of export markets in the 1970s. Such pressures moved the Governor to note the "urgency to the long term desirability of broadening our industrial base" (The Advisory

Committee on Diversification 1979:1) and in 1977 to appoint an advisory committee to look into the matter. The committee was asked to advise "whether the process of diversification of the economy, with particular reference to the manufacturing sector, can be facilitated by the modification of existing policies or the introduction of new policies" (The Advisory Committee on Diversification 1979:2). When the *Report of the Advisory Committee on Diversification* was finally published in late 1979, it "was out of date as soon as it was published because of the new role for Hong Kong as a result of China's opening up in 1977" (Chen and Li 1991:41). Firstly, China's open-door policy had brought about a revival of entrepôt trade. Secondly, the suggestions proposed by the committee were made redundant by the influx of migrants from China. The arrival of legal and illegal migrants from China since the mid-1970s had again, like previous waves of migration from the other side of the border, brought Hong Kong a new pool of low-wage labor for manufacturing production (Greenwood 1990; Skeldon 1986). Census statistics suggest that in the period 1976-1981, 58% of the population growth was composed of net immigration. With regard to the composition of this incoming population, there was a predominance of males (60.7%), and a large proportion of the immigrants in the age-group "5-34" (59.9%) (Census and Statistics Department 1982a:76). It is also noted that "[t]he unemployment rate of 3.4% for immigrants is significantly lower than the 4.0% recorded for the local population possibly because immigrants were more willing than local workers to take up jobs requiring lower levels of skill" (Census and Statistics Department 1982a:77). A large proportion of the economically active immigrants (73.9%) found their way to the local labor market as production operators.

What we find pertinent here is not only the fact that the arrival of immigrants has brought about an increase in the labor supply to Hong Kong's industries, but also that it has the unintended effect of perpetuating labor-intensive industries. The consequence is, as cogently put by Greenwood, that "the growth of Hong Kong's GDP in the 1960s and 1970s was made up, in significant degree, by the 'horizontal' expansion of the labor force, i.e. the arrival of large numbers of relatively unskilled workers, rather than by the 'vertical' upgrading of skills of resident employers and employees" (1990:21). Given the "timely" arrival of immigrants from China, local manufacturers quickly responded by turning to this fresh supply of cheap labor instead of taking up the more expensive option of restructuring the production processes. Also, with the re-emergence of entrepôt trade facilitated by the economic reforms in China and a change of business climate, public attention shifted to other concerns. The call for economic diversification gradually disappeared from the agenda of public discussion.

Triggers of Industrial Restructuring

As a consequence of the failure to achieve industrial upgrading in the 1970s, Hong Kong's manufacturing industries in the 1980s remained labor-intensive in character. Total value-added as a percentage of gross output of the manufacturing sector in 1981 was 26.4% and stayed at 26.3% in 1988, a figure far lower than the percentages of other major economic sectors (Industry Department 1991:21). In 1990, the percentage increased only slightly to 28.6% (Census and Statistics Department 1992:4). Moreover, compensation to employees in the manufacturing sector constituted 60.2% and 59.1% of value-added of manufacturing industries in 1981 and 1990 respectively (Industry Department 1991:21; Census and Statistics Department 1992:4). These statistics clearly show that local manufacturers continue to produce at low profit margins, leading to comments that there is a need for them to develop higher value-added products and processes.

It is in the context of the perpetuation of labor-intensive production that we can understand why rising production cost is a serious problem to local manufacturers. First, and most important, labor cost increased in both real and nominal terms in the 1980s. With regard to the nominal wage of "craftsmen and other operatives" in manufacturing, the figures were HK$73 and HK$163 for the years 1982 and 1989 respectively. In real terms, it was an increase from HK$73 in 1982 to HK$98 in 1989. Such an increase in wage level poses serious problems for Hong Kong's manufacturers because it makes it difficult to compete with producers from other NIEs on the grounds of low labor cost. In a study of Hong Kong's clothing industry (Kurt Salmon Associates 1992:A103), it has been found that in terms of labor cost in garment production, Hong Kong is the third highest among the major Asian producers. This problem of rising cost is especially pertinent in Hong Kong's case as its manufacturing industries fail to advanced to more capital-intensive production.

Second, the rising wage rate is only one among many issues related to organizing labor for production. Equally pertinent is the question of labor shortage (Ho et al. 1991; Joint Associations Working Group 1989; Ng et al. 1989). The problems here are twofold. In the first place, there are long-term causes behind the current shortage of labor, the most important being the trend of decline in population growth. But more interestingly, there is a vicious cycle in the failing attempt to restructure the manufacturing sector. Manufacturers are eager to keep wages low to maintain their competitiveness, and whenever possible, they will move their production to South China where there are abundant supplies of low-wage labor. These practices tend to discourage young workers from joining the manufacturing sector and this, in turn, creates further problems for labor recruitment (on problems related to the recruitment of women workers in manufacturing, see Ng et al. 1987:70-72).

Another critical factor contributing to the rising production cost is the "soaring" property market. Between 1981 and 1990, rentals for private flatted factories (those in high-rise buildings) had more than doubled and their prices had also increased by a remarkable 66.6% (Rating and Valuation Department 1991:15 and Table 44). The high costs of factory premises are obviously unfavorable for industrial development, especially for those industries competing in cost-sensitive, cut-throat conditions.

The rising cost of production constitutes the key factor that triggered the process of industrial restructuring since the mid-1980s. Of course, the problems of increased labor costs, labor shortage, and the rapidly increasing costs for factory premises are not new. Ever since the mid-1960s, local manufacturers have been calling attention to these issues (England 1989:60). However, problems related to labor supply and rising wage rates have repeatedly been alleviated by the inflows of legal and illegal migrants from China (Greenwood 1990; Skeldon 1986). As noted earlier, the fresh supply of cheap labor has the effect of delaying the need for taking positive action to cope with rising costs and increasing protectionism. However, with the cancellation of the "touch-base" policy in 1980 (Ho et al. 1991:10), illegal immigration was brought under control and local manufacturers were no longer able to rely on recent migrants as a source of low-wage labor.

The rising cost of labor and labor shortage have brought the Hong Kong government under tremendous pressure to consider seriously the call to import labor. In May 1989, the government introduced a scheme for importing guest workers. Then, in May 1990, the government took a step further and announced a new scheme of labor importation. However, as we shall see in subsequent discussion, the massive relocation of manufacturing industries to China in the late 1980s has eventually directed local manufacturers' attention away from the issue of importing guest workers. Compared with the abundant supply of cheap labor across the border, the option of labor importation has lost its attraction.

Industry Adjustments in the 1980s

It is interesting to observe that the garment and electronics industries managed to not only survive, but also do reasonably well in the face of rising production costs. The garment industry experienced a steady

TABLE 3.2   Industry Response to Economic Restructuring in Hong Kong,
1980-1991

Indicator	1980	1985	1987	1989	1991
Garment					
Establishments	9,499	10,307	10,556	9,672	8,837
Persons employed	275,818	292,789	298,377	274,732	224,925
Employment share (%)	30.9	34.5	34.1	34.2	34.4
Output (HK$ million)	27,425	46,891	73,910	81,652	85,095
Output share (%)	25.4	26.5	26.1	25.1	26.2
Electronics					
Establishments	1,316	1,304	1,949	2,009	1,815
Persons employed	93,005	86,115	106,835	99,455	71,466
Employment share (%)	10.4	10.1	12.2	12.4	10.9
Output (HK$ million)	17,209	30,462	54,376	61,208	55,487
Output share (%)	16.0	17.2	19.2	18.8	17.1

Source: Industry Department (1994:31, 33, 51, 68).

growth of gross output and throughout the 1980s contributed about one quarter of the output of all manufacturing industries (see Table 3.2). However, when we turn to look at the number of establishments and number of persons employed, the former started to drop in 1987 and the latter in 1986. These reflect the impact of plant relocation to China on the development of the industry.

With regard to the electronics industry, there had been a steady increase in gross output until 1988. Since then, the gross output of the industry had dropped both in absolute terms and in its contribution to the total output of the manufacturing sector. In terms of its contribution to employment, the number of workers started to fall in 1988-89. And the number of establishments in the industry had also experienced a fall in absolute terms since 1989. Again, these show the trend of going offshore, with a significant share of the production being carried out in relocated plants in China and other Asian countries.

The two industries continue to fare reasonably well in spite of rising production costs. The strength of the garment industry lies in its ability of being in touch with the ever changing fashion market. The fact that Hong Kong's garment industry has its origins in strong commercial ties is an advantage (Chu 1988), as it shapes the manufacturers' sensitivity to the needs of foreign markets, especially at the retail level. As a result of economic restructuring in advanced industrial societies, production has been increasingly conditioned by the needs of the retail market (Harvey 1989; Murray 1989). This is especially true for fashion and garments (Ward 1991). In this new world of consumption, an ability to handle such a volatile market is the basic requirement for success. Moreover, Hong Kong is still a very attractive platform in the region for international garment sourcing (Birnbaum 1993). Hong Kong's garment manufacturers can capitalize on such commercial linkages to secure orders from abroad.

To match the need to respond quickly to changes in the consumption sphere, Hong Kong's garment manufacturers have to be able to produce on time and to fit in with the fluctuating schedule of a volatile market. A study of garment manufacturing in Hong Kong in the mid-1980s (Kurt Salmon Associates 1987:143) showed that the time between a customer order being placed and the goods being ready for shipment was 14 days for small firms and 30 days for large firms. Typical lead times for knitwear production were 17.5 days for small firms and 35 days for large firms. On the whole, the manufacturers were internationally competitive in terms of manufacturing lead times, both in "cut and sew" and in knitwear (Kurt Salmon Associates 1987:144). In short, the continuing development of garment-making in Hong Kong depends on the strength of its commercial networks in international subcontracting and its flexibility in production. However, as noted earlier, with the opening of China and the availability of cheap labor across the border, plant relocation has also become a viable strategy for garment manufacturers. We shall come back to the issue of relocation in a later section.

With regard to the electronics industry, its strength lies mainly in its responsiveness and adaptability to changes in world demands. It is noted that Hong Kong's electronics production is:

> ... well known for its great adaptability and quick response to changes in external demand, which enables it to move rapidly into the production of many fashion products invented elsewhere. Typical examples were:
>
> | 1975 | calculators, watches, and clocks |
> |------|-----------------------------------|
> | 1977 | CB radios, walkie-talkies |
> | 1978-80 | hand-held and TV games |
> | early 1980s | telephones |
> | 1986-mid 1987 | talking and talk-back toys |
> | At present | fax machines and memory goods |
>
> Many of these products require purpose-built (or "dedicated") chips which have to be imported. The industry's strength is mainly its speed of investment and assembly. (Industry Department 1990:51)

That is, Hong Kong's electronics manufacturers survive by moving quickly from one fashion product to another, rather than relying on a strategy of enhancing the technological sophistication of their production. By importing purpose-built parts and components and concentrating on assembly, local manufacturers are able to respond swiftly to changes in product markets. The production of fashion electronics products shows that Hong Kong manufacturers can continue to find niches in the world market without the need for research and development to create technologically sophisticated products. They catch up with the current development of parts and components by acquiring them in the market instead of internalizing such production processes. Most producers can complete product designs in less than 12 months and can produce in less than 6 months from the time of order confirmation to shipment (Dataquest 1991:Appendix IV, 15). For survival, they are more reliant on market intelligence than on advances in core technological development. Local manufacturers are good at playing the role of subcontractors for the international market. But this is also to say that little has been done to go beyond the status of being international subcontractors. The constraints of electronics production lie in the structure of the industry:

> Apart from a few exceptions in the production of transfers, switches, and transistors, Hong Kong does not have a significant process industry for the manufacturing of electronic parts and components from raw or semi-finished materials.... The lack of precision metal working capability also restricts Hong Kong's entry into many value-added products such as micro-cassettes, disk drives and printers, which require precision mechanical parts and processing.... Hong Kong, while largely successful in competing in the international market as a subcontractor for many electronic consumer products, lacks well-developed supporting industries and a substantial re-search and development capability. This makes it difficult for the industry to diversify into other areas of knowledge-intensive and potentially high value-added production. (Industry Department 1989:48)

Given the fact that electronics production has made little progress in technological upgrading, local manufacturers are quick to capitalize on the abundant supply of low-wage labor in China. According to the study by Dataquest (1991:Appendix IV, 28), 67% of the 116 companies interviewed have production in China for the assembly of semi-finished products, finished products, and parts and components. Production cost and labor shortage are their major concerns when deciding to relocate (Dataquest 1991:Appendix IV, 28).

> The main reasons for their establishment of plants and the subcontracting of work in PRC were to solve the labor shortage problem in Hong Kong and to

lower the cost of production by making use of the cheap labour and the cheap and abundant supply of land in PRC.... They expressed that it was the only means for the electronics manufacturers to survive. In order to stay cost competitive, they have to move to PRC.

Environment and Firms' Strategy

In the above sections, we have briefly reviewed the historical development of Hong Kong's manufacturing, or more precisely the garment and electronics industries, from the 1960s to the late 1980s. Here in this section, we take the analysis a step further. As we have noted in Chapter 1 that our discussion of firms' strategy is based upon a matching survey of industrial establishments in Hong Kong and Singapore. The Hong Kong survey was carried out in 1992 and its findings of garment-making and electronics establishments allow us to dwell upon the strategy of restructuring at the firm level.[1]

Table 3.3 gives a brief description of the characteristics of our surveyed garment-making and electronics establishments. It is not surprising in terms of ownership of capital, reliance on exports, and the connection with international and local subcontracting, our samples are to be found consistent with the general depiction of Hong Kong's manufacturing in the existing literature (see Chen and Li 1991; Chu 1988; Ho 1992; Lui and

TABLE 3.3   Structure of Ownership and Source of Order by Type of Industry in Hong Kong (in percentage)

Characteristic	Industry	
	Garment	Electronics
Locally owned	94.2	82.0
Owner managed	92.8	74.0
Production for export: 50% or more	57.8	62.0
Order from overseas directly: 50% or more	10.4	42.0
Order from local import and export houses: 50% or more	47.9	28.0
Order from local factories: 50% or more	23.3	24.0
Order from own overseas outlets	2.8	8.0

Source: East-West Center Survey on Enterprise Strategy.

Chiu 1993, 1994; Sit and Wong 1989). That is, Hong Kong's manufacturing is connected to the global economy primarily through the international network of commercial subcontracting. Local manufacturing establishments are predominantly small, local capital. Moreover, these small establishments are export-oriented and rely heavily on the international and local subcontracting networks for survival. They receive their orders mainly from overseas buyers, local import and export houses, and local larger industrial establishments. In short, they are mainly OEM producers and subcontractors for international sourcing agents and local factories.

Perhaps two points are worth further elaboration. First, compared with garment-making, electronics establishments have a higher percentage of foreign ownership (also see Lui and Chiu 1994). Indeed, electronics is the local industry which has attracted a larger share of FDIs (82 out of the total of 472 overseas companies investing in Hong Kong's manufacturing in 1992, see Industry Department 1993). Second, garment-making is relatively more reliant on import and export houses as a source of order and receives less orders directly from overseas than the electronics industry. It is quite clear that both garment-making and electronics obtain their orders through the subcontracting network. Only a small fraction of our subsamples (8% and 2.8% of electronics and garment-making respectively) have their own outlets overseas. In short, in Hong Kong we are looking at how small, local manufacturing establishments cope with industrial restructuring in a changing business environment. Their limited resources and subordinate position in the subcontracting network are pertinent to our understanding of their restructuring strategies.

Technology Strategies

Compared with the electronics industry, garment-making is less likely to go after technological sophistication (see Table 3.4). Only slightly more than one-fifth (22.4%) of the garment-making establishments report they have applied new technology in their organization of work. Among those establishments which have introduced new technology, actually about one-tenth (11.8%) of the cases involve office automation. None of the respondents indicate that new technology has been applied to the process of quality control. Moreover, though most of the efforts of applying new technology are found in the areas of production and design (88.2%), as we shall see in the following discussion, the level of technological sophistication should not be overstated.

That garment-making has made limited effort in technological upgrading is perhaps no surprise. First, the industry itself has made little progress in applying new technology to the assembly process (Mody and Wheeler 1990:38). Most of the technologically sophisticated and automated

TABLE 3.4   Application of New Technology by Type of Industry
              in Hong Kong (in percentage)

The Use of New Technology	Industry	
	Garment	Electronics
Introduction of new technology	22.4	52.2
Type of new technology used [a]		
Production technology	70.6	76.0
Design technology	17.6	16.0
Office technology	11.8	0.0
Quality control	0.0	8.0

[a] Answers of those establishments which had applied new technology.

Source: East-West Center Survey on Enterprise Strategy.

processes (such as computer-aided design linked to marking and cutting) are found in the pre-assembly and post-assembly stages of production. In terms of computerization and automation, Hong Kong is no exception. Computer-aided pattern grading and marker making are commonplace. But "only limited automation of sewing operations has so far taken place" (Industry Department 1992a:39). Second, the application of linked automation to garment-making processes has the difficulty of matching the needs of volatile markets. In a case reported in the *Report on Industrial Automation Study* (Industry Department 1992b:19), the garment manufacturer has an integrated computerized system of pattern grading, marker planning and cutting. However, in order to realize the advantage of the automated system, the production has to be based on large batch orders and fabric-cutting has to avoid any pattern matching. Those producing fashion garments and working for small batch orders will not find such automation attractive (also see Bailey 1993:38-39). Third, very often the restructuring of garment production involves shopfloor reorganization rather than technological sophistication. For instance, the so-called modular production system, that is the formation of self-contained work units of 5 to 20 persons for the assembly of an entire garment, is essentially a new form of workplace organization which helps reduce in-process inventories, improve productivity by "between 10% and 40%," and reduce "throughput time to one or two days" (Industry Department 1992a:39; also see Bailey 1993:41-42). The modular production system has little to do with new technology. In brief, technological upgrading is not an important strategy for the restructuring of garment-making. And this is especially so to most Hong Kong garment producers because they are primarily small manufacturers producing for volatile markets of fashion garments in small batch orders.

Relatively speaking, the electronics industry is more likely to apply new technology than garment-making. About half (52.2%) of the interviewed electronics establishments suggest that they have used new technology. While, like the garment-making establishments, new technology is mainly applied to the areas of design and production, 8.0% of the respondents mention the application to quality control. Such stronger tendency for electronics manufacturers to apply new technology has to do with the characteristics of the industry itself. Rapid development of new products and the concomitant changes in production methods have pushed electronics manufacturers to follow, though not necessarily very closely, automation and new production processes developed in the industry. Indeed, in the *Report on Industrial Automation Study* (Industry Department 1992b:37), it was observed that:

> In the area of hard automation, the level of automation of the Hong Kong electronics industry lags slightly below the optimum. This observation is not based on what types of equipment are in use in Hong Kong, but on how this equipment is installed in local factories. Take for examples automatic component insertion machines and SMT placement machines. In the 1970s and early 1980s, through hole insertion equipment was installed by most manufacturers to reduce labour costs, improve quality, and eliminate operative error.... [A]s these ubiquitous machines become even more common, they are quickly becoming a "standard operative procedure" type of equipment demanded by customers of Hong Kong's contract assemblers (also known as OEM manufacturers). This is not merely the case where Hong Kong, because of the fragmented nature of its industry, is not in a position to try out new technology. For SMT placement machines, the adoption of which is driven by product technology and packaging technology rather than immediate direct labour savings, the situation is rather similar. On the whole, *the industry only invests in hard automation equipment if forced to by their buyers, instead of continually seeking out opportunities to add extra value for, and hence extra value from, their customers.* [original emphases]

For those establishments having introduced new technology, 48.0% of them apply imported technology, 28.0% use local-developed technology, and 12.0% use new technology developed in-house. As for the most important reason for them to use new technology, 40.0% of the establishments mention "to increase output" and 32.0% "to improve product quality." However, none mention the production of new products as the reason for using new technology.

About half (46.0%) of the interviewed electronics establishments suggest that they have carried out research and development (R&D) activities. But one should not jump too quickly to the conclusion that Hong Kong's electronics industry is largely research-based. When the interviewed establishments are further asked to indicate the number of researchers and engineers engaged in such R&D activities, 73.9% employ no more than three professional R&D staff in their production plants. This is consistent with our earlier descriptions of the state of development of the electronics industry in Hong Kong. As OEM producers, the R&D activities carried out by local manufacturers were likely to be product modifications as required by their overseas buyers or for catching up with changing demands for fashion products. In a review of the electronics industry in the late 1980s (Dataquest 1991:Appendix IV,20), it was observed that:

> Most of the respondents were involved in electronic system designs and the design of mechanical parts. In most cases, the designs were worked out according to the product specifications and product cosmetics provided by the parent companies or the customers. Only half of the respondents performed product cosmetic designs for some of their products, and design of tooling and molds were not widely provided by the respondents.

That Hong Kong's electronics manufacturers are subcontractors in the global division of labor clearly has its effects on the level of technological sophistication of their production. Equally pertinent is the lack of a supporting industry for electronics production (Industry Department 1992b:37-38). We shall not dwell upon these questions here. The point is to note the limited extent of technological upgrading in Hong Kong's electronics manufacturing.

Location Strategy and Industrial Relocation

In the above section, we have observed that both garment-making and electronics production have done little in terms of technological upgrading. And as we have noted earlier, local manufacturing is still largely labor-intensive in character. Given such a state of development of the manufacturing industries together with the pressure of rising production costs, local manufacturers find it increasingly difficult to run their production in Hong Kong. The major coping strategy since the late 1980s is that of relocation, mainly to southern China (Federation of Hong Kong Industries 1990, 1992, 1993), and this brings about the decline in the absolute numbers of establishments as well as employees in the two industries. However, there are differences between garment-making and electronics under this general response of relocating production plants to China. Generally speaking, though both industries look upon China as their source of cheaper labor and land, the electronics industry is more reliant on relocation while garment-making has a stronger tie to the production base in Hong Kong.

Although the garment manufacturers are losing their cost advantage, garment production is still largely locally based. Our survey findings show that only 30.4% of our respondents have offshore production and 78.3% still have their factory production in Hong Kong. Other studies of offshore investments in China by Hong Kong manufacturers also reveal that the garment industry is one of the least likely overseas investors (see, for instance, Federation of Hong Kong Industries 1992; the figure for garment manufacturers investing in the Pearl River Delta was 26.2%, well below the average figure of 40.7%). There are two major reasons why garment manufacturing has a stronger tie to its Hong Kong production base. First, while larger firms with retail outlets in Hong Kong and other Asian cities can rely on their relocated plants for mass production (see, for example, Giordano Holdings Ltd. 1991), there are still many garment manufacturers producing for local or overseas niche markets. Their small batch production and the need of meeting frequent changes in fashion and style make it difficult to realize the advantages of an expansion in production scale associated with relocation. Second, the reason behind many garment manufacturers' decision of not going offshore has to do with quota restrictions and the product origin rules enforced in Hong Kong. For those products exported to restrained markets, "[a] special outward processing arrangement is administrated by the Hong Kong government Trade Department to ensure that goods manufactured in Hong Kong but partly processed in China only qualify for Hong Kong origin status if they fully meet Hong Kong's origin rules" (Industry Department 1990:40). As a result of such institutional restrictions, unless products produced are targeted at local consumption or unrestrained markets, garment manufacturers will retain at least some parts of their production in Hong Kong.

While many garment manufacturers still retain their ties to Hong Kong as a production base, the leading restructuring strategy of electronics production is relocation to China, particularly the Pearl River Delta region (Dataquest 1991:IV-28) (Figure 3.1). Among our surveyed electronics establishments, 52.0% of them carry out offshore production (see Table 3.5). For those manufacturers who have moved offshore, all of them have their plants relocated to the Guangdong Province. More interesting is that 38.0% of the survey establishments do not have any production in Hong

TABLE 3.5   Overseas Investment by Type of Industry in Hong Kong
             (in percentage)

Overseas Investment	Industry	
	Garment	Electronics
Overseas investment in last five years	30.4	52.0
Lower labor cost as the most important reason for going offshore	85.7	92.3
Offshore investment in Guangdong	81.0	100.0
"Still running own factory production in Hong Kong"	78.3	62.0

Source: East-West Center Survey on Enterprise Strategy.

Kong and simply have all the manufacturing activities done in their plants in China. The aforementioned study of industrial investments in the Pearl River Delta conducted by the Federation of Hong Kong Industries also confirms such a trend of relocation. About 69.4% of the electronics establishments covered by that study have investments in the region (Federation of Hong Kong Industries 1992:63). And it is suggested that:

> Such a significant extent of investment can be explained by the labour-inten-
> sive nature of the industry. In Hong Kong, electronics products are turned
> out through many component-assembling processes which are mostly done
> manually. Since full scale automation is still uncommon, a large number of
> workers, particularly young workers, are needed. Faced with a severe
> shortage of labour in Hong Kong, which is complicated by the reluctance of
> the younger generation to enter the industrial workforce, the electronics
> industry has a strong incentive to take advantage of the abundant supply of
> labour across the border. (Federation of Hong Kong Industries 1992:63)

The same study reports that the average size of the relocated establishments is employing 905 persons (Federation of Hong Kong Industries 1992:69). However, in terms of investment, electronics firms in the Pearl River Delta tend to concentrate in two clusters (Federation of Hong Kong Industries 1992:67). At the one end, there are small- and medium-sized firms with capital size of less than five million Hong Kong dollars (39.2%). And at the other, there are larger firms with a capital size of more than 20 million Hong Kong dollars (20.8%). These findings suggest that the strategy of going offshore is by no means confined to

FIGURE 3.1   Hong Kong and the Pearl River Delta Region

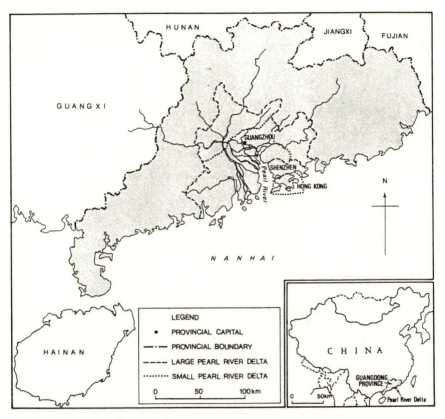

Source: Adapted from K. C. Ho and Alvin So. 1996. "Semi-periphery and Borderland Integration." *Political Geography* 15. Used by permission.

larger firms. Given the geographical proximity between Hong Kong and the Delta region, many small- and medium-sized firms can "make use of the abundant supply of labour there to reduce production cost" (Federation of Hong Kong Industries 1992:67).

Our survey findings also show that there is no significant association between the employment size of local establishments and that of offshore plants. In other words, there is no necessary connection that those running larger establishments in Hong Kong will have proportionately larger plants across the border. Although our survey data do not warrant us to go into a sophisticated statistical analysis of the strategic moves behind relocation, the answers solicited from our open-ended questions do allow us to discern, tentatively though, three possible strategic considerations in deciding relocation. First, it is the strategy of reducing assembly processes in Hong Kong, reorganizing the local plant into a R&D section, and sending the more labor-intensive processes to offshore plants. Among our respondents in the electronics industry, there is a significant association (χ^2=6.93570, df=1, p<.01) between investment overseas and conducting internal R&D. This suggests that manufacturers who have started offshore production are more likely to carry out R&D in their Hong Kong establishments. More sophisticated processes are retained in their Hong Kong premises while labor-intensive assembly is done in their relocated plants. However, it is important to note that only about one-third (34.0%) of our surveyed electronics manufacturers are estimated to have adopted this restructuring strategy. The extent to which local electronics manufacturers have adopted such a strategy should not be over-estimated. Indeed, in terms of technological sophistication, Hong Kong's electronics industry falls behind its East Asian competitors. Also, as noted earlier, most of the electronics manufacturers are OEM producers. They work on imported electronic components and their R&D activities are more related to product modification than core technology development.

The second strategy is similar to the above except that the concerned establishments concentrate on trading instead of R&D. In our survey of electronics establishments, 38.0% of the sampled establishments do not have their own factory production in Hong Kong. And among these establishments, 50.0% of them rely solely on their offshore plants for production, one-third carry out the production through relocated plants and subcontracting out to local or offshore factories, and the rest have all their production finished by subcontractors. While some of these establishments have retained the product development process in their local plants, many have changed into trading firms. In some cases, they assume the role of sourcing agent for MNCs. Given their business contacts with local subcontractors and manufacturers based in China, they can perform the function of commercial agents in facilitating international subcontracting.

Last, but not least, is the strategy of expanding production capacity by relocation. This is a strategy adopted by many medium-sized firms which see the advantages of the abundant supplies of cheap labor and land across the border and try to profit by expanding the scale of production rather than moving towards technological sophistication (Dataquest 1991:IV-61). For the electronics industry as a whole, this strategy has the danger of hindering the upgrading of production technology and will thus reduce the competitiveness of the industry in the long-run. However, for individual manufacturers, this strategy allows them to hold on to labor-intensive production and make lucrative profits by a significant increase in sales volume.

In brief, the relocation of electronics production is in full swing. And this, in turn, has its impact on the organization of production in the Hong Kong plants.

Labor Utilization Strategies

Differences at the level of industry between garment-making and electronics are also observed in matters related to labor utilization strategies. Table 3.6 gives a summary of the use of various labor utilization strategies. It is observed that, compared with those in electronics production, the garment-making establishments are more likely to use informal work practices and flexible workforce to maintain their survival in a competitive business environment. This, as we have seen in the above section, is related to the overall production strategies of the two industries.

Indeed, given the attractiveness and viability of relocation, it is not difficult to understand why various forms of informal work (like capacity subcontracting and outworking) are unpopular with local electronics manufacturers. If they are looking for production strategies to reduce costs and enhance flexibility, they turn to setting up their own plants in the Pearl River Delta or finding subcontractors across the border. A Hong

TABLE 3.6   Production Strategies by Type of Industry in Hong Kong (in percentage)

Production Strategy	Industry	
	Garment	Electronics
Organization of production		
Capacity subcontracting	46.4	22.0
Internal contracting	43.5	0.0
Outworking	47.8	10.0
Employment of flexible workforce		
Part-time workers	17.4	22.0
Temporary workers	40.6	26.0
Foreign workers	2.9	2.0

Source: East-West Center Survey on Enterprise Strategy.

Kong-based production strategy is losing its attractiveness. It is also in the light of this trend of relocation that we can understand why the employment of foreign workers as a source of flexible labor force is of little significance. Only 2.0% of the electronics establishments have employed imported labor. Their main sources of flexible workforce come from temporary and part-time workers.

Unlike the electronics industry, garment-making is still strongly tied to Hong Kong. Given the institutional restrictions on relocation and the structural constraints on technological upgrading, garment manufacturers find themselves increasingly locked into a system of flexible production for volatile export markets. Manufacturers who possess the required quota, who can obtain adequate orders for mass production, and who are capable of developing retail outlets in the domestic and East Asian markets, are the ones able to turn to offshore production or adopt full-scale automation to enhance their competitiveness in large-scale production. However, these are the exceptions and most local manufacturers have to make every effort to increase their production flexibility in order to keep pace with rapid changes in styles and tastes in fashion and garment retailing. This explains why the interviewed garment manufacturers use various forms of informal work quite extensively. Almost half (46.4%) of the surveyed establishments use subcontracting to enhance their quantitative flexibility, i.e., their capacity of expanding and reducing the production capacity in accordance with changes in demands. Among those who use subcontractors, 54.5% subcontract parts of their production process and 45.5% use subcontractors to handle both parts and the entire process of production. Another 43.5% of them employ internal contractors to work on cutting, pattern marking, and buttoning. Outworkers are also employed (47.8%) to handle various jobs in the assembly process.

In terms of the use of flexible workforce, the surveyed garment manufacturers tend to rely on temporary workers (40.6% have employed such workers) and part-time workers (17.4%), rather than employ foreign workers (only 2.9% did so). Given the fact that the garment-making labor process is fragmentable and women outworkers with working experience in clothing are available (see Lui 1994), garment manufacturers can rely on such domestic flexible workers rather than importing labor. However, that said, when the garment manufacturers were asked of their need of labor importation, 32.3% of them express interest. This clearly shows, given the institutional restrictions on relocation, garment manufacturers' need for enhancing production flexibility in order to survive in an increasingly competitive business environment.

Re-formation of the Industrial Structure

The impacts of relocation on the two industries are many. What interests us are the effects of industrial relocation on employment in the manufacturing sector. Earlier we have noted that the average employment size per manufacturing establishment decreased from 20 persons in 1980 to 13 persons in 1993 (Industry Department 1994:24). Such downsizing in employment reflects an absolute decrease in the number of persons employed in manufacturing. And in this process of labor market restructuring, it is interesting to observe that, despite a reduction of the employment of production operatives (a decrease of 43% between 1981 and 1991), most manufacturing industries have experienced an increase in their employment of non-operative employees (a growth of 11% in the period 1981-1991 for the manufacturing sector) (Census and Statistics Department 1993c:119). These non-operative employees are engaged in "supporting services such as sourcing of raw materials, product design, production management and engineering, marketing, and so on" (Census and Statistics Department 1993c:120). Such a change in employment mix shows the general trend of production reorganization in the face of changes in the business environment. Particularly, "[f]or industries where outward processing activities are prominent, this also reflects the increasing role of local industries of providing technical support to the production processes relocated to China" (Census and Statistics Department 1993c:120).

A clearer picture of the impact of industrial restructuring on manufacturing employment can be deduced from the changes in the workforce composition of the garment and electronics industries. Table 3.7 summarizes the shifts in the occupational structure of garment-making, electronics, and the entire manufacturing sector. It is evident that there has been a drastic reduction of the proportion of production and related workers in the composition of the manufacturing workforce. In 1981, 82.3% of the manufacturing workforce were engaged in production and related activities. In 1991, the figure fell to 68.2%. In the period 1981-1991, white-collar employees (broadly defined) have increased significantly. In 1991, 30% of the persons engaged in manufacturing belonged to professional, technical, managerial, administrative, and clerical occupations.

These patterns can also be observed in garment and electronics. With regard to the industry of wearing apparel (except footwear), the percentage of production and related workers fell from 85.0% in 1981 to 72.0% in 1991. Compared with the relevant statistics of the manufacturing sector (68.2% of the workforce in 1991 belonged to production and related activities), the garment industry still shows its tenacity in maintaining the

TABLE 3.7   Occupational Structure by Type of Industry in Hong Kong, 1981-1991 (in percentage)

Industry	PTAMW [a]	Clerical	Production and Related	Others
Wearing apparel				
1981	1.9	4.8	85.0	8.3
1986	2.7	6.6	83.1	7.6
1991	7.9	15.9	72.0	4.2
Machinery and electronics				
1981	5.8	7.7	81.5	5.0
1986	9.6	9.8	76.0	4.6
1991	22.2	21.7	50.4	5.6
Manufacturing				
1981	3.8	5.8	82.3	8.1
1986	5.5	8.0	79.8	6.7
1991	11.4	18.6	68.2	1.9

[a]   PTAMW = Professional, technical, administrative, and managerial workers.

Sources: Census and Statistics Department (1982b:78-79, 1988:58-59); unpublished 1991 Census data.

production base in Hong Kong. The trend of gradually reducing garment production (and the associated decline in the number of production workers) in Hong Kong continues, although at a slower pace compared with other industries.

Unlike garment-making, electronics manufacturing has undergone a drastic drop in the number of production workers (as a percentage of the entire workforce, it fell from 81.5% in 1981 to 50.4% in 1991). Part of the reason behind the restructuring of the workforce composition lies in the modest advancements in product design and technological sophistication of electronics production itself. Successful attempts have been made by local electronics manufacturers to enhance the marketability and competitiveness of their products. One example is the move towards product design (*Hong Kong Business Annual* 1993:58-59). With an emphasis on designs for emerging lifestyle, Eric Beare Associates produces executive toys, corporate presents (from pen sets, calculators to desktop accessories), and the so-called lifestyle products. Another strategy adopted by some local electronics manufacturers is to produce new, sophisticated, and high-end products for selected market niches. ABC Computer Company launched its home-grown subnotebook computer, targeted at the growing international market niche of portable computers. Recognizing the limitations of a small company, the strategy of ABC Computer is to "get and maintain a competitive advantage by being the first in the market" (Ward 1993:42-44).

However, and more importantly, the restructuring of the workforce composition is related to the resultant reorganization of production after relocation. As a result of developing offshore production in China, electronics manufacturers are able to expand production by utilizing the new supply of low-wage labor. The possibility of relocating parts or the entire production process to China provides local manufacturers with new options in organizing their business. We have discussed different strategies of production in connection to relocation in the above section and shall not repeat the points here. The increase in shares of professional, technical, administrative and managerial staff, and clerical workers (from 13.5% in 1981 to 43.9% in 1991) in the industry reflects the changing character of electronics production in Hong Kong. Production in Hong Kong and China are increasingly interconnected. This reinforces the current development of manufacturing fashionable goods and of staying at the relatively labor-intensive end of electronics production. But as a result of industrial relocation, Hong Kong becomes more of a strategic station for maintaining the business ties with the world market than as a production base for electronics. A growing proportion of its workforce is engaged in technical, administrative, and clerical duties supporting the production which has already gone offshore.

Although the garment industry has a stronger tendency (or, to put it differently, more restricted by existing regulations concerning product origins) of maintaining its production in Hong Kong, the trend of moving production processes to China, gradually in this case, inevitably means new arrangements in division of labor within the industry. For example, Yangtzekiang Garment Manufacturing Company Ltd. employed 1,500-2,000 workers in the 1980s.[2] By 1989-90 the employment figure fell to just above 1,000 workers. Contraction continued after 1990 and retrenchment was carried out in four stages. As of 1994, it employed only 50 production workers in the sample room. Among the 160 employees in its office, 80 were merchandisers and more than ten materials sourcing agents. Essentially the local office of the company was transformed into a garment trading firm distributing brand names such as Michele Rene, Pierre Cardin, Valentino, and Daniel Hechter. The company has long gone offshore, with investments in Sri Lanka, Burma, Malaysia, mainland China, and Macau. In addition to servicing customers around the world, it also serves as a buying office for Yangtzekiang Garment Manufacturing International Ltd. The Hong Kong office is now sourcing from countries like China, Indonesia, Mauritius, Poland, and Bangladesh. Another strategy practiced by local garment manufacturers is to move beyond manufacturing. That is, they work at three different levels: "manufacturing, wholesale and retail" (Keenan 1995:46). One notable example of local garment manufacturers moving towards high-end fashion retailing is Toppy International. Since its opening in 1986, the Episode line has "grown to more than 100 outlets in 16 countries" (Keenan 1995:46). And Toppy, spawned from the Fang Brothers knitting and textile group, also markets other brand names like Excursion, Jessica, and Colour Eighteen with varying styles for different segments of women's fashion market.

There is, then, the transformation of Hong Kong from a manufacturing base into more of a commercially oriented business networking center (also see Census and Statistics Department 1995). The findings of a survey of manufacturers and traders carried out by the Hong Kong Trade Development Council in 1991 largely confirm this view. When the respondents were asked of their future operations in Hong Kong, 83% mentioned "controlling headquarters," 81% "documentation," 73% "business negotiation," and 72% "trade financing" (1991:13). The Hong Kong Trade Development Council (1991:12) highlighted that:

> Apparently, operations performed by surveyed companies in Hong Kong in the future would concentrate on trade and manufacturing-related services, including marketing, merchandising, business negotiation, transportation, warehousing and distribution, quality control, testing and certification, product design, R&D, sample-making, prototyping, market research and after sale service.

In brief, the strength of the Hong Kong economy lies in business networking.

The aforementioned process of industrial restructuring can best be seen in the context of broader economic restructuring of the Hong Kong economy since the 1970s. Tables 3.8 and 3.9 give a brief description of the sectoral changes of the economy of Hong Kong in the period 1961-1991. They illustrate the emergence of Hong Kong as an industrial colony in the 1960s and then, from the 1970s onward, an expansion of the tertiary sector and the decline of manufacturing activities in the economy. The drastic decline of the manufacturing sector in the 1980s reveals the effects of deindustrialization discussed earlier. The point we are trying to show here is that such deindustrialization is embedded in the economic restructuring

TABLE 3.8   GDP by Industry in Hong Kong, 1961-1991 (in percentage)

Industry	1961	1970	1981	1991
Agriculture and fishing	3.3	2.0	0.7	0.2
Mining and quarrying	0.3	0.2	0.2	a
Manufacturing	24.7	30.9	22.8	15.5
Electricity, gas and water	2.4	2.0	1.4	2.2
Construction	5.3	4.2	7.5	5.3
Wholesale and retail trades, restaurants and hotels	20.4	19.6	19.5	25.4
Transport, storage and communication	9.4	7.6	7.5	9.7
Financing, insurance, real estate and business services	9.7	14.9	23.8	23.0
Community, social and personal services	18.0	18.0	13.3	15.4
Ownership of premises	6.5	NA	9.8	10.7
Nominal sector	NA	NA	-6.5	-7.4
Unclassified	NA	0.6	NA	NA

NA   Not available.
a   Less than 0.05%.

Sources: Chang (1969:66); Census and Statistics Department (1991:31, 1993a:39).

process, shaping Hong Kong into an international financial and commercial center. Relating this to our discussion of industrial relocation, one can argue that there exists a double-restructuring process. First, there is the general trend of a sectoral shift towards finance, trading, and services in the economic structure. In 1991, 10.6% of the working population were employed in the financing, insurance, real estate, and business services. Such an increase in employment in finance and business is largely an outcome of the development of Hong Kong into a world city within the global business network. As of 1993,

> Some 513 authorised institutions from about 40 countries conduct business under the Banking Ordinance and the presence of 81 of the world's top 100 banks has helped promote the territory as an international financial centre. The external assets of the banking sector were ranked the fourth largest in

TABLE 3.9   Distribution of Working Population by Industry in
Hong Kong, 1961-1991 (in percentage)

Industry	1961	1971	1981	1991
Manufacturing	43.0	47.0	41.2	28.2
Construction	4.9	5.4	7.7	6.9
Wholesale and retail trades, restaurants and hotels	14.4	16.2	19.2	22.5
Transport, storage and communication	7.3	7.4	7.5	9.8
Financing, insurance, real estate and business services	1.6	2.7	4.8	10.6
Community, social and personal services	18.3	15.0	15.6	19.9
Others	10.5	6.3	4.0	2.1

Sources: Census and Statistics Department (1982a:138, 1993b:95).

the world and the forex turnover was the sixth largest in 1993. Hong Kong
also has the second largest stock market in Asia outside Japan. (Government
Information Service 1994:64)

Second, as noted above, within the manufacturing sector itself, the
direction of change is towards a more commercially oriented center than a
production base. Manufacturers and traders are interested in maintaining
their controlling headquarters in Hong Kong (Trade Development
Council 1991). The major operations carried out by such headquarters are
likely to be trade and manufacturing-related activities rather than the core
production processes. Hong Kong is still "an irreplaceable location for
arranging trade financing and documentation" (Trade Development
Council 1991:vi). In this connection, the maturation of Hong Kong as an
international financial center gives the colony a leading edge in
strengthening the commercial component of its manufacturing sector. In
short, the two processes of restructuring are therefore inter-related. The
emergence of Hong Kong as a world city of global financial and
commercial activities has come to constitute a positive externality for the
future development of its manufacturing sector. The well-developed
financial and commercial business structures make it possible for local

manufacturers to retain their competitiveness by enhancing their market intelligence and strengthening their ties with the global trading networks and/or relocating production offshore.

Notes

1. The survey on garment and electronics industries was carried out in the period June-September 1992. The sampling frame was provided by the Census and Statistics Department. It consisted of a randomly selected 20% of all establishments in our chosen industries and an updated record of their addresses (as of December 1991). Manufacturing establishments of all sizes were included in this address list. Since not all the activities of the manufacturing establishments in the sampling frame were relevant to our research, for instance tailors were included as garment manufacturers, we removed inappropriate cases before sampling establishments for interview. Manufacturing establishments were selected by stratified random sampling according to establishment size. In other words, samples of different size categories were chosen in proportion to the size distribution of manufacturing establishments of the two industries. Altogether 211 establishments were selected for interview. A letter explaining the background of the survey was sent to the owner or manager of the selected establishments. This was then followed by a face-to-face interview with the owner or appointed managerial staff for the completion of the questionnaire. The numbers of successfully completed questionnaires for garment and electronics establishments were 69 and 50 respectively. Quite a number of the firm we approached had closed their business, relocated or stopped production, lowering the response rate to the range of between 67.6 and 73.5%.

Comparing our sample with the population, we found that the distribution of our sample is skewed towards the larger size categories. While electronics firms hiring 1-9 employees accounted for some 42% of the population, they constituted only 24.5% of our sample. In the garment industry, our survey also under-sampled the smallest size category by about 10%. This is not surprising, since the response rate of the smallest firms is likely to be lower than that of other size categories. Also, they tend to be the most unstable, such that though they may be listed in our sampling frame, they may also have closed down before the survey began. We also compared the sectoral distribution of the population with the sample within each industry and found that our sample consisted of a representative assortment of firms from each branch of the garment and electronics industries.

The following table provides a comparison of the distribution of establishments in population and sample (by number of employees, in percentage):

Number of Employees	Garment		Electronics	
	Population[a]	*Sample*	*Population[b]*	*Sample*
1-9	41.5	24.5	54.0	44.9
10-19	17.2	28.6	15.7	17.4
20-49	13.6	24.5	18.7	24.6
50-99	10.0	14.3	6.0	4.3
100+	17.6	8.2	5.6	8.7
(N)	(10,024)	(69)	(1,660)	(50)

[a] Employees of establishments in wearing apparel (HSIC 320 and 322) only. Size distribution of knitwear establishments is not available.

[b] Employees of establishments in HSIC 382, 383, 384, and 385 only. Size distribution of establishments in HSIC 3868, 3873, and 3893 is not available.

2. This section is based upon information gathered from interviews carried out by Stephen Chiu and David Levin for a research project on the impact on restructuring on labor.

4

Singapore:
Manufacturing Fortunes in "Sunrise" and "High Noon" Industries

The story of economic restructuring in Hong Kong can be understood as a continuation of labor-intensive production. Within this pattern of production, technological upgrading does not feature as an important strategy in adjusting to the problems of rising costs and increasing overseas competition. Rather, adjustment takes the form of sharpening abilities to respond rapidly to fashion and design changes. The major coping strategy of the late 1980s and 1990s has been to reorganize production lines by relocation to low-cost production sites in China while continuing to exploit the economic opportunities provided by an established commercial network centered in Hong Kong.

The Singapore story of economic restructuring is quite different because of two elements. Firstly, the state in Singapore intervenes actively in its attempt to manage the economy. As detailed in Chapter 2, much of the institutional groundwork was laid in the 1960s. This involved the setting up of specialized organizations to control the development process, particularly in the areas of finance, the transformation of land use needed for development, and in attracting FDI. The increase in administrative capacity worked alongside the restructuring of the unions, from being militant to being pro-business. This rapid transformation was achieved in a large part because of popular support from the people as a result of ideological gains from the government's reforms in housing, education, and health.

Secondly, to understand firms' strategy in Singapore, we have to take into account the contrast between multinational and local firms. Singapore's response to the regional political uncertainties of the 1960s (the Indonesian confrontation and the separation between Malaysia and Singapore) was to focus on attracting FDI as an industrialization strategy instead of regional economic cooperation. The 1970s was the period where Singapore increasingly locked into the global manufacturing circuit as MNCs invested in Singapore. Mirza (1986:46) estimated that in 1975, 48.6% of the FDI in Asia ended up in Singapore. The overwhelming presence of multinationals in Singapore's economy makes Singapore an anomaly among the Asian NIEs. Multinationals presently account for an over-whelming 90% of the manufactured exports and 63% of production (Hill 1990:25).

Thus, if we think of Singapore as a "manufacturing miracle," a term suggested by Gereffi and Wyman (1990), the miracle lies not so much in the transformation of indigenous manufacturing and the associated challenges in attaining export production status as in the dramatic case demonstrated by Japanese economic history. The central element in the Singapore story lies in the ability of the state to ensure the conditions of profitability for multinational capital through the various changes in Singapore's competitive conditions as a manufacturing site. The path of development under organized industrialism in Singapore has to do with the roles played by the state and capital and in the relationship between the two. These relationships are explored in two parts.

In this chapter, we focus on firms' industrial restructuring strategies. As the conditions of manufacturing competitiveness change in Singapore, how are these changes reflected in the strategic decisions contemplated by both multinational and local manufacturing firms? As in the case of Hong Kong, we examine the behavior of firms in two industries, garment and electronics, based on a matching survey conducted in 1992.[1] Unlike the Hong Kong case, the two industries have very different characteristics. The garment industry in Singapore is defined by local ownership, small scale production, high labor-intensity, and stable technology.[2] The electronics industry, on the other hand, is dominated by MNCs, large scale production, changing technology, and export orientation.

In understanding the behavior of firms, we analyzed them within a locational logic of operating in Singapore, which, as Massey (1984) points out, comes with it associated legacies of costs and benefits as well as possibilities structured by the nature of local institutions. Firms' behavior is also interpreted within a wider industry logic, which defines cost structures, regulation, nature of competition and cooperation, actual and potential markets, and the shape of technology.

By tracing developments in the garment and electronics industries, this chapter will focus on the different fortunes of small manufacturing concerns and large multinationals. The Singapore government has an important role to play in influencing such fortunes because of its ability to restructure the internal environment. This will be highlighted in the next chapter, where the state's management of Singapore's industrialization will be contrasted with the Hong Kong case.

Patterns of Industrial Development

Different industries played important roles in terms of employment share at different periods in Singapore's 30-year industrialization effort. The Singapore economy on the eve of industrialization was very much dominated by entrepôt trade. Manufacturing was limited to food and raw material processing. As shown in Table 4.1, food and wood products accounted for 15.5% and 9.2% of the manufacturing workforce respectively in 1961. Given Singapore's status as a regional port city, printing and publishing was also significant, accounting for 15.3% of the manufacturing workforce in 1961. In 1971, after the political situation has stabilized and FDI has begun in earnest, transport equipment, garment, and electronics showed rapid increases in labor-absorption. The growth in transport equipment in the 1960s was a result of oil discoveries in the neighboring region which fueled demand for marine vessels. The decline in employment shares of this industry in the 1970s and 1980s however hid the transformation within this industry, namely the growth of the aircraft servicing and the manufacture of aviation spare parts, which was capital intensive (Economic Development Board 1988:vii). The garment industry received significant boost from an influx of Hong Kong firms avoiding restrictions imposed by the British government on exports from Hong Kong in the 1960s (Lee 1973). From the early 1970s onward, the electronics industry started with the involvement of American, European, and Japanese MNCs. This industry continued to increase its dominance in the manufacturing sector in the 1970s as well as the 1980s, absorbing 24.6% of the manufacturing workforce in 1981 and more than a third of the workforce in 1991.

Although not showing any significant employment share, the petroleum industry was a major contributor to the manufacturing sector from the mid-1960s to the mid-1980s. In 1965, its manufacturing output share was 17.8%, reaching a high of 37.7% in 1975 before dropping back to 13.6% in 1988. The development of the petroleum industry in the mid-1960s was in part due to the island's long history of playing the entrepôt role in the region, and as a strategic refueling and repairs depot to

TABLE 4.1   Employment Share of Dominant Industries in Singapore,
              1961-1991

Dominant Industry	1961	1971	1981	1991
Food	4,112	9,705	10,075	11,104
(%)	(15.5)	(6.9)	(3.5)	(3.1)
Wood products	2,438	10,794	8,291	2,204
(%)	(9.2)	(7.7)	(2.9)	(0.6)
Printing and publishing	4,059	7,328	12,487	16,835
(%)	(15.3)	(5.2)	(4.4)	(4.7)
Transport equipment	1,128	18,529	28,491	29,737
(%)	(4.3)	(13.2)	(10.1)	(8.3)
Garment	583	13,389	27,870	25,915
(%)	(2.2)	(9.5)	(9.9)	(7.2)
Electronics	1,300	11,847	69,358	123,358
(%)	(4.9)	(8.4)	(24.6)	(34.4)
Electrical appliances	—[a]	6,659	16,141	20,768
(%)		(4.7)	(5.7)	(5.8)
Industrial machinery	1,542	6,624	23,963	24,113
(%)	(5.8)	(4.7)	(8.5)	(6.7)
Fabricated metal	1,945	9,128	19,481	30,593
products (%)	(7.3)	(6.5)	(6.9)	(8.5)
Total manufacturing	26,481	140,552	281,675	58,274
employment (%)	(100.0)	(100.0)	(100.0)	(100.0)

[a] Until 1970, electrical appliances was classified together with electronic
    components.

Sources: Department of Statistics (1983:84-85, 1991:114-15).

marine traffic. This development also occurred at a period when regional
demand for oil was growing and existing refining capacities were either
lacking or were incompatible with product demand patterns (Doshi
1989:82). Once in place, the spectacular growth of the industry in the late
1960s and 1970s was driven by the discovery of oil in Indonesia and the
South China Sea. According to a Ministry of Finance survey, three quarters
of the 186 companies in the oil industry established in Southeast Asia
during this period were based in Singapore. The Singapore-based

companies were largely service and supply companies handling activities which ranged from the supply of offshore vessels, crew boats, rig construction to seismographic services and helicopter services (Toh 1970:19). In more recent years, the contribution of this industry has been falling because of limits to expansion and escalating oil prices (S.Y. Chia 1989:257).

The manufacturing sector moved away from the small-firm-basic processing-for-a-local-market model by the end of the 1960s. From the 1970s onward, the increasing presence of foreign capital is best characterized by the electronics industry: dominated by large firms, and export-oriented. This industry grew more dominant, absorbing an increasing share of the manufacturing workforce. The flourishing of the electronics industry in turn boosted local subcontracting, notably the fabricated metal products industry, which registered systematic growth in the 1970s and 1980s.

Triggers of Industrial Restructuring

The demands made by rapid economic growth of the 1970s on the limited resources of the city-state affected labor costs and supply, strained land resources, and led to an appreciating Singapore dollar. Thus, along with the benefits that were described in Chapter 2 — a stable, efficient and pro-business government, a good infrastructure, and a set of incentives — came a number of costs. These changes came to define the competitive conditions associated with manufacturing in Singapore, and defined relative to an expanding set of manufacturing alternatives that were opening up in other parts of the Asian Pacific. These conditions affected the strategies of both the firms and the state, acting as pressure points for industrial restructuring.

As a production platform for MNCs, the fledgling manufacturing domestic base that existed during the colonial period was rapidly transformed into a substantial export-oriented sector that became entwined with the economies of Singapore's major investors. The rapid growth of the manufacturing sector in the 1970s quickly soaked up the surplus labor that had built up in the 1960s. The unemployment rate fell steadily from 6% in 1970 to under 4% in 1977 and by the late 1970s, Singapore had achieved full employment.

Given the chronic labor situation in Singapore in the 1980s, it was not surprising that labor cost in Singapore was among the highest in the region. According to a United States Bureau of Statistics survey, the average hourly labor cost for production workers in the late 1980s was US$2.67 for Singapore, lower than the $2.71 for Taiwanese workers, but higher than the $2.46 for South Korea and $2.43 for Hong Kong (*Business Times* April 26, 1989).

Compared to labor, the cost and availability of industrial land have been kept under control by an active land-use planning program despite the city-state's inherent land scarcity. For industrial land in particular, the promotion of industrialization has resulted in the systematic conversion of land into industrial uses by the government. This resulted in a 359% increase in industrial land and a 40% increase in warehouse land between 1967 and 1982 (Ministry of National Development 1983). Thus, while private residential property prices have been escalating throughout the 1980s and 1990s because of increased affluence, the supply and prices of industrial land have been moderated through state control.

With the rapid economic growth of the 1970s, Singapore began to enjoy consistent balance-of-payments surpluses. As a result, the official reserves grew from S$3.1 billion in 1970 to S$13.7 billion in 1980. The 1980s saw an even faster rate of increase, and by 1984, the reserves expanded to S$22.7 billion (Department of Statistics 1990). The growing size of Singapore's foreign reserves and the need to maintain a strong and stable dollar in order to develop the financial sector have led to a steady appreciation of the Singapore dollar. In 1970, the Singapore dollar was pegged at $3.09 against one US dollar. This exchange rate dropped to 2.14 in 1980 and 1.81 in 1990. For a city-state which imports most of its goods, this has generally been seen as a positive development. The strong Singapore dollar has also meant cheaper imports of raw and intermediate goods, lowering material costs. On the consumption side, the high exchange rate means lower costs of imported goods and lower costs of living, thereby reducing pressures for higher wage claims. However, for manufacturers, a strong Singapore dollar in relation to the currencies of major markets (the United States and Europe) means lower profits as a result of exchange rate losses.

Industry perceptions of a strong dollar as having an effect on exports seem mixed. The EDB quarterly surveys on business expectations revealed that while more industries were beginning to feel the impact of the strong dollar in 1990 compared to the early 1980s, the appreciating dollar was more likely to affect the export orders of textiles, garments and footwear, and food, beverages and tobacco. For example, taking the average of the four quarterly surveys, 19.8% of companies in textiles, garment, and footwear and 14.3% of companies in food, beverages, and tobacco felt that the strong Singapore dollar was the most important factor limiting export orders in 1990, compared to the average of 7.5% for all industries (Economic Development Board 1990). There have been suggestions (e.g., Bryant 1989) that the strong dollar contributed in an important way to the 1985-86 recession.

Coupled with the rising labor cost and the appreciating Singapore dollar is the competition from rival companies operating in new growth centers. These centers have also become increasingly attractive as alternative production sites for Singapore-based firms.

In terms of the relative weight of such factors, a 1992 survey by the Singapore Manufacturers' Association indicated that manufacturers were most worried about rising labor costs. The strong Singapore dollar was ranked third among manufacturers' main concerns. Keen competition in the foreign market, admittedly an indirect measure of the growing competition posed by other countries, was ranked fourth. The availability of various types of workers was also a concern (shortage of skilled workers [ranked 6th], production workers [ranked 7th] and technicians [ranked 11th]). Rising rental costs was ranked a distant 15th (*Business Times* March 6, 1992).

This, then is the new economic environment, and manufacturers in Singapore must constantly adjust to this rapidly changing environment or face serious problems in the near future. In terms of domestic factors, the increasingly tight labor market means, for foreign and local manufacturing capital alike, that the days of using Singapore as a low-cost production site are over and that new enterprise strategies need to be found. For the state, as the cushion of low-cost production gets steadily deflated, the pressure is on finding new ways of sustaining the pace of manufacturing, ways which have to take into account the attendant problems of Singapore's transformation into a NIE.

Industry Adjustments in the 1980s

For garment and electronics, these pressures led to different fortunes. As indicated in Table 4.2, both industries faced the downturn of the early to mid-1980s with a slowdown in output growth and by shedding labor. However, the electronics industry faced much faster recovery after 1985. The number of firms increased significantly, along with associated increases in workers and output. Except for 1983, the number of garment firms hovered in the 370-380 region throughout the 1980s, probably because of the quota system imposed by developed countries (see later sections for discussion) which restricted the number of new players in an already crowded field. The number of garment workers dipped in 1985, rose to a high of 29,105 in 1989 and dipped to 25,915 in 1991.

The story told by Table 4.2 reveals the very different environment faced by these two industries in relation to their specific production location in Singapore. Garment firms operating in Singapore have been struggling with three problems: increasing costs, increasing competition, and increasing regulation by the United States and Europe. The domestic

TABLE 4.2   Industry Response to Economic Restructuring in Singapore,
             1981-1991

Indicator	1981	1983	1985	1987	1989	1991
Garment						
Firms	373	391	370	373	372	351
Workers	27,829	27,234	24,782	27,718	29,105	25,915
Employment share [a] (%)	9.9	10.0	9.8	10.0	8.6	7.2
Output (S$ million)	922.9	938.9	1,035.4	1,562.3	1,790.4	1,739.1
Output share [b] (%)	2.5	2.5	2.7	3.4	2.8	2.3
Electronics						
Firms	158	166	167	202	233	243
Workers	69,367	65,837	65,617	84,910	116,080	123,358
Employment share [a] (%)	24.6	24.3	25.9	30.7	34.4	34.4
Output (S$ million)	5,679	6,891	9,014	16,409.6	24,692.3	28,957.7
Output share [b] (%)	15.4	18.5	23.4	35.6	38.8	38.8

[a]   As percentage of total manufacturing workforce.
[b]   As percentage of total manufacturing output.

Sources: Department of Statistics (1991:110-11, 114-15, 1993:104-07, 110-11).

problems which the garment industry had to grapple with had already begun in the 1970s. A labor-intensive industry comprising of small firms and operating on low profit margins, the garment industry had already complained of rising costs in 1970 (*Straits Times* April 20, 1970). The labor shortage and rising labor costs in the 1980s were especially painful for the industry which was unable to upgrade technology because of the nature of its operations (especially for women's wear, where intricate designs and style changes prevented sophisticated mechanization) and where small size increased the uncertainty in the financing of such ventures. It was therefore forced to compete with other industries for increasingly expensive labor. The industry had also repeatedly complained in the media that Singapore's dollar appreciation had reduced the competitiveness of Singapore-made garment products. The high labor component in total cost means that the garment industry is not in a position to benefit significantly from cheaper material imports, while the low profit margins increase the exposure of garment firms to losses due to foreign exchange fluctuations. Electronics firms, on the other hand, are relatively shielded from the appreciating Singapore dollar because of higher profit margins (which allow companies to absorb losses in order to maintain market share), lower labor intensity, and also because a significant proportion of the components used are imported. On the last two points, the manager of GM Singapore, a United States multinational, pointed out that "all our export sales are denominated in US dollars. And about 90% of our expenses are in US dollars as well" (*Straits Times* December 19, 1987).

The problems of the Singapore garment industry were reinforced by two other external forces. In the 1970s, textile merchants were affected by the Indonesian effort at developing its own textile and garment industries and, as a result, had been pushing for direct imports instead of getting re-exports of textiles from Singapore. By the 1980s, Indonesia, along with Malaysia, Sri Lanka, Thailand, and China were already competing effectively with the Asian NIEs in garment and textiles (see Ghadar et al. 1987; Hill and Suphachalasi 1992).

The textile and garment industry is a premiere example of how industrialized nations have exercised control on imports entering their markets. In the 1980s, this control was strengthened considerably. The 1981 Multi-Fibre Arrangement (MFA) allowed the European Economic Community (EEC) and the United States to unilaterally reduce quotas if exporters under-utilized their previous year's quotas. Other restrictions included imposing surveillance levels on items not included in the quota, and the fraudulent shipment ruling which penalized exporters if Singapore-made products were re-exported by a third country to the EEC and the United States. Three garment makers lost export quotas in 1984, nine in 1992, and another ten in 1993 under the fraudulent shipment ruling (*Straits Times* May 23, 1984, February 17, 1992; *Business Times* September 19, 1993). Apart from the MFA, the United States, the market for 70-80% of Singapore's garment exports, led by the American Textile Manufacturers Institute, the Amalgamated Clothing and Textile Workers Union, and the International Ladies Garment Workers Union, considered imposing duties on the imports of Singapore and 12 other countries on charges of unfair government subsidies to the garment industry. Although Singapore was cleared after subsequent investigation by the United States Commerce Department, this episode suggests that state selective action favoring the garment industry is unlikely to be significant in the future in the shadow of potential United States reactions. The effect of increased international regulation has therefore tended to muzzle Singapore garment exporters by restricting the range of strategic options available.

The problems faced by the garment industry in Singapore are serious. The deputy prime minister, in a 1987 speech urging the industry to upgrade in order to stay competitive, had referred to it in kinder terms: as a "high noon industry" rather than facing the "setting sun" (*Straits Times* April 4, 1987). While there has been some quibbling as to the economic future of the garment industry, there is no disagreement as to the "sunrise" nature of the electronics industry. Except for some minor dips because of economic downturns, the industry has been growing continuously and spectacularly since its inception in the late 1960s. This continuous growth masks several shifts. Singapore became linked to the semiconductor global production process in 1968 (Economic Development Board 1985:3), and by the early 1970s, Singapore was already becoming the preferred offshore assembly location (UNCTC 1986:339). As labor costs continued to rise in Singapore and labor became increasingly scarce, numerous MNCs expanded into Malaysia. By 1978, Malaysia had become the largest producer of semiconductors in the third world, a position it holds up to the present. While both Hong Kong and Singapore faced the transfer of lower-skilled, labor-intensive assembly activities out of the country in the 1970s, the state interventionist strategy adopted by Singapore allowed the Republic to move up the technology ladder to more technology-intensive operations. The movement of Singapore into this phase is indicated by a higher value to weight ratio of imports from Singapore compared to other offshore locations, reflecting the greater extent of final testing as well as more complex forms of testing (UNCTC 1986:353, 405); and the high volume of integrated circuits trade occurring between Singapore and other offshore assembly locations — Hong Kong, Malaysia, the Philippines, and Thailand, indicating the specialization of Singapore as a testing center (UNCTC 1986:398). In 1985, Singapore moved higher up technologically in the semiconductor production chain, when SGS, an Italian manufacturer, set up a wafer diffusion plant. Two years later, a second plant was added, arising out of a partnership between a government-linked company and two American manufacturers, Sierra Semiconductor and National Semiconductor. In 1991, another venture between the EDB, Texas Instruments, Hewlett Packard, and Canon resulted in a more advanced wafer fabrication facility. The chairman of the Semiconductor Equipment and Materials International, a trade group based in California with more than 1,400 member companies is quoted as saying that at least three more MNCs plan to set up wafer plants in Singapore in the next few years (*Straits Times* February 10, 1993).

These developments in semiconductors are matched by a number of related shifts. In the late 1970s and early 1980s, Singapore began hosting the production of disk drives. It rapidly became a major producer of Winchester disk drives, accounting for 45% of the worldwide output by the mid-1980s, thus earning Singapore the nickname "Winchester city"

(*Business Times* July 11, 1986; *Straits Times* November 18, 1988). The production of disk drives is still a significant force in Singapore's electronics industry, but there has already been some movement of production into neighboring countries, particularly to Penang, Malaysia.

By the 1980s, there was also considerable evidence (Salih et al. 1988; Henderson 1989; Todd 1990) that a major node in the global production of electronic consumer and industrial goods and components was being centered in Southeast and East Asia. Singapore has also emerged as the one with the strongest supporting industries for electronics in the region (UNCTC 1987:27). These factors, plus Singapore's good transportation, warehousing, and telecommunication support created conditions which led multinationals to center their purchasing arms in Singapore. Figures reported by Singapore's Trade Development Board suggested that the number of companies with purchasing functions in Singapore increased from 12 in 1985 to about 40 in 1988. For large electronics multinationals, the procurement budgets are hefty. Sony, for example, announced that it was buying 60% of the components needed for its factories worldwide from its office in Singapore with a $700 million dollar budget (*Straits Times* October 20, 1990).

Examining the organization of the electronics and garment industries in Singapore indicates that while the garment industry is weakening in the face of increasing costs, the electronics industry has been transforming successfully, moving to higher value-added activities in both manufacturing and service functions. Thus, firms' strategy is dependent on this environment which comprises of elements relating to the nature of industry, the associated costs and benefits of location in Singapore, and the challenges that stem from both regional and global forces. We take the analysis a step further in the next section, using the enterprise survey data to look at how industry-location interfaces impact on specific firm strategies.

Environment and Firms' Strategy

Firms in the two industries are quite different in their attributes: electronics firms are likely to be MNCs, large, foreign-owned, and operating at higher technology levels, while garment firms are likely to be smaller, locally-owned establishments with a low and stable level of technology. These characteristics define their export orientation and the nature of their marketing linkages. The survey data indicate that garment firms depend on intermediaries much more than electronics firms. About 23.7% of garment orders originate from local import/export companies, compared to only 12.3% of electronics orders. Another 17.1% of garment orders go to wholesale and retail establishments (this also indicates local market orientation), compared to only 5.7% for electronics. The presence of MNCs in the electronics industry means that the Singapore subsidiary is linked to other overseas affiliates in regional and global production chains. In the sample, 18.9% of the orders in the electronics subsample are in the form of supplying back to overseas outlets, compared with only 1.3% for garment firms. This is an established practice in Singapore. An early study of Japanese companies in Singapore indicated the extent of this interdependence. The Japanese companies interviewed relied almost exclusively on their parent or related firms for capital goods, components and other raw material imports as well as the parent companies' international sales networks for exports (Hirono 1969:97, 100).

As the electronics industry developed in Singapore, there has been a move away from this exclusive dependence and an increase in sourcing of components locally. Part of the explanation for this growth in the supporting industry is the tendency for subcontractors to follow their major clients over to Singapore (Lim and Pang 1982). More specifically, it is the large scale of operations of multinational electronics manufacturers which provides the volumes necessary for supporting industries. Thus, when Hitachi Electronic Devices expanded its operations in Singapore, Asahi Glass, which sold a third of its output to Hitachi, followed suit (*Straits Times* September 10, 1985). The scale of multinational production operations created a strong support base in the 1970s. The strength of supporting industries in turn acted as a key attraction for multinationals considering alternative sites. When Maxtor decided to set up a disk drive manufacturing facility in Singapore in 1983, its director of international operations pointed out that Maxtor could procure 80% of its materials in Singapore: "Where else can you get all your sub-contractors within 20 kilometres of your plant?" The growth in numbers of purchasing offices of multinationals in Singapore in the mid-1980s is another indication of the depth of the supporting industry.

From the sample, 18.9% of the orders in the electronics subsample go to local factories, compared to 10.5% for the garment subsample. Thus the electronics industry shows a balance between a high internal marketing arrangement, which is characteristic of multinational production net-works, and some local and regional sourcing as a result of the presence of local subcontracting firms, as well as the regionalization of the industry.

The early presence and critical mass of electronics multinationals allowed a support base to develop in the 1970s. The growth of this base means that support has broaden away from parts and components supply to subassembly services and design and product development, as subcontractor Amteck has done for Hewlett Packard, Phillips, and

General Motors. As suggested in the literature, the subcontracting advantage is not only in terms of cost. A mature network shows its value in terms of quality and rapid deliveries, essential features of the Just-in-Time (JIT) systems (Van Liemt 1992:16). There is some evidence of such emerging features in Singapore. As Seksun's marketing director points out, "Our customers know that we are willing to rush production for them if they should need certain parts urgently. We are very flexible in delivery time" (*Tradespur* March 1992).

The local orientation of garment manufacturers is seen in the fact that 18.8% of the garment firms do not export their products, while all electronics firms surveyed export a portion of their products. For those which export their products, the export destinations show an interesting contrast between the two industries. Electronics firms tend to supply back to their own subsidiaries and parent companies. This can be seen in the good coverage in the major markets (Japan [12.8%], North America [20.1%], and Europe [21.8%]). Their Singapore location also allows these firms to cover the Asian NIEs (Taiwan, Korea, and Hong Kong combined making up 14.5% of exports) and Southeast Asia (17.9%). The volume of exports going to Southeast Asia is particularly significant because this indicates the growing importance of Southeast Asia as a region for electronics manufacture (Henderson 1989). Garment firms export mainly to the North American (34.6%) and European market (35.9%).

Labor Utilization Strategies

As indicated earlier, one of the main problems faced by manufacturers in Singapore is labor. The problem is not only one of cost but also of supply. One consequence of a rapidly growing manufacturing sector has been the flood of employment opportunities for factory workers, thus setting up keen competition among prospective employers for a limited pool of labor. In a sellers' market, the tendency is for workers to switch jobs for companies offering marginally better pay and fringe benefits. In one survey covering 17 out of 18 firms operating in Bedok New Town, in southeastern Singapore, the 17 companies recruited 7,897 workers over a ten month period and lost 7,060 workers within the same period. This worked out to a loss of 7 out of 8 workers hired (*Business Times* January 25, 1989).

There is also a deeper side to labor turnover which is industry-based. Part of the reason for this high turnover has been the volatile nature of the electronics industry which goes through significant retrenchment cycles every four to five years. In the 1980s, there were two "dips" in the otherwise continuous expansion pattern of the electronics industry. The first downturn occurred in 1981-1982 and the second in 1985. In both periods, output fell between 5.5% and 7.5% over the previous year and the industry shed between 10,000 and 13,000 workers. In the earlier downturn of 1974-1975, retrenchment of workers was estimated at 15,000 (Lim 1978:18). Retrenchment and the threat of retrenchment weaken workers' attachment to any one company, and the labor response to this industrial environment has been to switch firms according to the financial incentives offered.

The enterprise survey indicates that about 22% of firms in both industries experienced a chronic turnover rate of 30% or more in 1991, and that marginally more of these firms are from electronics. Looking at the types of labor which are likely to be more mobile, the electronics industry is more able to keep the older, more skilled workers, compared to the garment manufacturers. The turnover of skilled workers with three or more years of experience is much lower in electronics than in garment (9.3% versus 21.4%). The ability of the electronics industry to keep skilled labor could very well be because of higher wages offered. Over one-third (39%) of firms in the electronics subsample mention experiencing steep wage increases, compared to only 24.5% of firms in the garment subsample.

How do firms cope with the labor problem in Singapore? The most direct form of coping with labor shortage and an unstable demand is the use of overtime. About 86.4% of the firms in the survey mention working their employees overtime (see Table 4.3). The reasons they give for overtime work is again another reflection of the fortunes of the two industries in Singapore. While both industries mention meeting deadlines as the most compelling reason for overtime work, garment firms are more likely to use overtime because they are not getting enough workers and have to work the existing pool for longer hours (34.8% versus 17.5% for electronics). Thus the result of having a smaller group of workers is a situation of having to rely on them more, as the volume of production ends up being shouldered by fewer workers. On the other hand, proportionately more electronics firms report an increasing demand for using overtime (32.5% versus 13.6% for garment). This is consistent with their more optimistic view of their market and their report of sales in the last two years. With a rising demand, and the difficulty of getting labor in a seller's market, a quick adaptation (though not necessarily a good long-term solution) is to use overtime to deal with the rush of new orders.

The labor shortage has also led to an increasing reliance on foreign contract workers. Foreign workers contributed to one-third of the growth in the workforce between 1975 and 1979 (Ministry of Trade and Industry 1986). In 1980, there were 80,293 foreign workers on employment passes (Saw 1984:26). This rose to an estimated 150,000 in 1985 and then doubled

TABLE 4.3   Labor Utilization Strategies by Type of Industry in Singapore
(in percentage)

Labor Utilization Strategy	Industry		Total
	Garment	Electronics	
Use overtime work			
Yes	84.3	88.1	86.4
No	15.7	11.9	13.6
(N)	(51)	(59)	(110)
Reasons for overtime work			
Meet deadline	48.5	43.8	45.9
Inadequate labor supply	34.8	17.5	25.3
Increase in demand	13.6	32.5	24.0
Other reasons	3.0	6.3	4.8
(N)[a]	(66)	(80)	(146)
Use foreign workers			
Yes	80.0	81.4	80.7
No	20.0	18.6	19.3
(N)	(50)	(59)	(109)
Reasons for using foreign workers			
Labor shortage	46.5	54.5	50.6
Work unpopular shifts	46.5	31.8	39.1
Lower wage and fewer benefits	7.0	9.1	8.0
More suited for job	0.0	2.3	1.1
Other reasons	0.0	2.3	1.1
(N)[a]	(43)	(44)	(87)

[a] Multiresponse question; total may exceed number of cases.

Source: East-West Center Enterprise Strategy Survey.

within five years to about 300,000 in 1990 (*Business Times* October 15, 1991). Within the survey sample, an equally high number of firms in both industries (80.7%) used foreign workers to supplement the local workforce (see Table 4.3). The current labor shortage is again mentioned as a major factor (50.6%). Another 39.1% of firms in both industries mention the willingness of foreign workers to work unpopular shifts and assignments as a reason for hiring foreign workers. Hiring foreign workers is not without its attendant problems, but interestingly, the problems mentioned by firms have not so much to do with the workers themselves (e.g., attitudes of workers). The main problems stem from the costs involved (e.g., levy and housing) and institutional restrictions on the flow of labor (e.g., approvals, quotas). Both problems can be traced to attempts by the state to control the absolute number of foreign workers in the country (which the government sees as a potential social problem) and, at the same time, to ensure sufficient flows to key industries. Thus the operation of the two goals implies not only a foreign worker levy to keep the cost of labor close to local wages, but also sector- and industry-specific policies in terms of quotas and differential rates which work to favor some, while discouraging other industries.

Technology Strategies

The difference in technology levels between electronics and garment is quite obvious. The garment and textiles remain the two most labor-intensive industries in modern economies with labor costs accounting for about 60% of total costs. Most of the technological innovations have been applied in textiles (in spinning, weaving, knitting) rather than garment. Sewing and assembly of garments accounts for four-fifths of all labor costs and there has been little automation in this phase of manufacturing. Several features of the industry — the delicateness and limpness of material, the intricate design and frequent style changes of women's wear — prevent sophisticated mechanization (Dicken 1992). The garment industry is still labor-intensive, as the subprocesses that are involved in the assembly of clothes can only be done by manual labor. The inherent difficulty of automating garment manufacturing process was highlighted when the president of the Singapore Textile Products Association responded to government pressures (through a high wage policy) for the industry to upgrade its manufacturing operations: "in our trade, upgrading means more automation for textiles and higher standards of workmanship for garments, which is what manufacturers are doing now. But this does not change the fact that the industry will remain labor-intensive. The new wage policy signals a reversal of fortunes in this highly competitive industry" (*Straits Times* July 2, 1979).

Electronics, on the other hand, is an industry which is characterized by a wide range of technologies and where the market grows by technological advances. In semiconductor production, for example, the technology range results in the geographical division of the production process where the labor-intensive assembly and packaging stages are in labor rich regions, and testing, wafer fabrication, chip design being located in regions of increasing skills and training (see Henderson 1989). In Singapore, the responses of the industry in the 1980s to increasing cost were to move out more labor-intensive operations and to upgrade existing activities.

Thus it is not much of a surprise that the survey data show that electronics firms lead garment firms in their efforts to introduce new technology, as 74.1% of the firms in the electronics subsample indicate that they have introduced new technology in the past two years, compared to 52.9% of garment firms (see Table 4.4).

The major considerations shaping firms' technology investment decisions are directed at responding to demand: increasing output and improving product quality. Labor cost is one of the several major considerations, while other costs such as material and energy costs are not as important. The different technology orientations and problems faced by the two industries also affect the reasons for investment. While both industries invest in technology to increase output and improve quality, garment manufacturers, faced with more serious labor problems, place greater concern on cutting labor costs as a reason for new technology. Electronics manufacturers, on the other hand, are particularly driven by the need to produce new products in their decision to introduce new technology (20.2% compared to 5.3% for garment firms).

These variations in technology investment decisions can be explained by referring to industry differences. Over 90% of the garment industry are, in a "specification market" where to clinch a deal, manufacturers have to sew to buyers' designs, size specifications, delivery time, and prices (*Straits Times* September 1, 1987). With this orientation, if competition cannot be waged in terms of cost, a factor which is increasingly against Singapore's favor, then the focus is on maintaining and increasing quality. The other option has been to use technology (which we noted has limited applications in garments) to reduce labor-dependency. In the case of Wing Tai Garments, this was the main motivation when it invested in a conveyor system which allowed it to redeploy some 80 of its workers and shorten the production cycle (*Business Times* May 26, 1989).

The electronics industry's footlooseness is encouraged by the high value to weight ratio (transportation being a small percentage of total costs). The consequence is a rationalization whereby activities are

TABLE 4.4   Technology Investment Characteristics by Type of Industry in
Singapore (in percentage)

Technology Investment Characteristic	Industry		Total
	Garment	Electronics	
Introduce new technology			
Yes	52.9	74.1	64.2
No	47.1	25.9	35.8
(N)	(51)	(58)	(109)
Reasons for new technology[a]			
Increase output	25.0	21.8	23.1
Improve product quality	23.7	19.3	21.0
Cut labor costs	22.4	16.0	18.5
Produce new products	5.3	20.2	14.4
Reduce skilled labor	9.2	5.0	6.7
Cut material and energy costs	7.9	5.0	6.2
Reduce wage costs	2.6	5.0	4.1
Reduce supervisory costs	2.6	0.8	1.5
Save space	1.3	1.7	1.5
Other reasons	0.0	5.0	3.1
(N)[b]	(76)	(119)	(195)

[a] Only those investing in new technology.
[b] Multiresponse question; total may exceed number of cases.

Source: East-West Center Enterprise Strategy Survey.

distributed according to the comparative advantages of locations. Within this logic, as Singapore's costs increases, the relocation and automation strategies occur simultaneously, with lower value-added activities moving out since the 1970s and existing facilities upgraded to handle more sophisticated operations.

Industrial Relocation Strategies

Historically, the movement of MNCs to Singapore in the mid to late 1960s was part of the big wave of foreign investments to third world countries. This movement of capital was, in part, a response to cost problems facing first world countries (Fröbel et al. 1980; Massey 1984; Dicken 1992). In the 1990s, with two decades of development and rising costs in the Asian NIEs (Hong Kong, Taiwan, Korea, and Singapore), the stage is set for further elaboration in the international division of labor in manufacturing as capital moves from the Asian NIEs to cheaper production locations.

Such pressures are faced by both garment and electronics manufacturers. The garment industry is a basic industry which has high shares in employment and value-added in developing countries (Choi et al. 1985). This high labor intensity and a stable technology imply that the manufacture of garments is often the ideal industry to begin the export-orientated phase of manufacturing for countries which want to have an increased presence in the global marketplace. In the 1970s, garment exports from the Asian NIEs were growing rapidly, penetrating both European and United States markets (Fröbel et al. 1980; Ghadar et al. 1987). By the 1980s, a new batch of competitors in Southeast Asia, particularly from Thailand, Indonesia, and Malaysia, have entered the global marketplace for garments (Hill 1990). This latter group of countries has become increasingly attractive to Singapore garment firms seeking relief from the high cost of manufacturing in Singapore as sites for the production of simpler items. By the 1990s, the president of the Singapore Textile and Garment Manufacturers estimated that almost half of the Republic's 180 garment producers had some offshore production facilities, or had farmed out some work to neighboring countries (*Business Times* March 24, 1992).

As mentioned earlier, the high value to weight ratio of electronics components has resulted in the industry having a production process which is spread geographically. From this vantage point, locations are being assessed for their potential in lowering cost, maintaining quality, and increasing delivery times. Thus, unlike garment where relocation is often done reluctantly (i.e., push factors are important), the very fact that the electronics industry is geographically dispersed worldwide encourages relocation as a key strategy in increasing or maintaining competitiveness (i.e., pull factors are important). Penang, in particular, with a growing supporting industry and a skilled workforce, has emerged as a competitor to Singapore for similar manufacturing activities. As the chief executive officer of Penang Development Corporation points out, "it is not true that this place (Penang) is for low-end products any more, we are talking about investors that Singapore wanted and did not get" (*Business Times* June 2, 1994). In the match-up of attributes, Penang holds the advantage in business costs: cheaper land leases, expatriate accommodation, and general costs of living which affect the wage index. The infrastructure strengths of Singapore become important when it comes to wafer production (which needs high levels of water purity and reliable power supplies), and sourcing functions (which require efficient transport and warehousing). Singapore's more educated workforce is also significant for wafer fabrication (where more than half the workforce are engineers and technicians) and chip design.

From the survey sample, the relocation process is more evident in electronics than garment. Nearly half (42.4%) of the electronics subsample and 32.7% of the garment subsample have set up factories in other countries in the last five years (see Table 4.5). The smaller size, the lower involvement of foreign capital, and a local market orientation are major limitations on garment manufacturers in investing overseas, while the footlooseness of electronics encourages this movement and the resultant division of labor.

For those who have established plants and factories overseas, labor (lower wage costs [29.2%] and fewer labor problems [23.3%]) is the main reason for moving overseas (see column total for section 2, Table 4.5). Land, either cheaper or more available, is mentioned as another major reason by 20% of the firms. Garment firms feel that the exchange rates of other countries also provided an incentive (17.0%). Electronics firms have also started locating plants overseas in anticipation of access to markets (16.4%). Access to markets should be interpreted not only in terms of final products as in consumer electronics, but also in terms of the tendency of component manufacturing networks and assorted supporting services to move in tandem, when contractors follow suit as their major clients move overseas. Examining the location of overseas production sites shows interesting differences for electronics and garment. Of the two, electronics shows a broader range of production sites. The investments in Malaysia, Indonesia, and the Asian NIEs reflect the growing importance of the region in electronics manufacture and the tendency for a regional division of labor to develop. One consequence is the emphasis on regional sourcing for components (Salih et al. 1988). Other than Malaysia, Indonesia, and the Asian NIEs, there is representation in North America as well as in Europe. A small number (10.8%) have already moved into China. The pattern of investment for garment is strongly regional, being concentrated particularly in Malaysia (48%), Indonesia (20%), and the Asian NIEs (12%).

Malaysia, Singapore's immediate neighbor, is the most popular choice for both industries, with 48% of firms from garment and 35.1% of firms in electronics investing in the country. Investment figures from the Malaysian Industrial Development Authority indicate that in 1989, Singapore was the second biggest investor after Japan for textiles and

TABLE 4.5   Foreign Direct Investment Characteristics by Type of Industry in Singapore (in percentage)

Foreign Direct Investment Characteristic	Industry		Total
	Garment	Electronics	
Investment in factories overseas in last 5 years			
Yes	32.7	42.4	38.0
No	67.3	57.6	62.0
(N)	(49)	(59)	(108)
Reasons for overseas investment[a]			
Lower wage costs	30.2	28.4	29.2
Fewer labor problems	26.4	20.9	23.3
Cheaper/available land	18.9	20.9	20.0
Currency advantages	17.0	10.4	13.3
Easier market access	3.8	16.4	10.8
Cheaper production	3.8	3.0	3.3
(N)[b]	(53)	(67)	(120)
Location of new plants and factories			
Malaysia	48.0	35.1	40.3
Indonesia	20.0	10.8	14.5
Asian NIEs	12.0	8.1	9.7
North America	0.0	10.8	6.5
European Community	4.0	8.1	6.5
China	0.0	10.8	6.5
Other countries	12.0	0.0	4.8
Philippines	0.0	8.1	4.8
Thailand	0.0	5.4	3.2
Brunei	4.0	0.0	1.6
Other Southeast Asian countries	0.0	2.7	1.6
Japan	0.0	0.0	0.0
(N)[b]	(25)	(37)	(62)

[a] Companies which mentioned investing overseas in last 5 years.
[b] Multiresponse question; total may exceed number of cases.

Source: East-West Center Enterprise Strategy Survey.

textile products, accounting for 28.6% of total investments in this industry. In electronics and electronics products, Singapore investments accounted for 9.4% of total investments in the electronics industry (Kamil et al. 1991).

The popularity of Malaysia and, to some extent, Indonesia as alternative production sites for manufacturing has been encouraged by efforts from the governments of Indonesia, Malaysia, and Singapore to jointly develop the subregion bordering Singapore. Thus, since 1989 when the cooperation was first announced, cooperation (in the form of joint development of infrastructure projects and the coordination of FDIs) has steadily grown between Singapore, Johor (in Malaysia), and the Riau Islands (in Indonesia). This region has ceremoniously been called the "growth triangle" (see Figure 4.1).

The movement of manufacturing into neighboring countries has resulted in a clear regional division of labor in firms' operations. A case study of Singapore firms expanding their operations into Johor, managerial/professional, engineers/technical, and clerical/sales/advertising workers form 27.1% of the workforce in Singapore-based operations, and only 5.2% of operations in Johor. As high as 93.1% of the workforce of Singaporean firms in Johor are production workers (Tham 1992). Thus, the data suggest that production operations are moving to Malaysia, with service, technical and management functions remaining in Singapore. This is a pattern similar to the Hong Kong-South China subregion.

Summary

The industrial restructuring of the 1980s has meant different fortunes for the garment and electronics industries. The garment industry in Singapore has been battered by rising labor costs, and problems of labor availability, and, compared to electronics, is harder hit by foreign exchange losses incurred as a result of an appreciating currency. It is also facing increasing competition from producers in lower cost countries and muzzled by an effective quota system set by major markets. Because the product has not been amenable to extensive mechanization, the industry has been unable to reduce cost by automation. Many firms are too small to consider relocation as a shelter. With the responses obtained from the survey, it may be suggested that in terms of competitiveness, the industry is past "high-noon" and is facing a "setting sun." The remnants that remain survive on existing quotas, upgrading the quality of their products with some experimenting on designing rather than on consignments. Others have moved most of their production functions to the neighboring countries of Malaysia and Indonesia and keep a small service base in Singapore.

FIGURE 4.1   The Growth Triangle: Singapore, Johor (Malaysia) and
the Riau Islands (Indonesia)

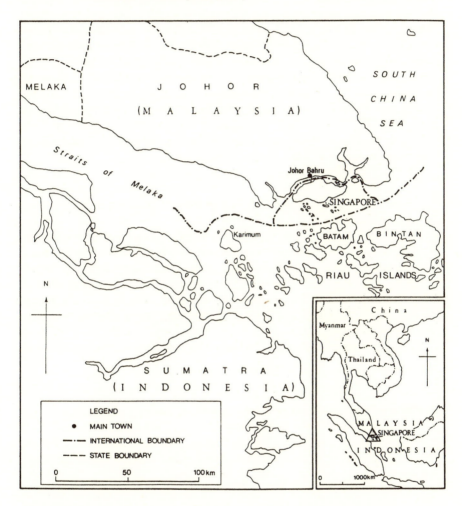

Source: Adapted from K. C. Ho and Alvin So. 1996. "Semi-periphery and
Borderland Integration." *Political Geography* 15. Used by permission.

Electronics, on the other hand, has weathered the same storms rather well. Facing a volatile but growing market, with large production volumes and active state support, upgrading into technologically more sophisticated operations has been occurring, with more less skill-intensive phases moving into lower cost parts of the region. Such restructuring of functions between Singapore and Southeast Asia has also led to a sectoral division of labor, with Singapore performing technologically advanced and service functions for the industry. In service functions, companies use the city-state's financial sector, and telecommunication and transportation infrastructure to maintain operational headquarters which perform functions such as treasury activities, marketing, component purchasing, and training manpower for regional subsidiaries.

Re-formation of the Industrial Structure

The different fortunes of our two focal industries reflect the reformed Singapore's industrial structure in the 1990s. The restructuring strategies undertaken by electronics firms show up in the occupational structure of the industry. The rapid increase in professional and technical staff (from 6.7% of staff in 1980 to 13.9% of staff in 1990, see Table 4.6) is indicative of the technological upgrading of the electronics industry, while relocation of some production facilities is probably responsible for the 5% decline in production workers between 1980 and 1990. In contrast, except for some

TABLE 4.6   Occupational Structure by Type of Industry in Singapore, 1980-1990 (in percentage)

Occupational Structure	Garment		Electronics		Manufacturing	
	1980	1990	1980	1990	1980	1990
Professional & technical	0.8	2.5	6.7	13.9	5.1	11.3
Administrative & managerial	2.7	4.4	2.5	2.7	4.5	6.0
Clerical	5.3	5.7	8.7	6.6	10.0	8.2
Service & sales	4.4	3.1	1.9	1.1	4.0	1.9
Production & related	86.8	84.3	80.2	75.7	76.4	72.6
Total	100.0	100.0	100.0	100.0	100.0	100.0

Sources: Department of Statistics (1981:214-18, 1991:119-24).

modest improvements in professional, technical, administrative, and managerial categories, the garment industry shows little change in the occupational structure.

The successful technical upgrading of the electronics industry, which accounted for 34.4% of the manufacturing workforce, 39% of the manufacturing output, and 42% of net investment commitments in 1991, to a large extent, contributes to the robustness of the manufacturing sector in the 1990s. As indicated in Table 4.7, the strength of the manufacturing sector in relation to other major sectors in Singapore can be seen in the dramatic increase in GDP share for manufacturing from 1961 to 1981, and stabilizing at about 29% between 1981 and 1991. Because of restructuring strategies that took into account especially rising labor cost, manufacturing operations in the 1990s tend to be more automated and less labor-intensive, and this accounted for the 2.2% drop in manufacturing employment share between 1981 and 1991.

The relative stability of the manufacturing sector should be considered together with another emergent pattern. Because of the industry shake-ups due to rising domestic costs, relocation, and the demise of more labor-intensive operations, electronics has grown to become the largest subsector in manufacturing. The manufacturing sector in the 1990s reflects a less diversified representation, compared to the 1970s and 1980s. The growing dominance of electronics in the manufacturing sector may be a cause for concern, since Singapore's manufacturing fortunes are now increasingly tied to this competitive and volatile industry.

Alongside the technical upgrading in some industries, the pressures to relocate costly labor-intensive activities overseas continues, for electronics, garment and other industries. Such movements are never total in the sense that companies do not pack up and move entire operations. Rather the relocation process should be conceived of as a geographical division, with labor-intensive activities moving, and more advanced manufacturing operations, and/or sales and service operations remaining in Singapore.

The latter has the tendency of reinforcing the finance and business services, as well as the transport and communication sectors. As indicated in Tables 4.7 and 4.8, the GDP and employment shares for finance and business services, in particular, have both shown significant increases from 1961 to 1981. Significantly, unlike the case of manufacturing, both GDP and employment shares for finance and business services showed no signs of slowdown between 1981 and 1991, increasing from 22.7% to 26.3% for GDP share, and 7.6% to 10.7% with regard to employment share.

Two parallel tendencies define the economic base of Singapore in the 1990s. Firms which see the value of maintaining manufacturing operations in Singapore have technically upgraded their operations to justify the

TABLE 4.7   GDP Shares of Key Sectors in Singapore, 1961-1991
              (in percentage)

Sector	1961	1971	1981	1991
Manufacturing	11.4	21.4	28.5	29.3
Commerce	33.4	27.1	19.9	18.7
Transport and communication	13.3	11.0	13.9	13.1
Finance and business services	11.8	14.6	22.7	26.3
GDP at current market prices (S$ billion)	2.3	6.8	29.3	73.0

Sources: Department of Statistics (1983:57-58, 1993:81).

TABLE 4.8   Employment Shares of Key Sectors in Singapore, 1961-1991
              (in percentage)

Sector	1961	1971	1981	1991
Manufacturing	14.2	22.0	30.4	28.2
Commerce	24.2	23.4	21.8	22.6
Transport and communication	10.6	12.1	11.4	10.0
Finance and business services	4.6	4.0	7.6	10.7
Total employed[a] (in thousand)	471.9	650.9	153.6	1,524.3

[a]   Employed persons 10 years and over for 1957 and 1970 and 15 years and
      over for 1981 and 1991.

Sources: Department of Statistics (1983:37, 1993:55).

higher costs of producing here and to continue exploiting the country's
economic advantages. These form the productive and higher value
manufacturing base. Unlike the case of Hong Kong, there is no signs that
manufacturing in Singapore is "hollowing out." However, the emerging
industrial pattern of the 1990s suggest that the industrial base seems to be
more homogeneous as less competitive industries are being forced out.
The second tendency is in the growth of services, prompted in part by
relocation and the regional division of labor. Of the two, this seems the
more dominant tendency, the direction of the near future. Singapore will
evolve to become a center supporting production sites around the region,
as more Singapore firms are driven to invest their economic surplus in

faster growing economies. As Southeast Asian countries develop, Singapore will also play host to companies wanting a base from which to exploit the growing Southeast Asian economies as sites for production and markets for goods and services.

These trends suggest that Singapore is now playing a stronger regional function in facilitating the integration of Southeast Asia (notably Malaysia and Indonesia) into the capitalist world economy. This reaffirms an earlier attempt by Friedmann (1986:74) to classify cities with regard to their role in the global economy, where he classified Singapore as a primary city within a semi-periphery region.

The nature of this function needs further clarification. In spite of Singapore's successful move into more sophisticated levels of production, the fact remains that Singapore has very little home-grown high technology manufacturing, and remains very much dependent on the production technology of MNCs. In the longer term, this condition will limit the ability of the city-state to host manufacturing innovation services (e.g., product design, prototype development, etc.), compared to cities like Tokyo and Seoul, where R&D networks exist for Japanese and Korean MNCs (see, for example, Fujita 1991; Park 1996). Moreover, while Singapore's role as a financial center has grown over the years, in terms of capitalization in stock market and as a center for banking, Singapore lags behind Hong Kong (see Sassen 1991:172, 176).

The increasing prominence of Singapore as a city in the global economy can be attributed to the transformation of the production functions of MNCs based in Singapore. Singapore's historic role as a production platform for multinationals has placed Singapore in a unique position to expand this role into a command center for foreign companies seeking a stronger regional presence in production and sales. This particular function is well served by Singapore's increasing dominance as a regional hub for air-travel (O'Connor 1995:101), supported by a strong telecommunication infrastructure (Keen and Cummins 1994:543-44) and seaport services (L.S. Chia 1989). Thus, companies with production subsidiaries in the region find Singapore advantageous as an operational headquarters, allowing easy access and communication between geographically dispersed subsidiaries, and as a transshipment center for both air and sea cargo. And as the market potential of Southeast Asia grows, Singapore's function as a center for marketing and sales should grow accordingly. Thus, unlike the truly global cities where their international ties link them to other global cities and pull them away from national and regional hinterlands (Gilb 1989:100-01), Singapore's role in the world economy is still very much tied to her role as a strategic node in the subregional and regional economy.

Notes

1. This survey is based on personal interviews with managers of the 109 firms which responded, 47 from the garment industry, and 62 from the electronics industry. The sampling frame was compiled from the garment and electronics manufacturers' directories and membership listings from the two industry associations and from listings supplied by the Singapore Trade Development Board. As was the case with the Hong Kong sample, the Singapore sample is skewed towards larger firms for similar reasons: larger firms are more stable (and therefore have current addresses). There is also a larger pool of managerial staff who would respond to our interview. Managers of smaller operations tend to cover all aspects of the business, and if could be reached after several phone calls, are still less likely to commit to an interview.

2. The data collected from the survey indicate that garment firms tend to be local-owned (70.2%) or joint ventures with foreign firms (23.4%). Electronics firms, on the other hand, tend to be foreign-owned (58.1%). Only 27.4% of the electronics firms surveyed are local, and 14.5% are joint ventures between local and foreign capital.

The greater participation of foreign capital in the electronics industry invariably results in larger operations. This is reflected in both the sales and the characteristics of the workforce. The average sales for 1991 for garment firms in the survey sample is about S$10.6 million, while the average sales for electronics is S$143 million. The average size of the workforce in the electronics subsample is about six times (622 versus 104) the size of the garment subsample.

5

Hong Kong versus Singapore:
Divergent Paths of Economic Change

The two previous chapters have discussed the dominant strategies undertaken by enterprises in adjusting to environmental changes. Before proceeding to an institutional explanation of these strategies in the next chapter, we shall take a step back here and compare them explicitly so as to put their differences and similarities into perspective. We shall first devise a quantitative analysis of the survey data that we have discussed separately for each city-state. Then the similarities and differences between corporate responses to environmental changes in Hong Kong and Singapore will be delineated. Path-dependence is observable as divergences in the restructuring process can partly be conceived of as a continuation of pre-existing patterns of economic and industrial development in the previous decades.

Comparative Overview of Restructuring Strategies

The previous chapters highlighted the "industry effect" on corporate response to environmental changes in manufacturing. In electronics and garment-making, two of the most important manufacturing industries in Hong Kong and Singapore, we found substantial differences in the configuration of their strategies to adjust to changes in the past few years. On the whole, electronics manufacturers are more inclined to introduce new technology, relocate production overseas, and invest in employee training than garment-makers. In this chapter, we are going further in our analysis by looking at the differences and similarities between the two city-states. Given the observable differences across industrial sectors in both economies, can these differences be traced to distinctive features of Hong Kong and Singapore? In other words, after controlling for the sectoral effect, can we still find a distinctive effect exerted by the locality? By putting corporate strategies under a comparative lens, we can prepare the ground for teasing out the impact of the institutional context on corporate decisions in the next chapter.

Effects of Locality versus Industry

In order to control for the inter-industrial differences, we first cross-tabulate the firms' responses in our surveys in the same industry across different localities. In effect, we compare the strategies of electronics firms in Hong Kong to their counterparts in Singapore, and the same for garment-making. In Figures 5.1 and 5.2, major differences between firms

FIGURE 5.1   Comparison of Restructuring Strategies in the Electronics Industry (in percentage of firms)

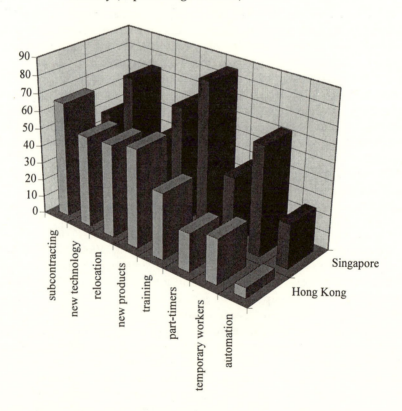

Source: East-West Center Enterprise Strategy Survey.

FIGURE 5.2 Comparison of Restructuring Strategies in the
Garment-making Industry (in percentage of firms)

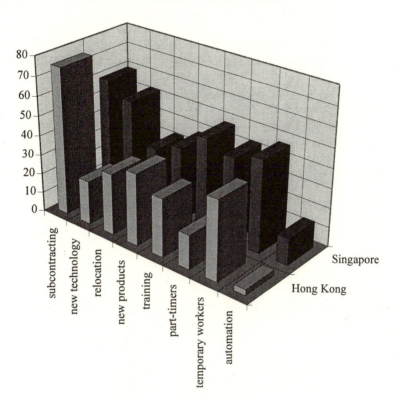

Source: East-West Center Enterprise Strategy Survey.

in Hong Kong and Singapore can be found in a few areas: the introduction of new technology and labor-saving machinery, training of employees, and employment of part-time workers. There are more electronics firms in Singapore than in Hong Kong which have extended their range of products and use temporary workers, while more garment firms hire part-time workers. Hong Kong electronics firms, on the other hand, have a higher propensity to relocate overseas, while Hong Kong garment firms do not seem to differ from their counterparts in Singapore in this regard. Garment and electronics firms in Hong Kong also rely more on subcontracting (which includes subcontracting to outworkers and internal contractors) in their production, but the differences are only modest.[1]

The last contrast in production strategies between Hong Kong and Singapore's manufacturing is best revealed by taking a closer look at the data taken from industrial production census on the weight of sub-contracting in production (Table 5.1). While slightly more garment firms in Hong Kong used subcontracting than in Singapore (as shown in our survey), its salience in the production process (in cost terms) was almost the same in 1990 in both economies. In both Hong Kong and Singapore, subcontracting (including both subcontracting to other firms and out-working) accounted for an increasing percentage of total cost in garment-making. Nevertheless, the increasing reliance of Singapore's garment-making industry on subcontracting is more remarkable than that of Hong Kong, as payment to subcontracting as a percentage of total cost almost tripled from 6.6% in 1980 to 17.1% in 1990. In Hong Kong, subcontracting accounted for some 11% of total cost in 1980 and 17.2% in 1990. This shows that the soaring cost of labor in both economies prompted garment-makers to turn to more flexible forms of production and the peripheral labor force, though garment firms in Singapore was affected more deeply than in Hong Kong. It does appear that the onset of

TABLE 5.1   Payment to Subcontracting Activities as a Percentage of Total Cost

	Garment		Electronics	
	Singapore	*Hong Kong*	*Singapore*	*Hong Kong*
1980	6.6	10.9	0.8	2.2
1981	7.9	NA	0.8	NA
1982	8.3	NA	1.4	NA
1983	11.0	NA	1.8	NA
1984	12.2	14.1	2.1	2.7
1985	12.0	14.0	2.0	2.5
1986	12.6	15.6	1.9	2.9
1987	12.7	16.2	1.7	3.8
1988	14.0	16.1	2.4	3.5
1989	15.9	17.1	1.9	4.3
1990	17.1	17.2	2.0	3.6

NA = information not available.

Sources: Unpublished data from the Census of Industrial Production, Singapore and the Survey of Industrial Production, Hong Kong.

restructuring has brought a major change in Singapore's garment production by making it as "decentralized" as in Hong Kong. On the other hand, the contrast between the electronic industries in Hong Kong and Singapore is consistent with our survey result. Again, in both industries, subcontracting increased during the 1980s, but Hong Kong electronics manufacturers were still more reliant on subcontracting than Singaporean firms.

To tease out the different effect of the "industry" and "locality" variable, we subject the data to further analysis by logistic regression. This has the merit of enabling us to look at effects of individual variables after controlling for other independent variables. To further explicate the effects of industrial environment and locality, we also controlled for the size of firms, as firm size is also commonly regarded as an important factor shaping company strategy. In the tests we performed, the data are recoded into dichotomous variables (see Table 5.2). A positive response to questions on restructuring strategies, that is, our dependent variables, is coded as "1" and a negative response as "0". In the "locality" variable, firms in Hong Kong are given the value of "0" and those in Singapore, the value of "1". The "locality" variable here is a proxy for the diverse effects flowing from the different institutional contexts in Hong Kong and Singapore. Garment-making and electronics firms are given the values of "0" and "1" respectively in the "sector" variable. Firms with 50 employees and more are coded as "1" and those with less than 50 employees are coded as "0" in the "size" variable.

The interpretation of the results are broadly similar to a linear regression equation. For example, in equation one, all three independent variables, "size," "sector" and "locality," have a significant and positive effect on "technology," suggesting that larger firms, electronic firms and firms in Singapore have a larger propensity to apply new technology in production, after controlling for the effects of other independent variables. The results from the logistic regression analyses therefore offer a nice overview of the effects of different variables on restructuring strategies. Except for two strategies, "new product" and "subcontracting," "locality" yields a statistically significant coefficient in all equations. Controlling for the effects of firm size and industrial sector, locality (Hong Kong versus Singapore) still has significant effects on various restructuring strategies. This means that irrespective of their firm size and industrial sector (electronics versus garment-making) firms in Singapore have a bigger propensity to pursue strategies of upgrading in production such as automation and training while Hong Kong firms adopt strategies of flexible production through relocation. This firmly testifies to the importance of institutional contexts which is embodied in the "locality"

TABLE 5.2   Logistic Regression of Restructuring Strategy

Dependent Variable	Independent Variables			Constant	-2 Log Likelihood Ratio
	Size	Sector	Locality		
Technology	.733** (.338)	1.07*** (.301)	.785** (.326)	-1.248*** (.256)	262.2
Training	.789** (.339)	.916*** (.305)	1.13*** (.325)	-1.275*** (.258)	257.8
Relocation	1.23*** (.352)	.509* (.297)	-.733** (.346)	-.834*** (.239)	274.8
Automation	1.13** (.554)	.736 (.496)	1.04* (.578)	-3.822*** (.575)	132
New product	-.259 (.334)	1.07*** (.291)	.282 (.316)	-.6143*** (.230)	289.5
Subcontracting	.26 (.334)	-.338 (.287)	-.449 (.318)	.6337*** (.229)	290.3
Temporary worker	-.835*** (.324)	.151 (.291)	-.593* (.309)	-.593*** (.231)	290
Part-timer	.818** (.351)	-.112 (.320)	.597* (.344)	-1.555*** (.274)	250.9

* p<.10,   ** p<.05,   *** p<.01.
Standard error of the coefficient in bracket.

variable. The statistical tests here serve an important heuristic purpose by pointing to the salience of certain variables, but they do not answer the more fundamental question of why these variables are significant. In particular, we need to unpack the "locality" effect. Why do firms in Hong Kong and Singapore respond to environmental changes differently, even after controlling for size and industry? To answer this question, we need to examine the effects of the divergent institutional frameworks, the origins of which may be traced to the early phase of Hong Kong and Singapore's industrialization. We will examine this later, but before we do that we need to turn to the more macro level changes in the two economies.

Contrasting Patterns of Structural Change

From the above comparison it is evident that the pattern of industrial change exhibits remarkable divergence between Hong Kong and Singapore, though a similar inter-sectoral difference between garment and electronics can be detected in both economies. The results of the restructuring in the manufacturing sector are also reflected at the macro-economic level in the shifting weight of manufacturing in the economy. While manufacturing contributed prominently to both Hong Kong's and Singapore's economy in the earlier decades in terms of contributions to GDP and employment, the restructuring process in the 1980s unleashed structural changes that divided the paths of the two economies.

In 1980, manufacturing accounted for 23.7% and 28.5% of Hong Kong's and Singapore's GDP respectively. In both economies, manufacturing was the largest contributor to the GDP as a result of rapid export-led industrialization. But the two parted ways in the 1980s. Hong Kong's manufacturing grew by about three times between 1980 and 1992, but the economy as a whole expanded by five and a half times (we will come back to the significance of this change in the concluding chapter). Consequently, the share of manufacturing in Hong Kong's GDP slid to 13.7% in 1992 (see Figure 5.3). Manufacturing also ceased to be the biggest employer in Hong Kong. It employed an overwhelming 46% of the labor force in 1980, but this has declined to 21.4% in 1993 (Department of Industry 1995). Manufacturing was not as important an employer in Singapore as in Hong Kong, hiring only 30.4% in 1980 (see Chapter 4). But in 1993, manufacturing firms were still engaging 26.9% of the entire labor force (Ministry of Trade and Industry 1994). As documented in Chapter 3, the massive relocation of production has triggered off major deindustrialization in Hong Kong in the late 1980s. The need to remain competitive has led Hong Kong manufacturers to places with a cheaper and more plentiful supply of labor. Although Hong Kong companies now controlled much of manufacturing production in South China, they were included under China's national account, not Hong Kong's. By contrast, Singapore's manufacturing showed a marked resilience to the rise in costs and competition, maintaining a rate of growth comparable to the rapid growth of the entire economy. In 1992, manufacturing still contributed about 28% to the national product. The technical upgrading of Singapore's manufacturing firms has at least temporarily arrested the decline of its comparative advantage as an export production platform. This supports our contention that comparative advantage is as much socially and institutionally constructed as it is dictated by economic laws. In both economies, a host of variables unfavorable to export manufacturing was evident in the 1980s, yet deindustrialization was only observable in Hong Kong but not Singapore. The radically different institutional frameworks shaped the different course of economic restructuring from the 1980s. In a sense, then, Singapore's institutional configuration enabled it to maintain its comparative advantage in domestic production, while a combination of the effects

114

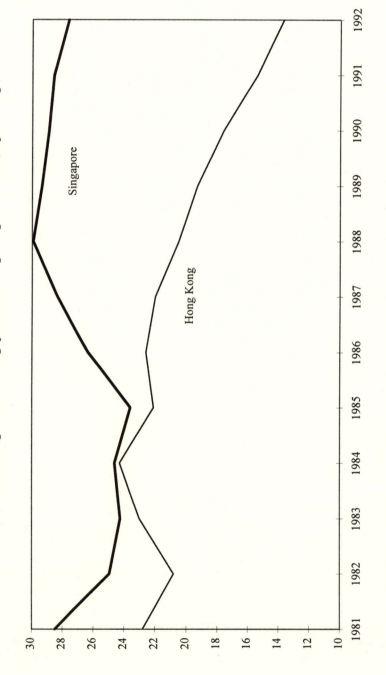

FIGURE 5.3   Share of Manufacturing in GDP in Singapore and Hong Kong, 1981-1992 (in percentage)

Sources: *Hong Kong Annual Digest of Statistics*, various years; *Economic Survey of Singapore*, various years.

of domestic industrial and societal structure and regional events (China's market reform) prompted Hong Kong's manufacturing industries to expand overseas.

As a concomitant of these structural changes, the economic complexion of the two city-states now shows some similarities as well as interesting contrasts. For similarities, finance and business services have now overtaken and become among the largest sectors in both economies. In 1992, the finance and business services sectors accounted for 26.9% and 24.5% of Singapore and Hong Kong's GDP respectively (Census and Statistics Department 1994; Ministry of Trade and Industry 1994) This represents an increase from the 1970 share of 16.9% for Singapore and 14.9% for Hong Kong.[2] It appears that both city-states have resumed their century-long role as the entrepôt of the hinterland and the region, but this time dealing with trading services in addition to commodities. The growing integration in industrial production between the city-states and their regional hinterland has also necessitated the growth of the financial sector in order to lubricate all the transactions between Hong Kong and Singaporean firms on the one hand, and their overseas affiliates, subcontractors, and foreign clients on the other.

Contrast shows up in another respect of their economic structures. In Hong Kong, the commerce sector (including wholesale, retail and import/export trades, restaurants and hotels) enjoyed a long-term increase in its share of the economy from 21.4% in 1980 to 26.2% in 1992. The same sector in Singapore, however, had remained more or less stable over the last decade. It accounted for close to 19% of GDP in 1980, and stayed at 18.4% in 1992. This is also reflected in another structural trend of the economy, namely, the importance of domestic consumption in total demand. In Hong Kong, domestic consumption (public and private) constituted a stable 66% to 67% of the GDP between 1980 and 1992. In contrast, Singapore's domestic consumption as a ratio to GDP declined from 61.2% in 1980 to 52.4% in 1992. Without further analysis it is difficult to ascertain the source of this divergence. Nonetheless, it does seem that with the deindustrialization in Hong Kong, internal demand has assumed a pivotal role in Hong Kong in the generation of growth. Repatriation of profit from Hong Kong investments in China has also fueled Hong Kong's domestic demand. The contrary is true in Singapore. With the continual dynamism of export-oriented manufacturing, external demand has consistently been a major source of growth in Singapore. By a preliminary analysis, exports of goods and services were the most important source of growth in 1993, accounting for 11% of the 14.6% growth in total demands (Ministry of Trade and Industry 1994:13). In sum, processes of restructuring in Hong Kong and Singapore have very different repercussions on the economic structure. Manufacturing continues to be one of the most important economic sectors in Singapore, along with the growth of business and financial services. In Hong Kong, on the other hand, manufacturing has experienced a long-term relative decline, only to be compensated by the growth of business and financial services as well as the commerce sector. Internal demand has become less important in Singapore, but the same is not true for Hong Kong.

Divergent Mechanisms of Growth

Given the difference in structure, it is not surprising that Hong Kong and Singapore's *mechanisms* of economic growth do not seem to be identical. Again, the imprints of the different institutional framework and developmental trajectory are significant. A few econometric studies attempting to disentangle the "sources" of growth in Hong Kong and Singapore have spotted a critical difference in the relative contribution of the growth in various "tangible" factors of production (labor and capital) versus growth in total factor productivity (TFP) or technical efficiency (which measures the effect of technical change or how efficiently the factors of production work net of changes in capital and labor inputs). Young (1992), for example, has made the observation that the rate of structural transformation in Singaporean manufacturing (measured by changes in the allocation of labor across two digit manufacturing sectors) during the 1967-1986 period has far exceeded that of Hong Kong:

> [I]n a short period of time Singapore passed through manufacturing industries previously traversed, at a more leisurely rate, by Hong Kong. By the late 1980s Singapore seems to have surpassed Hong Kong on the technological ladder, with Singaporean finance increasingly dominating Hong Kong finance and Singaporean manufacturing industries producing en masse hitechnology electronics goods which have eluded most Hong Kong entrepreneurs. (Young 1992:23-24)

While we have reservations about Young's valuation of the relative superiority of the financial sector in Hong Kong and Singapore, Young's depiction of the higher level of technological sophistication for Singaporean manufacturing over Hong Kong is consistent with our analysis so far. Young goes on to add, however, that such a rapid rate of structural transformation in Singapore has been largely a result of an equally rapid growth in factor accumulation from the 1960s onward. During the 1980-1985 period, in particular, growth of capital inputs accelerated once again after a brief slackening from 1975 to 1980. The surge in capital accumulation, in Young's model, explained all of the increase in output per worker in the Singaporean economy between 1980 and 1985.

Contribution of TFP growth was actually negative (-13%) in this period. Only in the following 1985-1990 period when growth of capital slowed down that contribution of TFP growth rebounded to 30%. Overall, in the 1980s, the contribution of TFP growth in Hong Kong to output growth was solidly positive and much higher than that of Singapore's. During 1981-1986, technical change contributed to 26% of output growth, and in 1986-1990, a massive 54% (Young 1992:33). This suggests that Singapore has pursued a more resource-intensive path of economic growth, fueling growth by plowing factors of production (principally capital and, to a lesser extent, labor) into the economy. Hong Kong, on the other hand, has chosen to economize on the slower growth of factors of production by using them more efficiently. As a result, the estimated real rates of return on capital in Hong Kong during the 1980s (23.1%) was much higher than that in Singapore during the same period (9.8%) (Young 1992:37). As can be seen in Figure 5.4, the ratio of fixed investment to GDP rose sharply in Singapore in the early 1980s, and was much higher than Hong Kong in most of the 1980s. In fact, Singapore by the mid-1980s had one of the lowest returns to physical capital in the world (Young 1992:36). This clearly testifies to the effect of state restructuring strategies in Singapore which sought to stimulate growth by intensified capital accumulation. The negative contribution of TFP growth suggests that the additional inputs were not allocated as efficiently as desired, hence leading to the slackening growth rates in the early 1980s and the recession of 1985. In Hong Kong, by contrast, the "slow but steady" pace of growth was a product of a stable growth in inputs and efficient allocation and utilization of these inputs by the private sector.

A recent World Bank study also corroborates with this observation (World Bank 1993). It estimates a cross-national production function relating variation in output to input changes. Output changes can then be decomposed into three elements: first, output changes due to changes in inputs (capital and human capital); second, the rate of technological progress of the international best practice, meaning the technological frontier of the world at a given time; and third, change in technical efficiency, which can be interpreted as the rate that individual economies approach the international best practice or technological frontier. For a given level of inputs and technological frontier, "a rapid shift from average practice to best practice — positive technical efficiency change — can provide a powerful engine of growth" (World Bank 1993:69). The result of World Bank's estimation shows that Hong Kong ranked among the highest in East Asian economies, while Singapore came out surprisingly as the least efficient economy in the past three decades (see Table 5.3).

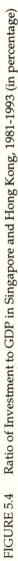

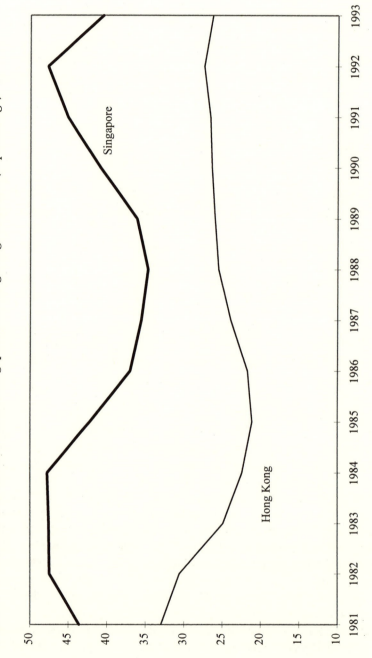

FIGURE 5.4   Ratio of Investment to GDP in Singapore and Hong Kong, 1981-1993 (in percentage)

Sources: *Hong Kong Annual Digest of Statistics*, various years; *Economic Survey of Singapore*, various years.

TABLE 5.3   Technical Efficiency Change Estimates for Selected
             East Asian Economies

Economy	Technical Efficiency Change, 1960-1989 (average annual percentage)
Hong Kong	1.9714
Indonesia	-1.2352
Japan	0.9876
South Korea	0.2044
Malaysia	-1.7767
Singapore	3.451
Taiwan	0.8431
Thailand	0.1067

Source: World Bank (1993:69).

The World Bank's method of estimating technical efficiency and productivity growth is not without its critics, so the above estimates have to be treated with caution. Kwon (1994), for example, has charged that the World Bank methodology is based on neoclassical assumptions which are unwarranted for growing dynamic economies, namely, competitive factor markets, long-run equilibrium, and constant return to scale. Consequently, the results of these TFP estimates have a built-in bias against state intervention to redress factor market imperfections and to promote economies of scale. These quibbles should not bother us too much for we are not using these TFP estimates to adjudicate, as the World Bank does, which type of growth is better. What these figures have clearly shown is that the modes of economic growth have been very different in the two city-states. Singapore has pursued a path of growth that hinged more on capital accumulation than technical efficiency, while Hong Kong tends to produce more outputs with a given level of inputs by better approximating the international best practice. At both the sectoral and aggregate level, therefore, we have discerned marked contrasts in the pattern of transformation and performance between Hong Kong and Singapore. How can we explain these differences?

Path-dependence and Economic Change

The institutional perspective advanced in this study maintains that a first explanation for such divergences must be sought in the historical starting point of Hong Kong and Singapore's respective restructuring. That is to say, at least some of the contrasts in their restructuring process must be comprehended in the light of their respective experiences of industrial takeoff which bifurcated in a major way Hong Kong and Singapore's trajectories of growth in the 1960s. Since their respective industrial structure was so different by the late 1970s when restructuring started, it was not surprising that such remarkable divergences could be observed in the process of economic change commenced in the 1980s. In short, we cannot ignore the path-dependent nature of economic change.

First of all, as outlined in Chapter 2, by the late 1970s in Singapore there emerged a manufacturing sector that was observably different from that of Hong Kong. It had a more balanced mix of heavy and light industries, the industrial structure was dominated by multinational firms, and the average firm size was ostensibly larger. Such an industrial structure conditioned Singapore's responses to environmental changes. The preponderance of large, more capital-intensive and foreign firms, we have argued, has contributed to a higher propensity to invest in new technology and automation, as well as to move up to higher value-added market niches. As documented above, size is indeed an important predictor of the adoption of restructuring strategies seeking to upgrade production. In addition, the presence of a critical mass of MNCs also facilitated the continual inflow of investment in the upgrading of Singapore's manufacturing industries. After the first half of the 1980s, investment commitments by foreign firms continued to grow and surpassed local investments. Between 1982 and 1991, local investments in gross fixed assets more than doubled, but foreign investments increased by almost 2.7 times. In 1991, foreign investments in gross fixed assets amounted to S$25.8 billion, but local investments were only S$9.8 billion (Economic Development Board 1992). Clearly the foreign firms that had already invested in Singapore by the early 1980s found it attractive to increase their investments there. The continual inflow of foreign investments has also facilitated the technological upgrading of Singaporean manufacturing, as when foreign firms made new investments, they typically invested in the production of more advanced products with a higher value-added content.

The converse was true in Hong Kong. Small local firms were the mainstay of the Hong Kong manufacturing sector. They started out in the earlier decades as producers of labor-intensive products in the lower end of the market. They were largely OEM makers, without their own design and R&D capabilities. They also typically operated with a shoe-string capital base and narrow profit margins. The key to their survival was agility in responding to market changes and exploiting market niches. In other words, due to the small resources (managerial and financial) available to them, they were not cut out for the job of transforming themselves into high-tech and capital-intensive enterprises. A small number of industrial firms had grown large by the late 1970s, but even for these firms their technological and financial capacities had not been very impressive. Innovation was just foreign to the industrial system in Hong Kong. So when manufacturers were confronted with the realities of rising cost and competition, their natural response was to look for new market niches that could enable them to continue their tested method of production. Thus fashion products were the lifeline of the electronics industry in much of the 1980s. Garment-makers also exploited the cheaper secondary labor market in order to cut costs. As discussed in Chapter 3, Hong Kong electronics and clothing manufacturers' predominant strategy from the 1980s was to pursue horizontal expansion, by investing in production facilities in other areas but keeping the method of production basically the same as it was in Hong Kong.

Nevertheless, the similarities between Hong Kong and Singapore in their earlier stage of industrialization also resurfaced to homogenize patterns of change in the two city-states. The pre-existing nexus with their respective hinterland, Malaysia in the case of Singapore, and China in the case of Hong Kong, has also produced a higher level of integration between the city-states and their immediate neighbor. The "growth triangle" was adopted as an official strategy to sustain Singapore's long-term growth, while the South China region has now become an organic and indispensable part of Hong Kong's production network (see Figures 3.1 and 4.1). The recent "regionalization" of the two economies therefore should be viewed in a historical perspective. Both Hong Kong and Singapore first developed as entrepôts of a vast hinterland and were not intended as self-sufficient and independent units of economic activity. Although geo-political forces in the immediate postwar period partially severed their ties with the hinterland, the economic and social logic of such ties remained intact. Hence, once political barricades were lowered, institutions facilitating economic exchanges were remolded, and the economic necessities of such exchanges became apparent, the economic (and political as well in Hong Kong) reintegration between the two city-states and their respective hinterland became inevitable.

The "inertia" in the industrial and economic development of Hong Kong and Singapore, however, tells only part of the story of path-dependence. While in one sense, economic change is "endogenous" so that past developments invariably shape current processes, the manufacturing sector should not be treated as isolated and self-contained. It has multifaceted ties and linkages to other institutional spheres in the society. A complete understanding of the continuities and discontinuities, therefore, must be sought also in the effects of the institutional framework of industrial development as a whole. A different institutional matrix emerged from Hong Kong and Singapore's industrial takeoff and is still in place to regulate the restructuring process. This will be the subject of Chapter 6.

Notes

1. Data from Singapore do not allow us to distinguish subcontracting to other firms and employment of outworkers and internal contractors.

2. All national income data on Hong Kong and Singapore in this section come from Census and Statistics Department (1994) and Ministry of Trade and Industry (1994).

6

Comparing Institutional Legacies and Trajectories

In the last chapter, the results of the logistic regression analysis of restructuring strategies indicated that the policies adopted by firms were significantly different not only in terms of the size of firm and industry, but more importantly in terms of whether these firms operated in Hong Kong or Singapore. The difference recorded for this third variable suggests an institutional context in operation. In other words, the two different ways of organization in Hong Kong and Singapore exert a significant impact on the way firms deal with industrial restructuring.

In this chapter, we will systematically specify this path by analyzing the institutional contexts of the two city-states in the 1980s. We will do so by delineating the points of divergence between the two city-states in their state-industry, finance-industry, and labor-capital relations. This chapter will complete the story of divergent paths which began in Chapter 2.

State-Industry Relation

Hong Kong: From Detachment to Hesitant Involvement

The relationship between the state and industry is the first point of departure in Hong Kong and Singapore's approach to economic management. In Chapter 2, we have described how the colonial state of Hong Kong pursued an arms-length approach to industrial development and resisted pressures for assistance from the manufacturing sector. The state mainly provided solid infrastructural supports, an efficient administrative and legal system, and even embarked on offering various social services (medical, housing, and education) which had the effect of facilitating the reproduction of labor power. However, it should be pointed out that these services are *universal* and *sector-neutral*. The state has anxiously guarded its policy of dispensing no selective incentives to the industrial sector.

This policy, however, was called into question when problems of international competition and growing protectionism had urged the Governor to appoint an advisory committee on diversification to look into the matter in 1977. The *Report of the Advisory Committee on Diversification* was finally published in late 1979. One of the results of the report was the formation of the Industrial Development Board, subsequently established in 1982 as a statutory body to advise the government on policies towards industrial development. The first action of the Board was to commission the Hong Kong Productivity Centre to conduct a study on the electronics industry, an industry rising rapidly in its importance in the Hong Kong economy. The report of the study was published in 1984 with recommendations, which, if followed, would entail a major revision of the "arms-length" policy long adopted by the state towards industrial development. The recommendations necessitated the state to devote public funds to foster the further growth of a particular industry. For example, the study's recommendation to establish centers for the diffusion of technology, consultancy, and equipment rental, would require at least HK$40 million per year, while the suggestion to start a venture capital company would need initially at least two to three hundred million dollars in order to have a noticeable effect. These recommendations were very bold within the Hong Kong context, since the total approved expenditure of the Industry Department was only HK$32.6 million in 1983-84 (Financial Secretary 1985). These suggestions departed significantly from the state's reluctance to interfere with the allocation of resources in different sectors by the market mechanism. It was also a policy of "industrial targeting" in disguise under which the state would attempt to anticipate market changes and "pick" and nurture the most probable winners in international competition.

The irony is that even if such "bold" measures were approved, increased state commitment would still be quite modest, compared with the magnitude of state support of industrial competitiveness in other Asian NIEs. Hong Kong's competitors, like Taiwan and South Korea, have substantially larger financial stakes in the development of electronics industry. Even Singapore, as we shall see later, has taken a much more active stance in the promotion of high-tech electronics industry. What is instructive in the Hong Kong case, however, is that even a modest accentuation of the state's role in industrial development has not been adopted. All of the above recommendations were eventually rejected by the state. Meanwhile the state also rejected a similar proposal by a number of electronics manufacturers to impose a levy on electronics export to fund a set of shared R&D facilities (Haggard 1990:153).

While industrialists continued to complain about the inadequacy of state assistance to industries, changes in China had reduced the urgency for overhauling the state's industrial policy. The influx of legal and illegal immigrants from the mainland eased the upward pressures on manufacturing wages. China's booming foreign trade also gave Hong Kong's entrepôt trade a big boost, contributing to much of the economic growth in the 1980s. The institutional reforms in China, and the opening up to foreign investment also gave Hong Kong manufacturers a welcome relief to local bottlenecks in land and labor. As a result, the state's emphasis changed from industrial restructuring to the facilitation of entrepôt trade with China as well as the development of Hong Kong as a financial center. The pursuit of these objectives did not require the state to depart from its established approach to economic management. To increase trade with China, it invested in port and highway development projects to speed up the flow of goods to and from China. The financial center concept, however, entails limited state financial commitment and regulatory changes, since this requires no more than a state-led publicity campaign to advertise Hong Kong's locational advantages and its favorable business environment for the development of financial services.

However, by the 1990s, the dramatic decline in the established labor-intensive industries had appeared to force the state to abandon its straight-jacket of non-interventionism in industrial development and to fashion a more active industrial policy. The Hong Kong Productivity Council (HKPC) has extended its scope of operation by providing a range of industrial consultancy, training, development, and bureau services to assist industry in moving up the value-added ladder. Under the HKPC, a host of demonstration centers have been set up to introduce advanced manufacturing technology such as CAD/CAM and surface mounting. Lately, the HKPC has also taken the lead in forming a consortium among private firms to develop more sophisticated products. The idea is to spread the sunk cost of R&D by enlisting investment from a number of firms in developing a particular product (*Ming Pao Daily News* October 5, 1991). Perhaps the most eye-catching departure from the *laissez-faire* rhetoric is the unveiling of a HK$200 million Applied Research and Development Scheme (ARDS) in 1993 under the administration of the Hong Kong Applied Research and Development Fund Company. Under the scheme, funding support of up to half of the cost of a single applied R&D project can be granted to a single locally-registered company or organization, either in the form of a loan or equity participation or a combination of both. In addition, in June 1993, the Hong Kong Industrial Technology Centre Corporation (ITCC) was inaugurated as a statutory body to encourage the growth of high-tech enterprises and to facilitate the transfer of technology from abroad. A total of HK$338 million in a mixture of grants and loans from the state was allotted to launch its operation. Since the start of its operation, it has provided incubation services to six technology-based companies.

Nonetheless, such efforts to assist technological upgrading were too little, and too late. The total government expenditure of Hong Kong on institutional support of industrial development and trade amounted to only 0.39% in 1987-88, which lagged far behind Singapore's 5.05% (Wong 1991).[1] Taking a broader view, in 1992-93, expenditures (recurrent and capital) on "economic services" accounted for some 6.1% of the entire budget, which was only about a third of the 16.4% level in Singapore in 1992 (Ministry of Trade and Industry 1994:126-27). It does seem that the Hong Kong state is far less willing to put in money for the purpose of economic development than its Singaporean counterpart.

In summary, the colonial state has refrained from pursuing a sectoral industrial policy that gives priority to manufacturing in the allocation of resources. It offers ample support and incentives for private capital accumulation in general while refraining from interfering with the flow and distribution of resources and capital across different sectors. Infrastructural provisions certainly serve this purpose well. Moreover, the Hong Kong state has also indirectly supported capital by intervening extensively in the "extended" reproduction of labor power through financing tertiary education, and the training of technicians and engineers by universities, polytechnics, technical institutes, and vocational schools. Applied research projects in tertiary education institutions are also promoted with public research grants.

An extended role for the Hong Kong state has been constrained by a limited resource base from which to launch interventions into the marketplace (cf. Chiu 1994). On the one hand, as a colonial state, the home government expects it to be self-sufficient without subsidies from the sovereign state. In recent years, the Chinese government has also watched Hong Kong's fiscal policy closely. The balanced-budget policy is actually written down in the Basic Law, the mini-constitution of the future administrative region of Hong Kong after the restoration of Chinese sovereignty after 1997. Muzzled by these external constraints, the colonial state must be very prudent in public spending. Apart from land sales and taxation, the state does not possess any other means (e.g., financial system, foreign aid and loans, and public enterprises) of acquiring resources to implement interventionist strategies. Besides financial constraints, Hong

Kong has historically developed a power structure in which the financial and commercial bourgeoisie have a commanding influence. At the early stage of industrialization, the commercial and financial interests had contributed to the emergence of a non-interventionist stance by the state towards the nascent industrial sector (Chiu 1994b). While over the postwar decades industrialists were gradually coopted into the power structure, the contour of the governing coalition had not changed radically.

Consequently, the state's support of industrial development is necessarily limited in scale and cannot involve a major increase in public spending or subsidies. Hence, the various public bodies (HKPC, Industry Department, and Vocational Training Council) geared towards assisting industrial development are either limited in their scale of operation, or operating on a self-financing basis. Most of the them serve as a medium of disseminating information to the private sector, with the non-governmental organizations like the Trade Development Council (TDC) and the HKPC being more successful in such undertakings than the Industry Department. The HKPC, in particular, has striven to serve the ever changing technological needs of local industrialists, such as propagating the ISO 9000 standard in quality control, and is virtually the only public organization in Hong Kong committed to the upgrading of local industries. Its scope of service, with a shoe-string budget, however, has naturally been more limited than its generously state-funded counterparts in Taiwan, South Korea, and even Singapore. Funding constraints have caused some projects to be held up or abandoned, and as the HKPC chairman expresses, "given our meagre resources and the severe financial constraints under which we operate, our hands are frequently tied" (*Electronics* 1992:117). The TDC also performs a valuable role in disseminating information on Hong Kong products and helping local manufacturers conquer new markets and widen existing ones. In this respect, the TDC is also essential for the garment industry to transform itself in the long run into a high fashion industry. But promoting designers and their works overseas are costly (one fashion show costs at least HK$500,000 in Paris), and the TDC can only bring over more local designers to fashion centers in Europe if more resources are available (McHugh 1994:17).

Singapore: Close Involvement with Industry

In the Singapore case, industrialization has, from the beginning, acquired the status of a national project with full government backing:

> From 1965, when Singapore became independent on her own, we have had to constantly review and revise our policies. The fundamental issue was how were we to make a living as a nation on our own. We have found one answer

to this in rapid industrialization, encouraging industrialists of the advanced countries to export not manufactured goods to Singapore for re-export, but their factories, technological management expertise and marketing know-how. (Lee Kuan Yew, in Koh 1976:44)

The independence of the Singapore state meant that it did not have the constraints which shackled the Hong Kong government. We saw, in Chapter 2, how the Singaporean state had forged a very different institutional framework in industrial development. The substantial involvement of the state in the economy means that "the key to understanding economic restructuring [in Singapore] is to understand the role of the public sector" (Lee 1992:34). The state often takes the lead in determining the direction and pace of the adjustment to various economic challenges.

In its attempts to manage the economy, the state has built on earlier policies to develop a set of incentives for targeted industries and its activities. For example, the following industries and key supporting services have been the recipients of state incentives: automotive components; machine tools and machinery; medical and surgery apparatus, and instruments; specialty chemicals and pharmaceuticals; computer, computer peripheral equipment, and software development; electronic instrumentation; optical instruments and equipment; precision engineering products; advanced electronic components including wafer fabrication; hydraulic and pneumatic control systems (Rodan 1989:148). To spur efforts at R&D in these industries, incentives such as double tax deductions for R&D expenditure and accelerated capital depreciation allowances for machinery, plants, and buildings are provided. On top of tax incentives, government funding schemes also provide more financial assistance to private enterprises for technological upgrading. For example, the Product Development Assistance Scheme received an increased injection of funds in 1981, from S$1 million to S$2 million. The Capital Assistance Scheme was also enlarged from S$100 million to S$150 million in 1980, and then to S$300 million in 1981. The intended objective is to develop higher value-added exports to the advanced countries as well as the regional market (Rodan 1989:150).

Not satisfied with this set of selective incentives, the government launched a major policy package in the late 1970s: the so-called "Second Industrial Revolution." This was a pro-active attempt, since the economy still appeared to be doing fine at that time. The program was designed mainly to force an increase in the pace of technological upgrading in Singapore, creating a more favorable environment for the development of high-tech, high value-added, and information-intensive industries. Significantly, the policy was also aimed at the phasing out of low-tech labor-intensive industries in order to release much needed labor for the new "sunrise" industries. Since the perceived drag to further economic growth by the late 1970s was attributed to a shortage of labor and low productivity growth, the core of the restructuring program was a three-year "wage correction" policy "that would encourage the more efficient use of scarce manpower through mechanization and automation" (Ministry of Labour 1992:xi). In the words of the Minister of Trade and Industry, this policy was seen as "a short term offensive weapon against slipping productivity and getting stuck in the quicksand of low value-added labor-intensive industries" (*Straits Times* June 1, 1980).

The shock of significant wage increases was immediately registered among various local business groups. The president of the Singapore Employers Federation labeled the government's pronouncement a "bombshell" (*Straits Times* June 28, 1979). Similar views and fears of inflation and the fate of small local firms were voiced from the Singapore Federation of Chambers of Commerce and the Singapore Manufacturers' Association. The problem was worsened by state policies in the 1970s. By maintaining moderate wage increases in spite of rapid growth, the containment of labor market pressures led to increasing pressures for restructuring, resulting in a significant jump in wage demands. Employers who had been used to a decade of moderate changes were caught by total surprise (Lim and Pang 1982). Even MNCs, usually reticent in public, found the shifts in wage scenarios disturbing. In the parsimonious remark of one Japanese electronics manufacturer when asked to comment on the situation: "We understand... but pain is pain" (quoted in *Straits Times* July 11, 1980a).

One major grouse has been that the wage recommendations were not pegged to increases in productivity or workers' dedication to the job. One executive director of a large shipyard commented that "workers appear to have accepted these higher wages as a reward for what they have already done and not prepared to do more" (*Straits Times* July 11, 1980b). This also reflected a basic difference between the perspective of industrialists, who were concerned with maintaining competitiveness within their respective industries, and the state planners, who saw the high wage policy as performing a redistributive function between industries.

The high wage policy was intended to restructure the economy by forcing industry to move up or move out and in the process redistribute scarce labor between industries. In the end, the higher wage bill did force some restructuring and increased productivity. But the transfer of labor was not as smooth as envisaged by state planners. It was very painful for some: "in our trade, upgrading means more automation for textiles and higher standards of workmanship for garments, which is what the manufacturers are doing now. But this does not change the fact that the industry will remain labor-intensive. The new wage policy signals a reversal of fortunes in this highly competitive industry" (president of the Singapore Textile Products Association, quoted in *Straits Times* July 2, 1979), while frustrating for others: "your prime minister, in his meeting with industrialists in Bonn last year, forecasted that industries such as textiles and shoemaking would close down and release their workers. We've used that forecast in our planning here. So far, we are still waiting for workers to be released. Nothing has happened" (a large German employer, quoted in *Straits Times* July 11, 1980a).

Despite the plethora of incentives for technological upgrading and the substitution of labor by capital, it was clear, by 1985, that the "Second Industrial Revolution" had not been a run-away success. Progress in the shift towards high-tech and high value-added industries, especially in electronics and machinery, had been remarkable. Nevertheless, the overall result of the program appeared to be mixed. As the government report reviewing the development of the Singapore economy in the first half of the 1980s shows, while the overall GDP growth between 1980 and 1984 (8.5%) reached the target of 8-10%, productivity growth lagged (4.9%) behind the targeted 6-8% (Ministry of Trade and Industry 1986). Though investment indeed shot up by an average of 14% each year during 1981-1984 and reached 46% of GDP in 1984, most of them went to construction and property development. The state's generous investment incentives did not seem to work; investments in equipment and machinery increased by a meager 3% (by Singaporean standards). Export growth also slowed down from 30% during 1976-1980 to 21% during 1981-1984. As the report observes: "Not only has trade with our neighbors declined, we have also lost our export competitiveness in major markets such as the EC" (Ministry of Trade and Industry 1986:27-29). The most critical problem facing the Singapore economy in 1985 was, however, the jump in labor costs unmatched by productivity growth. As a result of the wage correction policy, increases in total labor costs (i.e., wages plus Central Provident Fund [CPF] and other benefits) exceeded productivity growth by an average of 3% in the 1979-1981 period, and by a further 9% between 1982 and 1984. As a whole, unit labor costs rose by 40% each year during 1979-1984. In 1985, the erosion of international competitiveness finally converged with the slump in construction and weak domestic demand to produce a 1.7% decline in real GDP.

The unprecedented recession in the mid-1980s came as a shock to Singapore, which had not seen one in two decades after the onset of industrialization in the 1960s. In March 1985, the government announced the formation of the Economic Committee to "review the progress of the Singapore economy, and to identify new directions for its future growth."

The release of the report of the committee, entitled "The Singapore Economy: New Directions" marked a reorientation of state restructuring strategies from the phase of "Second Industrial Revolution." Unlike the Hong Kong situation where government-commissioned industrial recommendations were rejected because the hands of the state were constrained by Britain and China, the key suggestions of the committee were followed through.

For example, an ambitious reorientation suggested by the report was the move to develop an external economy. With two decades of rapid growth, the impending resource exhaustion which stemmed from Singapore's small size and maturing economy, had kept costs climbing. In this sense, by the mid-1980s, the government had done all it could to keep domestic business conditions from becoming even more adverse. A logical move for the state to maintain competitiveness was to take some of the pressure off its resources by encouraging a regional division of labor where labor-intensive and low value-added activities were relocated to lower-wage, land-rich neighboring countries, while maintaining control (i.e., management operations), and keeping services (e.g., sales, training, advertising) and higher-end production activities at home. This strategy operationalized a series of state initiatives that began in the mid-1980s.

A major component in the strategy to develop the external economy was to encourage local business to become "internationally oriented." Under the catch phrase, "the world as hinterland," the state envisaged a series of concentric circles with Singapore in the middle. To this end, the state pledged to provide support for local companies to invest overseas, and in particular, in the Growth Triangle development venture involving Singapore, the Riau Islands of Indonesia, and Johor of Malaysia (see Figure 4.1). Subsequent policy changes included the provision of fiscal and tax incentives, equity financing of overseas ventures as well as infrastructural facilities like better information links between Singapore and the world. By June 1993, the state (through the EDB) had approved S$18 million in loans to finance overseas projects of 12 local companies.

Government-Linked Companies (GLCs) and statutory boards have also extended financing for overseas ventures by taking equity stakes in such projects. For example, in 1989, Temasek Holdings, the state's investment arm entered into a partnership with local company Yeo Hiap Seng to purchase an American food company Chun King (*Business Times* September 25, 1991). In the same year, Singapore Airlines, Singapore's biggest GLC, invested about US$180 million in America's Delta Airlines (*Business Times* December 13, 1991). More recently, spurred by its success in the Growth Triangle projects, the government announced its intention to develop an industrial estate in Fujian, China, about ten times the size of the one it developed in Batam, Indonesia (*Business Times* November 29, 1992).

These examples illustrate an emerging policy of the 1990s. While the emphasis on managing the state's financial resources continues to be on portfolio assets (shares, bonds, and debentures) in order to ensure a good rate of return to Singapore's foreign reserves, attention is now focused on the use of direct investments overseas to maintain Singapore's competitiveness (*Straits Times* August 2, 1991). The EDB describes this as strategic investments, defined as those that increase business opportunities for Singapore. Between late 1988 and 1991, about S$2 billion of international direct investment was made. It is estimated that 70% could have come from the Singapore government and GLCs (*Business Times* December 13, 1991).

Overseas ventures are by their nature risky, which is why the state has to take a leading role in the first place. There is no guarantee, therefore, that the state's overseas forays are an instant success, despite its financial power and entrepreneurial experiences at home. Foreign markets are as much a strange place for private and state enterprises alike. For example, in the early 1990s, the Singapore state had invested nearly US$300 million in high-tech ventures in the United States. Acting as a venture capitalist financing high-tech start-ups in the Silicon Valley, the state's investment arms sought to obtain in return the transfer of advanced technology and assembly-line operations to Singapore from the United States. In 1991, therefore, two government agencies, Singapore Technologies Ventures and the EDB invested more than US$40 million in venture capital in Momenta International, a California company that develops pen-based computing technology. By the end of 1992, however, the company was said to be ready to file for bankruptcy and the Singapore state was likely to lose as much as US$8 million. While the Singapore government has a deep pocket, it is simply "not intimately attuned to Silicon Valley" (Burton 1992:60).

While offering assistance and incentives to local enterprises to venture overseas appears to be a straightforward matter, promoting entrepreneurial spirit among Singaporeans is not. The *Final Report of the Committee to Promote Enterprise Overseas* is almost entirely devoted to this subject. The report points to a number of institutional features in Singapore society that are hindering the spread of the entrepreneurial spirit: the CPF and the social safety nets that discourage individual ambitions and adventures, the school system that breeds conformity, and the availability of well-paid, secure jobs in the MNCs, GLCs, and the public sector that crowds out entrepreneurial talents. Nevertheless, even with these realizations, the report does not seem to be able to offer a ready solution to these problems. In fact, some of the problems it identified does seem to be integral to the institutional matrix of Singapore's economic miracle. The report points out that a more creative and less conformist society is the key for the emergence of entrepreneurs, and students should be encouraged to become more inquisitive and to exercise their creativity. Yet the extensive presence of the state may reduce the space necessary for individuals to acquire a creative and less conformist outlook. It is also doubtful whether administrative actions by the state would be successful in fostering entrepreneurship.

Section Summary

It is clear from the analysis that the state-industry arrangements in Hong Kong and Singapore are very different. The state in Hong Kong, as a result of historical legacies in the composition of the governing coalition as well as on-going financial constraints, tends to adopt a detached approach to the economy. While the Hong Kong government has been active in fostering the reproduction of labor in terms of education, training, and housing, it generally steers clear of direct involvement in industry, therefore avoiding the "distortion" of the market allocation of resources across different sectors. When there has been pro-industry initiatives, like the starting up of the ITCC, such efforts tend to be too little and too late, compared with those of Taiwan, Korea, and Singapore.

In contrast to the detachment of the Hong Kong government, the Singapore state has intervened systematically and extensively in its attempt to increase the competitiveness of the economy. However, as accounted in this chapter have shown, the implementation process has not always been smooth. The vision of state planners to restructure the economy means prodding favored industries to upgrade their operations, discriminating against lower value-added industries, and pushing all industries to move their more labor-intensive phases to neighboring countries so as to free up land and labor resources for more productive uses. Opening up an external economy also means exploiting economic opportunities abroad, with state linked enterprises leading the way. Restructuring, therefore, involves a painful trial and error learning process for all, state bureaucrats and company executives alike, even if there are attractive incentives only for some.

Finance-Industry Relation

A second component of the institutional context of industrial restructuring is the financial system. It has been argued that the banking system has been the pillar of the development of manufacturing industries in East

Asia (Wade 1985). Under the state's selective credit policy, banks in Japan, Korea, and Taiwan channeled large amounts of funds to the industrial sector. This has allowed industrial companies to have easy access to resources for expansion, R&D of new product lines, and for new companies to be nurtured.

Hong Kong: Institutional Separation

Hong Kong bears limited resemblance to this active partnership between finance and industry in other East Asian countries. For example, there is no industrial bank in Hong Kong. Indeed, Hong Kong's situation appears to be closer to that of Britain, characterized by an "institutional separation of finance and industry" (Ingham 1984). As shown in Chiu and Lui (1995), the share of loans and advances to the manufacturing industries accounted for less than 20% of the total in the 1960s and declined further in the 1970s and 1980s. The meager share of Hong Kong manufacturing industries in bank loans obviously does not commensurate with their contributions to the national product, and is far below corresponding figures in the other Asian NIEs (Lau 1994).

The inadequacy of support from the banking sector is most noticeable when we look at the medium and small manufacturing firms. Only larger firms with substantial collateral manage to solicit assistance from the banks; smaller firms are often denied financial assistance. As a study conducted in the early 1960s observed, "The degree of self-financing in Hong Kong industry is indeed abnormally high; a number of substantial firms rely exclusively on their own resources" (Economist Intelligence Unit 1962:16). The same study also pointed out that even for the larger firms, long-term capital investment tended to be self-financed and most bank loans were directed to the financing of short-term working capital. Later studies also reveal the same pattern of the "institutional separation" of the small scale manufacturing sector from the financial sector (cf. Goodstadt 1969). This institutional feature discourages restructuring strategies which require heavy capital investment and encourages capital-saving strategies, especially among the smaller firms. In fact, in the 1980s, the share of manufacturing in bank loans had declined further and hovered at about 10% of the total (Figure 6.1).

We are not, however, saying that the banking system is altogether irrelevant to industrial enterprises. In terms of general banking services, Hong Kong's banking sector is one of the most advanced in Asia. Both the range and quality of banking services in Hong Kong are impressive. Industrialists in general hold positive views of the banking sector. It is in the area of lending, especially long-term lending for capital investment, which local manufacturers find the banking sector most unforthcoming.

FIGURE 6.1   Share of Manufacturing in Bank Loans to Non-bank Customers, 1982-1993 (in percentage)

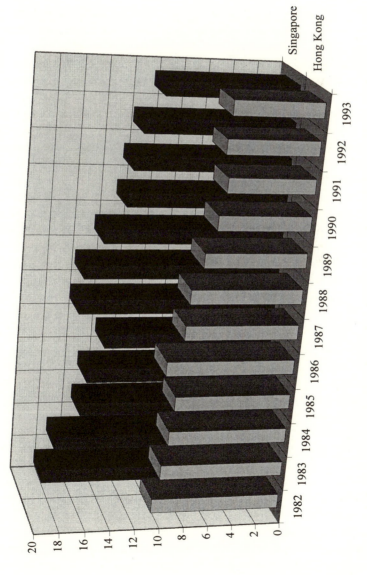

Sources: *Hong Kong Annual Digest of Statistics, various years; Economic Survey of Singapore, various years.*

Again our survey findings testify to the same relationship between manufacturing firms and the banking sector. The vast majority of the responding firms were founded with a combination of the entrepreneurs' own fund and loans from friends and relatives. Only three electronics firms and five of the garment-makers started with 50% or more of the capital from banks and finance companies. Since then, more than 50% of the electronics manufacturers had successfully borrowed money from banks. Garment-making firms were less fortunate, with only about one-third of the firms managing to borrow from the banks. More revealing is the fact that only some 40% of all responding garment firms had ever attempted to solicit finance from the banks. Forty-four percent of the electronics firms in the sample indicated they had never borrowed from banks.

We also asked our respondents to evaluate the adequacy of banks' assistance to different aspects of their operation: working capital, trade credit, and fixed capital. Given that most of them had no previous experience in soliciting banking assistance in some of the three areas, the number of "no answer" response was rather high in the survey. As shown in Table 6.1, among those who had a opinion about these banking services, they were more satisfied with banks' assistance in providing trade credits. This is not surprising, given the origin of Hong Kong's banking sector in financing entrepôt trades. The self-liquidating and short-term nature of trade credits also minimizes the risk bore by the banks. The evaluation of the banks' assistance in the lending of working capital was mixed, splitting between positive and negative assessments. The majority of the firms, however, regarded the banking sector's assistance to the lending of fixed capital as inadequate. On the whole, electronics firms had more positive ratings of the banking sector than garment-making firms. In all three areas, the proportion of electronics firms viewing banking assistance as adequate outweighed those having a negative evaluation. The majority of garment-making firms in our sample, on the other hand, regarded banks' assistance as inadequate in the lending of both working capital and fixed capital. The size factor is evident here. As shown earlier, electronics firms were larger on average than garment-making firms in our sample, as well as in the population as a whole. Typically smaller firms in the sample felt more left out of the banking sector's services to the manufacturing industries. Hence, while larger firms enjoyed international standard banking services, small-scale firms found few channels to obtain funding for restructuring and upgrading. The lack of long-term funding perhaps explains to a large extent why industrial automation has been progressing so slowly in Hong Kong.

TABLE 6.1   Hong Kong Industrialists' Evaluation of Supports from the Banking Sector (in percentage)

Support	No Comments	Adequate	Netural	Inadequate
Working capital				
Electronics	8.3	43.8	22.9	25.0
Garment	22.2	20.6	20.6	36.5
All	16.2	30.6	21.6	31.5
Trade credit				
Electronics	14.6	50.0	18.8	16.7
Garment	28.6	27.0	15.9	28.6
All	22.5	36.9	17.1	23.4
Fixed capital				
Electronics	18.8	35.4	25.0	20.8
Garment	34.9	12.7	11.1	41.3
All	27.9	22.5	17.1	32.4

Source: East-West Center Enterprise Strategy Survey.

If the banking sector is not providing manufacturers with the much needed long-term finances that would allow the latter to invest in R&D and labor-saving production, equity financing should normally serve as an alternative source of long-term capital. But the problem for Hong Kong is that even the capital market has not been playing a major role in industrial investment. A number of large textile and garment firms such as Nanfung Textiles, Windsor Industrial Corporation, Yangtzekiang Garment Manufacturing, and Lai Sun had utilized this channel before the 1980s. Many of these firms had since diversified into real estate development which dwarfed their manufacturing operations. The fact is that only a very small number (11) of the 13,144 textiles and garment firms in 1980 were listed in the stock market (Stock Exchange of Hong Kong 1987). The picture is even dimmer for the nascent electronics industry, as the *1982 Electronics Industry Report* points out:

> The public stock markets have essentially no role in financing the Hong Kong electronics industry. Only three electronics companies are currently traded on Hong Kong stock exchanges: Conic, Atlas and Chuang's Holding. The recent public offering of Conic stock was the first industrial offering in

Hong Kong in eight years. The Hong Kong stock market comprises mainly property companies (estimated at 75% of the capitalization), shipping, and banking. The industrial sector is extraordinarily under-represented. (Hong Kong Productivity Centre 1984:72)

Towards the late 1980s, more and more manufacturing enterprises were using the capital market as the source of financing. The buoyant and the relatively well-organized stock market had made it easier for larger manufacturing firms to offer their shares to the public in exchange for fresh capital. In the 1980s, more garment and electronics firms had raised capital through this channel. Electronics makers were more active in becoming listed. As their volume of business expanded in the late 1980s with the establishment of production facilities in China and other low-cost areas, it became economical for them to raise cash through the bourse. The number of industrial stocks almost doubled from 36 in 1984 to 64 in 1989. In 1993, as the China-based productions were in full swing, the number of listed industrial companies shot up to 145.

Nevertheless, the share of industrial firms is still a small fraction of the total volume of capitalization in the Hong Kong stock market. Industrial stocks accounted for around 17% of the total market capitalization of all listed companies in 1977. By 1993, in spite of the vastly increased number of industrial stocks, their relative share of total market capitalization had actually shrunk to 6% (Stock Exchange of Hong Kong 1994). The market seems to prefer firms in the public utilities and service sector which tend to have more stable earning growth. The Hong Kong stock market was heavily weighted towards the properties sector, with close to 29% of total market capitalization in 1993 coming from it. Consolidated enterprises and finance came in second and third in terms of market value. As Gao (1992:58) observes: "Unlike in the NYSE and TSE, no industrial company is listed among the top 20 in the Hong Kong stock market. Moreover, industrials remain relatively under-represented by the Hang Seng Index with only two industrial among the 33 constituent stocks." A recent reshuffle in the Hang Seng Index also reflects the shifting of balance further away from industrial stocks, when a few industrial players (mainly garment and textile firms) are excluded.

Industrial stocks have tended to under-perform relative to the overall trend of the market, and their stock prices have been hampered by a relative lack of interest from institutional investors due to their poor liquidity (Taylor 1991:36). Also, industrial stocks also tend to have a lower market price and pay less dividends (Gao 1992). Earnings of industrial growth tend to depend overwhelmingly on the export market which is vulnerable to dramatic swings (cf. Karp 1994). Since manufacturers typically have very volatile earning streams and it is difficult for industrial firms to maintain a steady growth in profits, institutional investors usually prefer the blue chips in trading, banking, and property to industrial stocks. Large scale R&D projects undertaken by manufacturers often require a protracted period of pay-off which will inevitably reflect in a period of depressed profits. Shareholders, especially institutional investors like mutual funds, have a low level of tolerance towards this kind of long-term strategy. Therefore, while industrial firms have been able to obtain capital through the stock market, such a strategy is not very conducive to investment in R&D and technological upgrading. Instead, capital raised is often used to expand production along existing lines, exploiting low wages and land prices overseas. A typical case is Tomei Industrial which became listed in 1988. It was a star performer among industrial stocks in 1991, and a stock analyst describes its strategy like this:

> Not a company that believes in hefty investment in research, it has historical-ly pitched for the Sony Walkman-lookalike market with considerable suc-cess.... Tomei fares better in a slump than its competitors because it concentrates solely on being the cheapest producer of commodity-type con-sumer electronics. (Taylor 1991:36)

For many listed electronics company, the capital obtained by public offering is basically an opportunity for the founders to earn a hefty return from their initial investment and entrepreneurship, and most of the spare cash would then be used to expand their production bases in China or buy up other firms with a similar technological level. Typical of the strategies described in Chapter 3, R&D is always not high on their agenda.

Recognizing the inadequacy of the supports from the banking sector and the stock market, the *Electronics Industry Report* recommended the setting up of a Venture Capital Company to supply equity financing to high-tech companies (Hong Kong Productivity Centre 1984:74). The report pointed to the significant contribution made by the American venture capital funds in fostering the extraordinary development of high-tech electronics firm. Now world-class companies like Intel, Apple, and Digital Equipment are all financed initially by venture capital. Unfortunately, the idea of a semi-public venture capital company is not followed through by the government. Also, private venture capital companies are not making major inroads into the incubation of manufac-turing firms, preferring "to see tangible assets first—a factory or an already established business—before sinking funds into a new enterprise" (*Electronic Components* 1993:A23). Few Hong Kong venture-capital firms will bet their money on early-stage businesses. At this fledgling stage, if only an idea, an intellectual property, or a prototype exists, the chance is slim for financial backing from venture capitalists. Programme Research and Software Corp., for example, has to sell the intellectual property rights of IC logic systems to radio manufacturers such as Matsushita and Sony rather than developing them itself (*Electronic Components* 1993:A23). In sum, long-term external financing for industrial firms, especially those used in R&D and technological upgrading, will continue to be quite limited in the near future.

Singapore: Guided Involvement

The Singapore financial sector had a head start in the earlier decades of development. As outlined in Chapter 2, the development of the Singapore financial system after independence has given the state a major presence through the state-owned Development Bank of Singapore (DBS), the operation of the CPF, as well as the administrative guidance of the Monetary Authority of Singapore (MAS). Consequently, in Singapore, we find a financial system in which a partnership exists between the state and the banks, with the latter being more responsive to the state's policy initiatives. The thrust of such initiatives in the 1980s was the development of Singapore as a regional financial center. As Bryant (1989:337) points out, the approach taken by the government has been to attract financial institutions to Singapore by regulating and taxing certain aspects of financial intermediation in Singapore less heavily compared to other nations. At the same time, it also takes great pains to erect a fence between the domestic economy and the international activities of financial institutions so that fluctuations in the world economy would not easily spill over to Singapore.

Besides the growth of the financial system itself, the impact of the financial system on the restructuring process also has to be gauged in terms of its effects on industry. As early as 1976, the state set up the Small Industry Finance Scheme (SIFS, later renamed the Local Enterprise Finance Scheme, LEFS) to help small and medium enterprises (SMEs) "gain access to financing through the provision of soft but credit-worthy loans for equipment and machinery, industrial buildings, working capital and export factoring" (SME Committee 1989:45). Although the EDB is responsible for the administration of the scheme, loans are actually given out by several participating banks and financial institutions on a joint risk-sharing basis.

The SIFS demonstrates the effectiveness of the state in initiating the scheme as well as in establishing a high level of trust by financial institutions with the state's administrative competencies in screening applicants and their previous experiences in lending to manufacturing. When the SIFS first started, the only participating bank was the state-controlled DBS. When the SIFS was opened to other banks in 1977, only the Overseas Chinese Banking Corporation was interested. The prevailing opinion in financial circles was that the risk was too high for lending to small businesses, and that the administrative cost per dollar of such loans was also higher than normal loans (*Straits Times* October 28, 1978). Several years passed by before Hong Leong Finance participated in 1980, followed by Chartered Bank in 1982. The other financial institutions jumped on the bandwagon only when the scheme had proven that such loans were a relatively safe undertaking.[2] By 1986, there were 15 participating financial institutions in the scheme.

The amount of loans made under the scheme grew unevenly between 1976 and 1993. Initially the SIFS was found to be too stringent in its screening policy, and its interest and application fee were too high.[3] Between 1976 and March 1980, only S$34.8 million were disbursed. Local enterprises, especially SMEs, were not satisfied with the financial support both from the state and financial institutions. They felt that their needs were ignored by the banks. With more participating institutions in the 1980s, total loans made between 1981 and March 1985 was S$414.1 million. The 1985 recession forced a turnaround in state policy towards local enterprises and SMEs. This resulted in a major expansion in the magnitude and scope of financing available to them. In 1986 alone, 929 cases and S$250.1 million were approved (SME Committee 1989:43). In 1992, LEFS loans totaled S$338.7 million (Ministry of Trade and Industry 1993:59). While such loans only accounted for some 4% of all loans to the manufacturing sector, it had been able to redress the bias of bankers towards SMEs, and helped local enterprises to upgrade and automate their production facilities.

Thus, while in Hong Kong bankers had been reluctant to lend to manufacturers due to the perception of risk, in Singapore, market inertia was partially overcome. The state created the initiatives by assuming the lender's risks initially through the DBS, and by its demonstration effect attracted other financial institutions to participate in the LEFS.

The apparent success of this scheme must however be weighed against the primary orientations of the banking sector. As in the case of Hong Kong, the most lucrative opportunities remain outside manufacturing. The growth in loans have been in building and construction, and to private individuals. These have outpaced the sluggish growth in manufacturing loans (Ministry of Trade and Industry 1993:152). For the banking sector as a whole, the weight of manufacturing loans in all bank loans still declined from 21.5% in 1980 to 12.1% in 1992.

Compared to Hong Kong, the Singapore capital market seems to be more conducive to the upgrading of industries. The share of industrial stocks accounted for some 30% of total market capitalization (Singapore-based firms only) in mid-1992, while the financial sector and properties companies accounted for only 39%. In contrast, financial and real estates stocks in Hong Kong had a lion's share of 47% of total market capitalization while industrial stocks amounted to only 6% (Stock Exchange of Hong Kong 1994:44).

The presence of the Stock Exchange of Singapore Dealing and Automated Quotation System (SESDAQ), a secondary stock market, also enables smaller scale firms to have fresh capital injection at a lower cost. Following the recommendations of the *New Directions* report, the state launched the SESDAQ in 1987 to encourage entrepreneurship and to allow start-up firms access to long-term equity capital. The SESDAQ was modeled after similar second-tier stock markets in the United States (Nasdaq) and the United Kingdom (USM). Its main advantages to local firms are that it carries less stringent listing requirements, less expensive, less time-consuming, and less complicated than compared to the process of listing on the main exchange (Chia and Wong 1989). Since its inception, 39 companies have offered their shares to the public through the SESDAQ, representing a capitalized value of S$989.5 million (*Stock Exchange of Singapore Journal* September 1994). Of the 27 firms in this group which have published company information, nine are electronics companies manufacturing computers and computer peripherals, and electronic components. Another five are engineering companies which provide various services (for example, conveyor-based integrated automation systems [Material Handling Engineering], material handling systems [Inter Roller Engineering], and precision engineering service [Horiguchi Engineering]) (Tan 1994).

The establishment of the SESDAQ is a boost to venture capital activities. It gives venture capitalists more options to exit and cash in their investments in start-up firms, as the "ultimate objective of most venture capitalist is to take profits from subscribing to the liquidity route through flotation or acquisition by another company" (Chia and Wong 1989:141). The origin of the venture capital industry in Singapore can be traced to 1983. In 1985, the government gave it a boost by the EDB's establishment of a S$100 million venture capital fund. It also created the Venture Capital Club to provide a venue for local entrepreneurs to interact with members of the venture capital community and potential financial sponsors (SME Committee 1989:46). To encourage the growth of the venture capital industry, various fiscal incentives are also conferred upon venture capital firms such as the pioneer status, which exempts them from paying corporate taxes for a period of five to ten years. A Venture Capital Incentive was also installed to give investors write-offs against their other income, the full amount of capital loss arising from the disposal of shares in an approved project. It is hoped that this will embolden venture capitalists in supporting highly risky but sophisticated technology projects. By 1992, the pool of venture capital funds in Singapore had approached S$2 billion, and more than 120 local enterprises had benefited from venture capital funding (Ministry of Trade and Industry 1993:61).

Section Summary

It is clear from the above discussions that on the whole, the financial system in Singapore is much more conducive than that in Hong Kong for the development of high risk, high-tech, and highly innovative industries and firms. In this respect, the financial system facilitates the restructuring process by allowing the entry of new firms or bankrolling the company restructuring process (e.g., automation, expansion of product lines, etc.).

Smaller local firms with a commitment to high technology have much less difficulty than their Hong Kong counterparts, especially after 1985, in getting access to loan and equity capital. To be sure, the system is still in its infancy and the SESDAQ has its teething problems. We have yet to see a burgeoning venture capital industry as in the United States.

However, questions of demand must also be posed alongside questions of capital supply. No matter how much financial support is given by the state, there is no substitute for thousands of innovative entrepreneurs willing to put their own money into a business idea. On this, the institutional legacies in Singapore have both its advantages and disadvantages. An activist state bent on bankrolling industrial upgrading and a financial system more attentive to industrial needs can be traced to the early periods of industrialization. Yet the channeling of savings away from prospective entrepreneurs to the public sector (CPF, tax, etc.), and the lower entrepreneurial drive which can be traced to the presence of secure and gilded careers in MNCs and the public sector, are also institutional legacies from the past which cannot be done away with overnight.

Labor-Capital Relation

Hong Kong: Unions as Pressure Groups

Although firms in Hong Kong have not received much direct assistance from the state and the banking sector, they are given a free hand in restructuring their production by their employees and the trade unions (on recent development of unionism, see Levin and Chiu 1993). While private firms are not required by the state to bear any "social responsibility" that limit their options, they are also not constrained by a strong labor movement in making decisions on restructuring production. Hong

Kong's union movement is numerically weak, with less than 20% of all employees belonging to unions. Union density in the manufacturing sector is even lower — less than 10%. Unions are also organizationally fragmented into three "federations" of different political persuasions. Shopfloor organizations of unions are particularly weak, and unions have very limited power in mobilizing collective actions such as strikes (Levin and Chiu 1993). Consequently, in devising various strategies of restructuring, industrial firms are almost completely free of resistance or interference from unions. Hence, they are rather flexible in their production strategies. In particular, unions are unable to resist the relocation of production to China. There is no need to negotiate with workers for the schedule of relocation, and employers do not have to honor or to be bound by the union contracts. Not surprisingly, then, most respondents in our survey (74% in garment-making and 71.4% in electronics) reported "cooperative" labor relations within their firms. The overwhelming majority (over 95%) of the respondents also regarded unions as having negligible influence on the management of their enterprises.

While unions are ineffective at the firm level, they have increasingly become a potent pressure group in the community. True, unions are often incapable of mobilizing collective action at the enterprise level, but they are the rare breed of interest groups which have a more grass-root orientation. As 1997 approaches, Hong Kong's political system becomes more liberalized, with a higher level of popular participation. Political parties of all political shades, which lack a solid popular base, naturally see trade unions as their critical link to the local people, or at least as a stamp of popular approval for their organization. The Democratic Party has developed strong links with the Federation of Independent Unions and the Confederation of Trade Unions, while left-wing political organizations have relied on the Federation of Trade Unions as its arm of popular mobilization. The system of functional elections also guarantees two seats representing trade unions in the legislature. Under such circumstances, the labor movement has gained valuable access to the political arena which was closed to unions in the past. While the political clout of trade unions is still limited relative to the weight of business interests, the "noise" of unions both inside and outside the policy-making arena is a factor that the state can no longer ignore.

A key area of concern for the unions since the 1980s has been the importation of foreign workers.[4] As noted in Chapter 3, beginning from the early 1980s, business organizations started to highlight the problem of labor shortage in order to pressure the government to look for possible solutions. Initially the government resisted calls for labor importation, and preferred increased automation, greater productivity, and improved wages and more attractive working conditions as the longer term solutions to the labor shortage. This official policy had the support of the trade unions which were strongly opposed to labor importation because of perceived threats to their own employment and standard of living.[5]

In April 1989, however, as pressure from business mounted, the government announced that it would adopt a more flexible stance on the importation of labor. During 1989, some 11,409 professionals and other persons with technical expertise or administrative and managerial skills from over 30 countries were admitted for employment. In addition, due to the general shortage of skilled labor in the local market, a special scheme allowing employers to recruit skilled workers from outside Hong Kong was introduced in May 1989. The scheme provided for the importation of 3,000 workers at technician, craftsman, and supervisory levels on contracts not exceeding two years. This scheme was then expanded in 1990 to a maximum of 14,700 skilled workers (Commissioner for Labour 1991:8). Subsequently in late 1991, facing double-digit inflation which the business community argued as wage-induced, the government announced that it was considering further expanding the labor importation scheme to allow the import of up to 25,000 skilled and semi-skilled foreign workers on two-year contracts but without specification or allocation of quotas to any particular industry (Skeldon 1995).

Fearing foreign workers would suppress local wages and hurt employment opportunities, 219 labor unions representing some 200,000 members from both the left and right wings of the union movement agreed to put aside ideological differences to form a coalition. In mid-January 1992, a Joint Committee Against Importation of Labor was established and a decision was made to set up a strike fund.[6] Plans were made for a mass rally and demonstration outside the Legislative Council chambers in late January when labor representatives in the Legislative Council planned to move a motion to debate the issue. A signature campaign, public hearings, and demonstrations were also planned to maintain momentum. Despite labor's mobilization, the motion in Legislative Council calling for shelving of labor importation schemes was defeated by a vote of 35 to 23. However, no general strike followed. This is not surprising since, firstly, it is not clear that substantial numbers of workers would respond to a call to strike over the imported labor issue and, secondly, the threat of a general strike is probably intended more as a signal to the government and business of the potential loss of labor's goodwill and of future labor relations problems if the labor importation scheme were to be expanded further. What organized labor had succeeded in achieving was to sensitize the government to the potential explosiveness of policy changes that did not take into account the interests of labor.

Partly to pacify the unions over the imported labor issue, the state announced in 1992 to retrain workers previously employed in manufacturing sectors. Before that, the state had maintained that there was a problem of alternative employment for displaced manufacturing workers because the overall unemployment rate was very low. Moreover, demand for workers in the service sector had been expanding rapidly. When non-interventionism became indefensible after massive labor importation, the state established a Employees Retraining Board (ERB) to provide training to workers who were adversely affected by the industrial restructuring. In 1993, an "On-the-Job Training Scheme" was launched to subsidize employers who hired and provided training to retrainees. Employers participating in the scheme could then pay retrainees lower than the prevailing market rate, with the shortfall covered by a retraining allowance paid by the ERB. By the end of 1993, 342 employers had joined the scheme which offered more than 4,200 vacancies (Commissioner for Labour 1994:69).

Unions continued to criticize the scheme for its small scale and for the lack of real skill acquisition in these employers' provided "training schemes" (*Ming Pao Daily News* June 7, 1995). They preferred to see large scale unemployment benefits installed to give displaced manufacturing workers a reasonable standard of living while they were looking for alternative employment. The state, on the other hand, argued that the scheme was a model for public-private cooperation in tackling the retraining problem. In taking such a course of action, the state was determined to avoid transforming retraining into a disguised unemployment benefit. At the same time, it steered clear of a centralized state-administered scheme that would be too inflexible to keep up with the ever-changing demand for new skills. By 1994, when the labor market began to cool down and the unemployment rate rose again, the trade unions demanded for a termination of the labor importation scheme in order to reduce competition against local workers.

While Hong Kong trade unions are not as powerful as those in other industrial countries and have largely failed to establish collective bargaining relations with employers, their presence as a pressure group and social movement at the community level is one factor shaping the course of restructuring. Unions have not been capable of stalling the importation of foreign workers, but they have kept foreign workers at a level much lower than what the business associations demanded. While union opposition was not the only, and perhaps not even the most important reason behind the state's restrained "liberalization" of immigration controls, the concerted and consistent efforts of the unions to keep the issue alive in public debate certainly played a significant role. The autonomy of the union movement in Hong Kong *vis-à-vis* the state hence makes it a countervailing force, albeit a limited one, to industrial restructuring forces which jeopardize workers' interest. This can be traced to institutional legacies from the early industrialization period which created adversarial relations between the state and organized labor, inhibiting close cooperation between state and unions in tackling the human resource problems in the restructuring process. This autonomy and the adversarial element in state-union relations are missing in the Singapore case.

Singapore: Unions as Partners

The trade union movement in Singapore continues to be a central actor in the PAP's development strategy. The subordination of the trade union movement to the state had enormously facilitated the latter's juggle between the sometimes contradictory needs of upgrading the industrial structure and maintaining economic growth at the same time in the 1980s. Of course, the smooth cooperative role of Singapore trade unions did not come from the "natural" evolution of labor movement under the logic of industrialism. It was instead a product of conscious statecraft. As discussed in Chapter 2, bitter struggles were waged between the PAP and the militant unions in the 1950s. The PAP finally tamed the unions, and established new unions and federations that are friendly to management and the government, as well as revamped the entire institutional framework of industrial relations with the legislative initiatives in the 1960s.

The relationship between the state and labor unions can be described as paternalistic: the interests of workers are protected by the state in exchange for labor cooperation. One crucial mechanism in this arrangement is the National Wages Council (NWC), a tripartite body of state, management, and labor established in the early 1970s which provided guidelines for wage changes each year. While the guidelines are not mandatory, the government as the largest employer accepts and follows recommendations, and so do most large multinationals, producing a demonstration effect on other employers. More significantly, in a tight market situation, those that do not follow will be faced with a significant exodus of workers. Moreover, the publicity accorded to the recommendations in the media also means that workers tend to see such recommendations as their entitlement (*Straits Times* July 11, 1980b).

The NWC also recommended the setting up of a Skills Development Fund (SDF) to promote skill-upgrading, mechanization, and automation (Ministry of Labour 1992:xi). It is to be financed by a compulsory levy on employers amounting to 4% of the wage bill for workers earning S$750 or less per month. The rationale, therefore, is to tax employers of low-earning, and hence low productivity operations, and use the fund accumulated to assist skill-upgrading. In order to discourage labor-intensive production, employers' contribution to the CPF was also increased by 4%. The SDF would be used to subsidize training programs offered by enterprises to their workers. In 1980, only 200 enterprises received subsidies of S$14 million. By 1984, the scope of the SDF had expanded to 2,800 enterprises with a total assistance of S$113 million (Hayashi et al. 1990:189). Apart from subsidizing private training programs, the state also established the Vocational and Industrial Training Board (VITB) to provide public training facilities on applied technology in commerce, industry, and services. The VITB was to coordinate the training efforts of 15 training centers, 52 full-time courses, as well as 4 part-time courses. Between 1980 and 1988, enrollment in the VITB courses rose sharply from 9,520 (6,895 full-time and 2,625 part-time) to 29,688 (Hayashi et al. 1990:187).

A pliable union movement has been the key to the success of tripartite wage determination through the NWC in controlling the upward wage spiral in the 1970s. Despite the increasingly tight labor market, the NWC guidelines of wage increases continued to fall behind productivity and GDP growth. As the state realized that the low-wage policy had been counterproductive in moving the economy towards a higher league, the role of the union movement was transformed accordingly to make labor more responsive to the restructuring efforts of firms. In 1979, the government reorganized the union movement from cross-industry general unions to smaller industry-based unions. One reason for the restructuring was to enable the smaller unions to acquire more knowledge of their industries and to develop a closer relationship with their employers. This would allow managers to tailor-make industry-specific restructuring plans with the cooperation of their respective industry unions. However, the move would also weaken the power base of the union movement since the restructuring invariably meant an end to the numerically large unions previously possible (Rodan 1989:157). In 1980, two of the largest general unions in Singapore, the Pioneer Industries Employees' Union and Singapore Industrial Labour Organization representing over 90,000 workers (or about 40% of NTUC membership), were dissolved to form nine industry-based unions. State supervision of these unions was exercised through the advisory councils to these new unions, which consist at least one government MP, loyal union cadre members, and PAP-related "founding members" (Rodan 1989).

The reorganization of the union movement was taken a step further after the publication of the 1981 *Report of the Committee on Productivity*. Since the objective of the Second Industrial Revolution was to upgrade the industrial structure from labor-intensive to high-tech production, workers' skills and productivity had to increase quickly. To this end, the report recommended reforms in industrial relations institutions in order to reinforce workers' identification with employers, which include discretionary annual bonuses, long-service awards, company welfare funds, work excellence committees and quality circles, and most important, the formation of enterprise unions. These measures would eventually lead to what Leggett (1988) calls the "Japanization" of industrial relations in Singapore.

As the Labor Minister explains,

> The formation of house unions or enterprise unions is being considered for a few union branches where the Branch Committees, workers and managements felt that such an arrangement will strengthen the close relationship that already exists. In these companies the track record of management's attitude towards its employees and the workers' loyalty to the enterprise has [sic] been good. The prevailing mutual trust and confidence means [sic] that setting up a house union there is not only logical but will also help cement the harmonious relationship that exists and perpetuate the climate of mutual concern and cooperation for the common good. (quoted in Leggett 1988:248)

As a corollary to the formation of enterprise unions, the state also made a pitch to promote the COWEC (company welfarism through employers' CPF contributions) scheme. The scheme enables portions of the employers' CPF contributions to set up workers welfare funds. The interest payment accrued to such funds is to be administered by the employers for the purpose of providing better welfare benefits to employees (Cheah 1988:267). Again, this is modeled upon the Japanese employment system in order to foster the dependence of employees on the enterprises rather than on the state. Employers, however, have been lukewarm to the government proposal and the scheme is not widely adopted.

All these efforts to restructure the union movement consummated in the 1982 amendments to the Trade Union Act. The aim of the amendments was to ensure that the new objectives of the trade union movement fitted the new development strategy: "promote good relations between workers and employers; improve the working conditions of workers or enhance their economic and social status; and achieve increases in productivity for the benefit of workers, employers and the economy of Singapore" (Rodan 1989:159). In a way, a strait-jacket was imposed on union activities, so that unions deemed by the state as having "oppressive or unreasonable" constitutions, or pursuing activities inimical to the new objectives, and especially to union-management harmony, would face the prospect of being legally deregistered from the registrar of trade unions (Leggett 1988).

The state-NTUC's overhaul of the union movement and industrial relations institutions had not enjoyed unanimous support from the rank and file and the NTUC-affiliates. No ballots were held to ratify the reorganization into enterprise unions, so rank and file members had no opportunity to voice their discontent (or approval). Decisions to reorganize were taken by executive councils of individual unions, but some unions resisted the state initiatives. The best known instance was the strong Singapore Air Transport Workers (SATU). Certain union members and officials, under the lead of Doraisamy, the SATU secretary-general, resisted NTUC pressure to split the union into three enterprise unions representing the employees of Singapore Airlines, the airport, and terminal services respectively (Leggett 1988:249). The SATU eventually gave in after substantial NTUC pressures.[7] The United Workers of the Petroleum Industry also unsuccessfully opposed the NTUC efforts to split up the union (Rodan 1989).

A reformed union is obviously important in the state's plan of restructuring the economy. As the chairman of the NWC notes,

> The most important role of the trade union movement in Singapore in the restructuring of the Singaporean economy is undoubtedly that of ensuring not only that the restructuring is carried out effectively, but also that it is carried out in an orderly manner with the minimum of disruption and inconvenience. In particular, the wage adjustment has to continue to be orderly, and the maintenance of industrial peace and harmony has to continue to be uppermost in the priority schedule of trade union leaders. (Lim 1984:100)

The restructured unions became an important vehicle for increasing worker productivity. At the workplace, union officials were supposed to promote "positive" productivity attitudes, including a willingness to learn new skills, use new technology, take up new tasks, and of course work hard. To achieve these tasks, the state sought to borrow other features of the Japanese model of industrial relations. Union officials and employer representatives formed small groups like the Work Excellence Committees or Joint Productivity Councils to achieve teamwork, motivation, commitment, and organizational effectiveness. Where managers resisted this idea, union leaders should convince them of the importance of such joint consultative efforts, although they also had to take care not to allow such bodies to erode managerial prerogatives on such issues like remuneration (Lim 1984:100). Unions also organized participatory groups among employees to promote productivity consciousness: Quality Control

Circles in the private sector, and Work Improvement Teams in the public sector.

The state regarded negative work attitudes on the part of workers as an important roadblock to be overcome on the road to high productivity. The union, therefore, played an important part in the campaign to convert workers to the new productivity ethos by moral persuasion. Individualism, for example, had been highlighted as a hindrance to teamwork, and an intensive campaign was launched to redress such bad work habits (Leggett 1988). "Job-hopping" by "choosy" workers, on the other hand, was similarly criticized by a media campaign (Cheah 1988). On the issue of wage increases, although the NWC awarded hefty increases to workers, the Productivity Movement would also be jeopardized if across-the-board increases were granted to all workers irrespective of their individual performance or merits. In order not to blunt workers' motivation, unions were expected to side with employers to discriminate the better workers from the "undeserving" employees in pay adjustments.

As we have seen earlier, the wage correction policy backfired and triggered off a recession in 1985. When the problems of the high wage policy surfaced in 1985, the state's reaction was to push through a wage restrain policy. This time, again, the NWC's role was pivotal. The Economic Committee report recommended that "decisive action be taken to reduce wage costs and introduce more vigorous wage restraint in 1986 and 1987." Three concrete proposals were made:

1. a reduction in the employers' CPF contribution from 25% to 10%, for two years in the first instance;
2. a freeze in wage increases in 1986 and 1987; and
3. the public sector taking a leading role in wage restraint. (Ministry of Trade and Industry 1986:100)

A subsequent subcommittee on wage reform under the NWC then proposed the following principles for a more flexible wage system in which wage adjustments should reflect the company's profitability as well as productivity and should aim at rewarding loyalty and long service (Ministry of Labour 1992:xiii). In effect, the wage reform ensured that, in practice, wage increase should lag behind productivity growth and should be determined by individual companies according to their performances. With the state's full support, employers naturally jumped on the opportunity to regain the initiative in wage adjustment. By 1992, 71% of all companies in Singapore had done so.

The implementation of the flexible wage system, however, has only mixed successes. First of all, soon after the wage freeze of 1986 and 1987, real wage increases exceeded productivity growth for five consecutive years (Flexible Wage System Review Committee 1993). Between 1988 and 1992, real basic wage increase averaged at 5.4% annually, but productivity growth was only 3.5%. It appears, therefore, that the tight labor market situation has defied the state's desire to control wage costs. More importantly, as Cheah (1988) observes, there is an internal contradiction in the state's measures to reform the wage system. For example,

> the efforts to create a more flexible reward system have already been undermined to some extent by the imposition of a general wage restraint in 1986/87, which amounted to a large extent to an attempt to enforce a wage freeze or wage cut. This retarded the formulation and implementation of differentiated rewards by the individuals and firms directly concerned. (Cheah 1988:281)

Though the state is trumpeting the merits of market mechanism and the need for individual firms to adjust their wage policies flexibly according to their own performance, the state still cannot shake off its *dirigiste* legacies. It can be argued that if the state continues to "distort" the market in this manner, the "artificial" low-wage business environment is likely to discourage firms from pressing for productivity improvements. Fortunately, or unfortunately, the weight of market forces in this case is too heavy for the state to arrest wage growth.

Section Summary

We see, in the state-labor relationship, another important point of divergence between Singapore and Hong Kong. In the case of Hong Kong, the unions had maintained its autonomy from state control early in the industrialization phase. This autonomy did not result in a strong unified union movement that was capable of reversing decisions made by the business sector and the state which affected labor. Nevertheless, it has shown itself able to put aside ideological differences and put pressure on the colonial government to slow down labor importation by pressuring for retraining schemes, thereby improving the job prospects of local labor displaced by restructuring.

The Singapore case is quite the opposite. The period of the 1980s saw a further consolidation of what was already a close state-union relationship. Within this period, the government was able to reorganize the unions such that in the 1990s, the latter become more responsive to the economic restructuring process. Thus, unions are now charged with promoting worker productivity and labor has accepted the condition that wages are to be pegged to the respective companies' productivity growth and earnings. Thus, a union "captured" by the state has meant yet a closer alignment of interests between state, capital, and labor.

With comparative hindsight, we can perhaps say that the labor movement in Hong Kong lost an opportunity in the mid-1980s to strike a compromise with the employers and the state to anticipate the impact of restructuring on the labor market. Rather than one-sidedly resisting the importation of labor and insisting on a statutory minimum wage for foreign workers equivalent to the median wage, trade unions could perhaps concentrate on retraining and ensuring that local workers get upgraded in manufacturing or transferred to other sectors. The Hong Kong state could then follow Singapore's practice and extract a larger share of the wage differential between local and domestic workers and use it for aiding industrial restructuring and retraining. Manufacturers could then also have access to a steady supply of unskilled foreign workers, thereby easing the pressures for wage inflation and relocation. But of course this had not happened. Without a tradition of corporatist policy-making and tripartite coordination, trade unions could not trust the state and employers. They could only adopt an adversarial approach to the state and employers' attempt to bring in foreign workers. In the end, foreign workers were admitted to Hong Kong only when relocation and deindustrialization had proceeded apace; they are also too small a number to have significant effects in arresting the industrial exodus. Of course we could not ascertain whether deindustrialization would have been slower if more foreign workers had been admitted earlier and in greater numbers, but the Hong Kong-Singapore comparison clearly suggests how the burden of history facilitated or hindered the adoption of a particular corporate and public strategy towards the process of industrial restructuring.

Concluding Remarks

In this chapter, we have examined the institutional configuration of divergent paths of industrial restructuring in Hong Kong and Singapore. We look at the effects of state-industry, finance-industry, and labor-capital relations on restructuring strategies in the two city-states. Indeed, institutional legacies matter. They shape the trajectories of industrial development, open opportunities, and impose constraints on future growth.

Notes

1. "Institutional support" here includes expenditures on Industry and Trade Departments, and subventions to various programs and statutory bodies related to industrial development.

2. For example, while the ratio of bad debts normally amounted to 70% for small firms, that for the SIFS loans was less than 1%. The extremely low rate of bad debt reflected a very stringent screening policy on the credit-worthiness and collateral of applicants (Choy 1985:72).

3. For a sample of such complaints, see the proceedings of the "Symposium on Small Industries in Singapore" jointly organized by Department of Trade, Institute of Banking and Finance, and Singapore Manufacturers' Association in 1977.

4. This discussion of importation of foreign worker is based on Chiu and Levin (1993).

5. A number of stop-gap measures were proposed: relaxing restrictions on overtime work by women, examining ways of inducing more people to enter the labor market, and expanding the advisory services of the Productivity Council.

6. The independent Confederation of Trade Unions initiated an organization called "All Circles Against Importation of Foreign Labour" one day before the Joint Committee, but it appears that the left and right wing unions decided to isolate the Confederation in subsequent actions. See *Hong Kong Times* January 17, 1992; *Ming Pao Daily News* January 12, 1992 reproduced in *Labour Movement Monthly* (No. 95:2, 27).

7. Doraisamy's right to work full-time on union matters was repealed, and the union's check-off rights was withdrawn on a technicality.

7

Conclusion

In this concluding chapter, we want to shift from the more narrative style of the previous chapters by posing the main issues discussed in this book as a set of questions. This allows us to provide a more focused summary discussion relating empirical details to broader conceptual issues central to the development literature. It also enables us to address specific problems and consequences of economic restructuring, and the future of Hong Kong and Singapore.

Our questions are:

- Do history and institution matter? How do historical and institutional factors mold the paths of development?
- In what ways does geo-politics form part of a broader social context in which strategies of economic development are taken?
- How does size impact on governance and development?
- How does state intervention make its impact on the course of economic development?
- Will industrial restructuring lead to rising unemployment and labor redundancy? What are the impacts of restructuring on labor market adjustments?
- Will industrial restructuring "hollow out" manufacturing?

These are the questions we shall attempt to answer in each of the following sections respectively. In answering these questions, we shall once again show the importance of probing into the trajectories of industrial development in the two city-states.

History and Institution

Few researchers of economic change would have failed to recognize the significance of history in shaping economic processes. North argues: "[p]ath dependence means that history matters" (1990:100). Arrow also discusses the relevance of history in his analysis of the effects of established codes in organization (1974:55-56). And in the literature of economic sociology (see, for instance, Swedberg 1993; Weber 1978; Granovetter and Swedberg 1992; Friedland and Robertson 1990), the emphasis is placed on the social and historical constitution of economic action. In our study of Hong Kong and Singapore, the effects of history are analyzed at three different levels. First of all, the colonial connection with the British empire has significant impact on the incorporation of Hong Kong and Singapore into the world economy. As port cities, Hong Kong and Singapore became the focal points of British commercial interests in East and Southeast Asia. Both city-states developed as centers for the collection of regional produce for shipments to the West, and centers for distribution of Western manufactures to the region.

Secondly, subsequent political developments in the two port cities also have their imprints on the configuration of the state-economy relationship. The legacy of British colonialism does not determine the timing of export-oriented industrialization in the two city-states. Thus, the active intervention of the state in shaping economic development in Singapore has to be understood in the context of national independence and the search for an economic strategy for national development. Industrialization comes to be defined as a national project in the years immediately after the independence movement. In the case of Hong Kong, economic development in the postwar decades can be seen as a continuous process under the rule of British colonialism. While national independence marked a critical conjuncture in Singapore's shift towards a national economic strategy for economic development, the economy of Hong Kong changed from an entrepôt to an industrial colony not so much out of the direction of the colonial government, but rather from the entrepreneurial efforts of local capitalists. The fact that local capitalists had no other alternatives than manufacturing for export became the driving force behind the rapid development of export-oriented industrialization in Hong Kong.

Thirdly, after Hong Kong and Singapore have developed their manufacturing capacities, each phase of industrial development comes to constitute both the enabling and constraining structures for the development of manufacturing in the following phase. In other words, the development of manufacturing industries in one phase is constituted by what have been done in an earlier period. That Hong Kong and Singapore have great difficulties in shaking off their labor-intensive industries and still have to struggle in the league of the NIEs is by no means accidental. Indeed, the strategy of utilizing resources in neighboring regions for industrial development both in Hong Kong and Singapore is essentially the accumulated outcome of previous practices of labor-intensive production processes. When the capitalists in Hong Kong finally came to feel the pain of rising labor and production costs, they looked for a short-term strategy of relocation rather than extensively upgraded the production processes. Offshore investments by Singaporean manufacturers were facilitated by an entrepreneurial state which opened opportunities in the neighboring countries. The point is that the development path itself imposes constraints on the course of further development. A perspective which captures this process is in order.

Indeed, one may further add to this discussion of the impact of history by pointing out how the existing paths of industrialization will shape the patterns of future economic development. In Chapter 3 we argue that Hong Kong is undergoing a process of "double restructuring." First, there has been a trend towards sectoral shift from secondary to tertiary activities since the 1970s, reflecting Hong Kong's development into a financial center in the East Asian region. Second, concomitant with the relocation of production processes to South China, many local manufacturing firms are becoming offices for product design, marketing, commercial, and trading functions. As a result of such structural changes, Hong Kong is undergoing a process of socio-economic transformation through which it has become a financial center and a subregional node for "triangle manufacturing" among Hong Kong, Taiwan, and mainland China (Gereffi 1994:224). It is interesting to observe that Hong Kong manufacturers have capitalized on the commercial, financial, and trading network of the city-state. The future direction of manufacturing development in Hong Kong is towards a commercially oriented center than a production base, that is manufacturing increasingly embedded in the institutional structure of a world city driven by financial and commercial activities. The case of Singapore is very different. Given its success in attracting foreign investments to start manufacturing production there, Singapore is connected with the world urban hierarchy through multinational articulations (Friedmann 1995:24,36). It works as a regional headquarters for coordinating production activities of MNCs in Southeast Asia. The fact that Singapore continues to operate as an attractive manufacturing and coordinating location for MNCs makes an impact on how it is articulated with the global system of world cities.

Thus, the industrial development in Hong Kong and Singapore can best be described as stories of different "logics" of economic growth and divergent paths to industrialism. Our two cases clearly demonstrate the complexity of East Asian development, an issue which many comparative studies have, surprisingly, failed to recognize.

In our study of industrial restructuring in Hong Kong and Singapore, we emphasize the path-dependent nature of economic change. Through an analysis of the constitution of two development paths and the unfolding of two different "logics" of industrialization, we explain how Hong Kong and Singapore, two city-states with a common background as British colonies and port cities, have come to their present positions in the world economy.

For analytical purposes, we make the distinction between two parallel, and often interactive, processes: path-dependency at the societal and corporate levels. At the societal level, we discuss how contextual and institutional factors (operationalized in terms of state, finance, and the industrial relations system) have shaped the structure of industries in the two city-states and the paths of industrial growth in an increasingly competitive environment. At the corporate level, we draw on the findings of matching surveys carried out in Hong Kong and Singapore to elaborate the organizational responses to the changing economic environment. Without repeating what we have said in the earlier chapters, the conclusion is that Hong Kong and Singapore are struggling in the "middle league" of the world economy by very different strategies. While the industries in Singapore have come to upgrade their technologies and capitalize on the resources of its neighboring region with the assistance of a developmental and entrepreneurial state, Hong Kong's industries remain labor-intensive, by turning to South China for cheap land and labor, and restructuring their local stations into headquarters for trading and commercial activities.

Our study shows that these paths of economic change are both constituted and constitutive of the developmental experiences in Hong Kong and Singapore. It illustrates how Hong Kong and Singapore bifurcated from their similar political and economic backgrounds and developed their own "logics" of economic development in their own respective industrial systems. They also show how their present institutional configurations of industrial restructuring will impose constraints on the future course of development.

Geo-political Context

In understanding the divergent paths of industrial development in Hong Kong and Singapore, it is important to recognize that the effects of history are geographically embedded. At the same time, it is also true to say that the relevance of geography is historically structured. This interplay between history and geography is appreciated at the global and regional levels.

The attention of super-powers to different parts of the world has resulted in particular geo-political legacies which in turn have influenced the economic destinies of smaller nations caught in these webs. Access to markets, foreign aid and military support, restraints to capital movements, and trade embargoes are consequences of super-power regional intentions. These in turn affect in a crucial way domestic security and choices in economic development.

Historically, linkages with British imperialism have brought both Hong Kong and Singapore to the global economy, first, as entrepôts for commercial activities within the British empire and the neighboring regions and, subsequently, as modern city-states in the developing sector of the global economy with well-developed economic ties with core countries. Such economic linkages, on the one hand, are contributive to the development of export-oriented industrialization, and, on the other, have facilitated the subordination of Hong Kong and Singapore to the core capitalist economies.

Moving to more recent phases, Cumings (1987) has shown how the East Asian policies of the United States have helped Korea and Taiwan develop. While the focus of our discussion is not on a systematic analysis of how super-power relations impact on the domestic policies of Hong Kong and Singapore, our study does recognize the significance of international politics to the economic development of the two city-states. The influence of the international environment is, to some extent, affected by the size of the two city-states. The "importance of being unimportant" means that many external economic policies such as tariffs and foreign exchange regulations are not subject to much scrutiny (Demas 1965; Saul 1982). Moreover, since both city-states have open economies, there is very little to contend with in terms of international economic relations. In terms of international politics, being small also means that when it comes to super-powers' perception, small countries are often seen as parts of a larger configuration. They are not perceived as major strategic sites of international geo-political maneuvers. In the case of Hong Kong, super-power relations are mediated through Britain, and presently, increasingly, through China. Similarly for Singapore, except for a brief period in the 1950s through the mid-1960s, where there were intense concern by the United States, Russia, and China on Indonesia and its expansionary tendencies, present United States action is mediated through Association of Southeast Asian Nations (ASEAN). Morrison (1985:2) suggests that even as a region, ASEAN is more distant and ranks low among United States foreign policy and international economic priorities.

Lastly, the path-dependency approach we adopted logically requires a corresponding argument that incorporation into world capitalism as a result of super-powers' support does not in turn explain how particular nations have responded to the opening of these opportunities. Thus, embracing path-dependency implies that we abandon an emphasis on the broad strokes of the international level in favor of finer details at the regional, national, and corporate levels.

At the regional level, a common entrepôt history means that both Hong Kong and Singapore are closely connected with their neighboring countries. In the case of Hong Kong, its hinterland is mainland China. The fact that Hong Kong is a British colony on the border of communist China has not deterred local industrial capitalists from utilizing resources from the mainland for their own profit-making purposes. Prior to the opening of China for foreign investments, China facilitates industrialization in Hong Kong by supplying food and daily necessities at low cost and providing industrialists with repeated waves of refugee laborers through legal and illegal migration. When economic reform was carried out after the fall of the Gang of Four, there was further opening of the socialist economy for capitalist offshore production. China, especially the region around the Pearl River Delta, became the destination of Hong Kong's relocated plants. As we have noted earlier, Hong Kong manufacturers are largely left on their own. Relocation of production across the border is a strategy which fits in well with the needs of the manufacturers. While they maintain their connections with global capitalism through their established bases in Hong Kong, actual production is carried out in China for the purpose of reducing production costs. Indeed, it is fair to say that southern China and Hong Kong, at least in terms of economic connections, are increasingly tied up. The future development of the Hong Kong economy is largely embedded in the continuation of economic reform in China.

The case of Singapore also shows the relevance of geo-economics and geo-politics at the regional level. Its status as a port city in colonial Malaya resulted extensive commercial linkages in trade, finance, and industry during the inter-war years. These linkages originated from Singapore and were linked particularly to Malaya Peninsula (see Huff 1994). After the Second World War, political uncertainties and nationalistic fervor kept neigboring countries from working out regional economic cooperation programs. After Singapore's rapid industrialization in the 1970s and 1980s, the higher cost of manufacturing in Singapore is pushing firms into the neighboring countries. The new regional economic reality is being accelerated by various inter-state cooperative efforts between Singapore, Malaysia, Indonesia, and Thailand. Thus, the economic integration of

Hong Kong and South China is being repeated within the Southeast Asia region. Unlike the Hong Kong-South China case where integration efforts are largely initiatives of businessmen relying on cultural ties (Smart and Smart 1991), the Southeast Asian integration is enhanced through regional forums such as ASEAN and inter-government bilateral and tri-lateral arrangements.

Size

In the East Asian development literature, when writers point out that Hong Kong and Singapore are "atypical," the accusation is often that these two countries are city-states. This observation is valid, but the unfortunate part is that the analysis stops there. First, typicality or atypicality should not be abstracted from the broader context. When Hong Kong and Singapore are so described, they are actually types, with their specificities though, within a continuum. They are not types which fall out of the range and, therefore, are irrelevant for comparative purpose. More importantly, the distinctiveness of city-states and its contrast to countries is a combination of two basic traits that can be separated analytically, but not empirically: both Hong Kong and Singapore are *cities*, and they are both *small* in terms of land area and population. These two traits bring about a host of issues which are both advantageous and problematic. For example, the absence of a hinterland and countryside inhibits the growth of the local economy but this absence reduces the scale of various problems. Also, they do have to encounter issues such as rural development, rural-urban problems (e.g., migration), inter-regional and inter-city rivalries, and the politics and associated inertia of a federated government structure.

There is now a growing European literature on small states and development which has resulted in a number of insights into how size has shaped the organization of the economy, domestic politics, and foreign relations. According to Saul (1982), the economic histories of small countries in Europe in the nineteenth century have suggested that by being small,

1. it is possible to achieve a more rational and intelligent economic policy where there are fewer interests to reconcile;
2. development is achieved by specialization (driven by lack of natural resources and limited options of development strategy available) in niches created by neighboring and overseas markets;
3. such niches are either not attractive to larger countries, but sufficient to smaller ones, or such niches are in areas where smaller countries can and do compete; and

4. governments are forced to play a larger role in supporting industry because of the imperatives of size.

Katzenstein (1985) suggests, also from the evidence of small European states, that there are commonalities:

1. in domestic politics, the acute awareness of the fragility of small states, their open economy, and their dependence on overseas markets have helped shape the kind of democratic corporatist structure which emerged in small European states; and
2. in external relations, small states rely heavily and participate actively in regional and international organizations.

The reason why geography is so important to Hong Kong and Singapore has to do with the dynamics that originate from their city-state status. Being small city-states, both Hong Kong and Singapore have to be outward-looking. One can say that, by default, import-substitution is simply not a viable development strategy for such small city-states. Export-oriented industrialization is the option which they have to adopt. A small domestic market is simply not able to support the local industries. The survival of these industries hinges upon their ability to export. Moreover, being small, urban, and without a larger hinterland, the city-states have to rely on resources from the neighboring countries for their own consumption and development. These hinterlands are created through geo-politics and geo-economics and the two city-states have tapped on resources from China and Southeast Asian countries for the development of their manufacturing industries.

Saul's insight into the problem of size and the diversity of industrial options is also applicable to the industrial restructuring experiences of Hong Kong and Singapore. Hong Kong and Singapore concentrate on a few industries instead of developing a broad industry base. Extensive forward and backward linkages exist only in a few major industries, for example, garment in Hong Kong and electronics (this should be considered as emerging) in Singapore. The constraint of size, in a large measure, is responsible for the movement of Hong Kong capital into South China. Similarly, but under the different Singaporean institutional configuration, small size and the accompanying constraints on land and labor resources, account for the expansion of MNC-dominated and government-supported industrial sectors at the expense of traditional and labor-intensive sectors.

Katzenstein's relation of size to local and regional politics is certainly applicable to Singapore since one can arguably take the position that

Singapore has maintained a corporatist structure which incorporates both business and organized labor. And at the regional level, Singapore has, especially since the 1980s, worked with its neighbors within the ASEAN forum to achieve collective economic objectives relating to trade, and with multilateral arrangements with Malaysia and Indonesia, to achieve a higher level of FDI. The case of Hong Kong is, understandably, a variation from the Katzenstein model since foreign policy and domestic politics are dictated by Britain and China.

State Intervention

The question concerning the effects of state intervention on economic development of the two city-states comes directly out of the state-market debate. The attempt to polarize the constructs of state and market simplifies a complex issue because it ends up abstracting both concepts.

Our study tells a story of different *types* of state involvement. While it is true that, quantitatively, Singapore is more state interventionist than Hong Kong, this is not to say that the colonial state stays aloof from economic affairs. As we have emphasized in earlier chapters, the colonial state actually plays an active role in providing mass public housing, education, and medical services. The debate concerning whether the colonial state of Hong Kong is interventionist or otherwise is basically misplaced. The contrast between Hong Kong and Singapore lies in the role of the state in directing the development of industry. The colonial state gives no incentives to any particular industry. Nor does it assume a leading role in shaping and reshaping the structure of local industries. Industrial capitalists in Hong Kong are very much on their own in competing with competitors from other NIEs. In short, the response of individual manufacturers to the changing business environment and their strategy of restructuring are instituted by the existing configuration of state-economy relationship. The organizational bifurcation in the two industrial systems is the outcome of such instituted processes. What is also important is that both circumstances have enjoyed successes which accompany these varied forms of state involvement.

The same can be said of free market liberalism. Given differences in the role of the state in economic development, one can hardly imagine how free market liberalism can be applied to both Hong Kong and Singapore. The market does not operate in a vacuum. Rather, it is embedded in specific institutional settings. In the two city-states, there are no abstract market mechanisms creating economic growth in the same manner. To abstract the market out of its context is simply begging the question of how state and market interact in the two city-states.

It is quite clear that our analysis is critical of any sweeping generalization of a mono-casual explanation of East Asian development. Our discussion above suggests that the attempt to look for a general thesis, should it be developmental state, free market liberalism or changing international division of labor, is basically misplaced. Our answer is to examine the structural and institutional configuration of the path to industrialism. We emphasize the interactions between global and local factors. Also, our analysis requires us to look at the dynamics of industrial development at the institutional level. That is, the institutional setting has its independent effects in shaping industrial organizations. Our analysis of industrial restructuring is an examination of the organizational strategies of manufacturers in a concrete historical and instituted contexts.

Consequences of Industrial Restructuring

Following our discussion of the role of the state in the above section, our argument is that different paths of economic development and varying modes of state intervention will bring about different labor market outcomes in the process of industrial restructuring. We ask: what are the impacts and implications of industrial restructuring for Hong Kong and Singapore labor markets? Will the city-states follow the footsteps of other advanced industrial societies in restructuring their labor markets, particularly in terms of rising unemployment and human resource redeployment, during the process of reorganizing manufacturing production? Our path-dependence approach alerts us to the important fact that while both Hong Kong and Singapore are working hard to cope with the rising pressures of industrial restructuring, the prospects of manufacturing labor in the two city-states can be very different.

Between 1988 and 1993, 336,442 employed persons in the manufacturing sector had been displaced as a result of the process of industrial restructuring in Hong Kong. Further reduction of the size of manufacturing employment is projected because of massive relocation of industrial plants to mainland China. Workers displaced by industrial restructuring tend to be female, older, less-educated, and less-skilled workers (cf. Census and Statistics Department 1994).

The impact of industrial restructuring on the local labor market is mediated by existing social divisions. Local labor organizations have expressed their concerns of rising unemployment among marginalized workers. Given their lack of formal educational credentials and restricted experience of working outside the manufacturing sector, displaced industrial workers have experienced great difficulties in finding new jobs. Up to now, there are no official statistics that would allow us to comment on the pattern of job shift in the context of recent restructuring processes in the manufacturing sector. But tentative findings (see, for example, Ngo 1994; Chan et al. 1994; Lai et al. 1995) suggest that many retrenched women workers can only find new jobs in the lower tiers of the labor market of the service sector. Quite a number of them have become part-timers in fast-food chain stores or cleaning *amahs*. Their experiences of transition from manufacturing to services often mean moving down to lower paying and insecure jobs in a casualized labor market.

For those who remain in manufacturing, they experience slow improvement, if not deterioration, in their incomes (Chiu and Levin 1993:20-25). Furthermore, one should note that there has been a widening of income disparity between production workers (i.e., craftsmen and other operatives) and middle-level employees (i.e., supervisors, clerical, and technical staff) in many manufacturing industries (for textiles and garment, see Chiu and Levin 1993). A growing income gap between men and women employees in manufacturing goes along with the internal stratification of the workforce noted above.

Manufacturing jobs have not only become badly paid, they have also become more insecure. The share of industrial disputes caused by insolvency and cessation of business increased from 39.2% in 1989 to 61.8% in 1993 (Commissioner for Labour 1990:141, 1994:57). These figures suggest that manufacturing workers have to confront the harsh realities of plant closures and abrupt terminations of production. Many other workers suffer from underemployment as local plants reduce production quotas and subsequently choose to leave their jobs.

The response of the colonial government towards labor market adjustment problems is the establishment of a retraining program. Whether such a retraining scheme will be effective in helping workers cope with industrial restructuring is a matter for further investigation. At present, the effectiveness of retraining is a contentious topic between local unions and the government. Unions are vocal in criticizing the inadequacy of the retraining scheme, particularly in the areas of its restricted scope of training and limited commitment to assisting trainees in finding new employment.

As Hong Kong is increasingly integrated into the economy of South China, further restructuring of the local labor market will be expected. Some white-collar jobs, such as typing and other clerical work, can easily be relocated to Shenzhen and other special economic zones through the use of fax modem and new information technology. While it is still too early to access the full range of the impacts of industrial restructuring on the labor market, it is clear that the Hong Kong labor market is increasingly embedded in the Hong Kong-South China economic region.

While the manufacturing workforce in Hong Kong is being battered by the movement of manufacturing capital to southern China, the situation in Singapore is quite different. As indicated in Table 4.8, the employment share of manufacturing has remained fairly stable through the 1980s and 1990s, at close to 30% of the total labor force. Thus, at the aggregate level, there is little evidence to suggest labor displacement on a scale indicated in Hong Kong towards the late 1980s. A closer examination is possible by using the Labor Force Survey figures for labor retrenched and workers affected by the cessation of business in Singapore as a rough indicator of the number of workers displaced by industrial restructuring. The number of workers displaced by company retrenchment and company closing its operations in Singapore hovered between three to four thousand workers per year, between 1981 and 1993. The exception was between 1985 and 1988, where the number of workers displaced by the recession rose very sharply. The highest was in 1986, with the figure at 28,781. The characteristics of displaced workers also show some variation from the Hong Kong case. Women, for example, are not adversely affected. The percentage of women workers who were displaced dropped from 30.7% in 1981 to hover around the mid-20s percentage points between 1983 and 1993. Similarly, in the years where the age of displaced workers are reported (i.e., from 1989 onward), the percentage of displaced workers 40 years and above varied between 15% and 18%. The variable which has a significant influence is the education level of displaced workers. Displaced workers who had primary school education and less (i.e., up to six years of formal education) represented between 65% and 75% for the period 1981 to 1988. This figure started to decline after 1988, to 53.7% in 1991, 38.9% in 1993, and 29.7% in 1994. Thus, if we make the reasonable assumption that low education and low skill are closely connected, then the low skilled jobs were the targets of the industrial restructuring of the 1980s, where the rapid wage increases initiated by the government essentially forced firms to restructure their operations by substituting low skilled labor for machines, or move their operations overseas. Moreover, the figures suggest that this process of shedding the lower value-added components of manufacturing operations was essentially completed by the late 1980s.

The effect of industrial restructuring on the labor market is, therefore, the systematically displacement of lower skilled workers as firms restructure their operations. As elaborated in Chapter 4, this restructuring also has an inter-industry dynamic. In an increasing cost and competitive environment, industries in Singapore end up experiencing different fortunes. For example, we see how the garment industry in Singapore has been hard hit by a set of local and international economic factors. Domestic problems of rising labor and land costs, problems of labor availability and, foreign exchange losses incurred as a result of an appreciating Singapore dollar confront all manufacturers in Singapore. However, these problems are more serious for the garment industry since the product does not allow extensive mechanization as a labor saving strategy. Unlike the case of Hong Kong, many firms are also too small to consider plant relocation as a shelter. Aside from operating within an increasingly restrictive international economic regime controlled by quota systems set by the West, Singapore garment exporters are also facing stiff competition from the newly developing countries. Thus, since the 1990s, the number of garment manufacturers has fallen steadily, with a corresponding declines in output and employment shares for the garment industry.

The electronics industry in Singapore, on the other hand, has successfully managed the same set of domestic problems. With an selective state policy favoring electronics, the industry has, from the 1980s onward been restructuring its operations, making use of government incentives to automate, retrain workers in upgraded operations while moving the more labor intensive phases into the neighboring countries. The manufacturing which remains in Singapore is essentially in higher skilled and technological operations, notably in wafer fabrication. The regional division of labor which results from manufacturing relocation has also made the electronics industry in Singapore more service oriented. There is the tendency for companies to maintain administrative regional headquarters in Singapore to perform producer services such as marketing, component purchasing, manpower training for manufacturing subsidiaries scattered in the region.

The differential impacts of industrial restructuring on various industries mean that the surplus labor created by unemployment and labor redundancy faced by one industry tend to be absorbed by more vibrant industries. This movement of labor has been facilitated by an active labor retraining program that is sponsored by the government and trade unions. It may be suggested that the percentage of displaced workers having primary education and less has been declining since 1989 because of such schemes.

Hong Kong and Singapore in the Global Economy

What are the prospects for NIEs like Hong Kong and Singapore in meeting the challenge of the changing business environment? Are the two little dragons in distress? Can they continue to compete competitively with other NIEs? Of course, these questions can become topics for separate research projects. In the following sections, we shall look at these issues and give our tentative thoughts about the future economic development of Hong Kong and Singapore.

In the earlier chapters and the sections above, we have pointed out the pressures on industries in the two city-states for restructuring. Rising production costs have already driven manufacturing industries in Hong Kong and Singapore to look for new strategies for survival. Our question here is whether they can survive and compete with other NIEs in the context of changing domestic economic environment and increasingly fierce competition. Will they wither as a result of more NIEs from the same region entering the economic competition? Will the economies of the two city-states be restructured and come to assume new leading roles in the growing East Asian economy?

In our discussion of industrial relocation in Hong Kong, we have underlined the trend of further economic integration between the city-state and South China. The economic linkages between Hong Kong and the special economic zones in the Pearl River Delta are well documented (Sit 1991; Federation of Hong Kong Industries 1992; Ho and Kueh 1993). Recent studies have pointed to the further extension of investments from Hong Kong into other parts of China and areas of economic activity other than manufacturing (such as retail, services, property, and finance) (see, for example, Federation of Hong Kong Industries 1993). If tension eases across the Taiwan Strait, earlier optimism (e.g., Chen and Ho 1994) on the prospects of a "Southern China Growth Triangle" which consists of Hong Kong, Taipei, and the special economic zones of South China may be revived. The advantageous position of Hong Kong in this emergent economic subregion lies in its status as a world city. The global connections of local business through trading and financial activities will place Hong Kong in a competitive position *vis-à-vis* Taipei and other cities within this subregion. Indeed, as we have argued in earlier chapters, Hong Kong is undergoing a process of economic restructuring through which the city-state has assumed the important role of regional headquarters for commercial and "manufacturing related services." Many firms find Hong Kong the ideal location "for their controlling head-quarters and for arranging trade financing and documentation" (Trade Development Council 1991:12).

However, it is not difficult to see that the continual growth of Hong Kong as a center of commercial and "manufacturing related activities" hinges upon two main factors. First, it concerns political uncertainty related to the 1997 issue. The eventual return of Hong Kong to China means a change of political and economic environment. Though the maintenance of the capitalist system has been guaranteed in the Basic Law jointly signed by the British and Chinese governments, there is still the uncertainty concerning the autonomy of the economy from political intervention. A relevant issue here concerns the scope of political intervention in daily socio-economic life. Even without an imposition of socialist ideological control over economic activities, it remains to be seen how a system which works effectively in an environment of free information flows and free markets can be maintained. In other words, it is a question of institutional compatibility between a socialist political system and a capitalist economy. Also pertinent is whether the "Hong Kong style" entrepreneurship will continue to flourish after the return to China. Of course, any projection of the Hong Kong economy after 1997 is necessarily speculative. But few observers would have failed to notice that the success of the Hong Kong economy rests on its ability to incorporate market capitalism along with the demands of the Chinese mainland government. The crux of the matter is, therefore, whether two economic systems (Hong Kong and China) can actually work within one overarching political regime.

Second, as Hong Kong is increasingly integrated into the regional development of South China, the prospects of its economy depend much on the future of economic reform in the Chinese socialist system. Through the process of economic integration, it is now difficult to conceive of Hong Kong as a separate economic entity from South China. As we have noted in our discussion of industrial relocation, it is clear that the future development of Hong Kong's industries depends significantly on the utilization of land and human resources in South China. South China serves as a hinterland for the industries of Hong Kong. Such a trend of economic integration is expected to continue and, increasingly, Hong Kong will be connected to the economy of China through a wider spectrum of economic activities. Furthermore, after 1997, both in terms of the construction of the infrastructure and the traffic of economic activity, Hong Kong will be fully embedded in the regional development of South China. Whether Hong Kong will continue to prosper is much affected by the conditions of the Chinese economy.

The manufacturing industries of Hong Kong are primarily outward looking. The future of Hong Kong industries will continue to depend on trade and export. In addition to their connections with markets of advanced industrial societies, Hong Kong industries are capable of tapping into the expanding markets in the East Asian region. Hong Kong manufacturing products are renowned for their trendy outlook. Such an image has helped Hong Kong entrepreneurs to develop their retail markets within the region. They are very capable of developing regional brand names which have the ability to reach markets of developed countries, and also the sensitivity to adjust to the taste and consumption habits of Asian consumers. How Hong Kong industries are going to capitalize on the growing economies and the concomitant expanding markets for consumer goods within the region will be an important issue for manufacturers' consideration.

While the future of the Hong Kong economy will be increasingly shaped by political conditions and economic consequences in larger China, the Singapore economy faces a different set of challenges. There is considerable evidence that firms have relocated labor intensive manufacturing operations into neighboring regions, a process which started in the mid-1980s. In the resultant division of labor, Singapore like Hong Kong, ends up with more service functions overseeing and supporting manufacturing operations in the region. However, unlike Hong Kong which will see a natural evolution to a service and commerce base because of the political and economic integration with the mainland, a regional integration process with Singapore and its neighbors cannot be taken for granted. Thus, the Singapore government will have to continue its diplomatic efforts within regional bodies like ASEAN and in strengthening bilateral ties in order to ensure economic integration.

Unlike Hong Kong, the Singapore government also continues to accord priority to manufacturing. Indeed, the major difference between Hong Kong and Singapore has been state leadership in industrial development — from the fashioning of selective industrial policies to attempts at building institutions (e.g., finance, labor) that are supportive of the industrialization program. The challenge for Singapore within the context of a more competitive global economy is whether a state regulated economic regime that continues to be reliant on MNCs will be as conducive to growth as the Singapore economy matures.

Such a model faces several challenges. First, Singapore's small size continues to pose constraints in the deepening and widening of the industrial base. It is uncertain whether Singapore's industrial base can remain competitive without the continued involvement of MNCs. Second, the strategy of attracting MNCs to use Singapore as an production export platform, a strategy which has worked well in the past, will become more difficult to put into practice. As Singapore has already priced itself out of low-cost, labor-intensive manufacturing operations, successive efforts at attracting manufacturing operations at the mid to high-skill and capital-intensive levels will be more costly, as the wafer fabrication project has shown. On this issue of attracting foreign manufacturing capital, Singapore's edge has been in the ability of the state to foresee technology trends and stay ahead of the competition by making it attractive (not just tax incentives, but through joint ventures and equity financing and through efficient resource mobilization [e.g., rapid labor training and retraining programs, land conversion schemes]) for multinationals to come and manufacture on the island. In such efforts, the state has really gone beyond the "developmentalist" label and a strong case could be made for an "entrepreneurial state." But herein also lies a crucial difference between Hong Kong and Singapore. In the Singapore case, the task and the talent for spotting technology trends and picking the "winners" tend to lie in the bureaucracy not in industry. The flexibilities, accordingly, are quite different. To summarize and somewhat simplify the argument made by Young (1992), Hong Kong's growth has been achieved by a learned maturity (learning by doing) while Singapore's growth has been through technology transfer by a changing mix of MNC activities. While Young's argument on the superiority of the Hong Kong over the Singapore model is open to debate on several methodological points (see Chapter 6), there is no question that the strategies are quite different. Thus, while the flexibility in the Hong Kong case lies within the industry, with Singapore, the initiative lies in the hands of the state.

Chapters 2 and 6 have shown that this flexibility is embedded in the institutional framework of Singapore, especially in terms of the responsiveness of finance and labor to state initiatives. Our comparative analysis has also demonstrated that the state has made a difference in dampening the effects of deindustrialization and fostering technology upgrading. However, the success of earlier industrial targeting and resource mobilization efforts will be more difficult to duplicate when rising domestic production costs dictate more expensive capital-intensive ventures. Perhaps the most fascinating question in the Hong Kong and Singapore comparison is the question of how is industrial restructuring best handled. It remains debatable whether this exercise is better managed by bureaucrats or industrialists. The Hong Kong story shows how industrialists are better placed to handle adjustments within industry (through relocation into China and by incorporating the latest designs and fashions), while the Singapore side illustrates how bureaucrats are able to stage inter-industry shifts and are better placed to mobilize the finance and labor systems to achieve such shifts.

Our study of the trajectories of industrial development in Hong Kong and Singapore shows how the two city-states have grown and prospered in the global economy. In the face of growing pressures from rising production costs and fierce competition from other NIEs, the two city-states are finding different ways of restructuring their industries and making the necessary adjustments. Our emphasis is placed on the interactions among history, institution, and the global economy in shaping the paths of industrial development. And we argue for a path-dependent explanation of changes in industrial development in the two city-states.

Our efforts in disaggregating the Asian NIEs and probing the historical and institutional configurations of industrial development show the direction of a more fruitful and rigorous approach to the comparative analysis of Asian capitalism.

Appendix:
Survey on Enterprise Strategy[1]

Preamble

This survey is part of a comparative research project on industrial restructuring in the Asian NIEs. The project is sponsored and coordinated by the East-West Center's Population Institute in Honolulu. At the local level, the project is being conducted by the institutions listed in the acknowledgements. The aim of the project is to better understand the changing conditions facing local companies and enterprises, and the kinds of responses of businesses to those economic pressures. The survey asks questions related to technology, labor costs, labor supply and turnover, investment decisions and future plans in relation to market conditions.

Information obtained from the survey will be treated as CONFIDENTIAL. No information will be released to the public which could identify particular companies or enterprises. Your participation in this survey is gratefully appreciated. Copies of the final report will be available upon request.

I. Basic Firm Data

1. Name and address of your firm:_____

2. Year of establishment: _____

3. Type of industry:_____

4. Principal products: 1. _____   2. _____   3. _____

5. Is your firm: 1. Fully locally owned 2. Fully foreign owned 3. Joint venture

6. Is your firm: 1. Listed   2. Unlisted

7. Is your firm: 1. Independent firm
                  2. Branch/subsidiary of another organization

     7-1. If independent, is it owner managed: 1. Yes   2. No

     7-2. If a branch or subsidiary, where is the headquarters of the parent company located?

     _____

8. How large was your enterprise as of the year end 1991:

     1. Total sales _____

     2. Number of Employees _____

II. Enterprise Size and Markets

9.   How many persons including management are working in your enterprise as of July 1992 (include those temporarily absent and on sick leave)?

	Male	Female
1. Full-time	_____	_____
2. Part-time	_____	_____
3. Total	_____	_____

10. What is the distribution of employees by occupation?

	Male	Female
1. Managerial/administrative	_____	_____
2. Professional/technical	_____	_____
3. Clerical/sales/service	_____	_____
4. Operatives	_____	_____
5. Others (e.g., apprentices, janitors, etc.)	_____	_____
6. Total	_____	_____

11. What is the proportion of production for export?

_____%

11-1. If any "export," where does your enterprise export to (percent of total exports):

	Region	Export (%)
1.	_____	_____
2.	_____	_____
3.	_____	_____
4.	_____	_____
5.	_____	_____

12. What are your principal sources of order?

	%
1. Direct order from overseas buyers	_____
2. Local import/export firms	_____
3. Local factories	_____
4. Wholesale/retail business	_____
5. Own overseas sales outlet	_____
6. Others (e.g., own local outlet)	_____

12-1. What proportion of your total orders/jobs come from the largest contractor/customer?

_____%

12-2. Has the largest contractor/customer been a steady source of orders in the past two years?

1. Yes   2. No

12-3. Do you have a stable market for your production in the past three years?

1. Very stable   2. Stable   3. Average

4. Unstable   5. Very unstable

III. Business Conditions and Plans

13. In the last two years, how has your business changed in terms of sales volume?

1. Increased   2. Decreased   3. Remained same

14. If business has decreased, what factors are responsible? (If more than one, list them in descending order of importance)

_____   _____   _____

15. If business has increased, what factors are responsible? (If more than one, list them in descending order of importance)

_____   _____   _____

16. Has your enterprise extended its range of products (including diversification of products, multiple products, and new products) in the last two years?

1. Yes   2. No

16-1. If yes, has that led to any changes in employment?

1. Increased   2. Decreased   3. No change

16-2. If yes, have the new products changed skill requirements in production?

1. Increased   2. Decreased   3. No change

17. In the last five years, has your enterprise invested in overseas plants / factories?

1. Yes   2. No

17-1. If yes, what year/years has the investment been made?

_____   _____   _____

17-2. If yes, what were the main reasons for investing overseas? (If more than one, list them in descending order of importance)

_____   _____   _____

17-3. If yes, where were those investments made?

_____   _____   _____

18.   For the next three years, is your enterprise planning to invest in overseas plants/factories?

      1. Yes   2. No

      18-1.   If yes, what is the main reason? (If more than one, list them in descending order of importance)

      _____   _____   _____

      18-2.   If yes, where will those investments be made?

      _____   _____   _____

IV.   Labor Market Conditions

19.   In the last three years, the wage rates of production workers in your enterprise have had:

      1. Steep increases   2. Moderate increases

      3. Decreases   4. Remained the same

20.   What was the rate of labor turnover (percent of workforce per year) in your enterprise in 1991?

      1. 0-9%   2. 10-29%   3. 30-49%   4. 50-69%   5. 70% and more

21.   Which groups had higher labor turnover rates?

      1. Male _____ or Female _____

      2. Skilled (more than 3 years of experience) _____ or Unskilled _____

      3. Young (less than 25 years old) _____ or Old _____

V.   Enterprise Strategy (Technology)

22.   Has your enterprise introduced new technology in the last two years?

      1. Yes   2. No

      22-1.   If yes, what kind of new technology?

      _____

      22-2.   If yes, were those technologies imported, domestically developed, or in-house developed?

      _____

      22-3.   If yes, has that caused any change in employment?

              1. Increased   2. Decreased   3. No change

23.   What were the main purposes of introducing new technology?(See below codes and list three major ones in descending order)

      _____   _____   _____

VI. Enterprise Strategy (Contract Work, Part-time, and Shift)[2]

24. Does your enterprise contract-out the following activities?

	Yes/No	No. of Contractors
1. Maintenance (including security)	_____	_____
2. Employees' welfare (e.g., transport, canteen)	_____	_____
3. Component/parts production	_____	_____
4. Others	_____	_____

24-1. If yes, what are the main reasons for contracting-out work?

_____   _____   _____

24-2. What is the proportion of your production expenses spent on paying your subcontractors?

_____%

24-3. If yes, is contract work mainly done on your enterprise's premises or in other locations?

_____   _____   _____

25. In the last two years, has your enterprise hired temporary or casual workers?

1. Yes   2. No

25-1. If yes, for what types of work?

_____   _____   _____

25-2. If yes, what are the major reasons for employing temporary or casual workers? (List three major ones in descending order)

_____   _____   _____

26. Does your enterprise employ more or fewer part-time workers compared with two years ago?

1. More   2. Fewer   3. Same

26-1. If more, what are the major reasons for that? (List up to three major ones in descending order)

_____   _____   _____

26-2. If fewer, what are the major reasons for that (List up to three major ones in descending order)

_____   _____   _____

27. Does your enterprise operate shifts for workers?

1. Yes   2. No

28. How many shifts has your enterprise been operating?

In July 1992: _____ per week

29. If the number of shifts changed in the last year, what was the direction of change?
     1. Increase   2. Decrease   3. Same

     29-1.   If increase, what was the main reason?
     _____

     29-2.   If decrease, what was the main reason?
     _____

30. Does your enterprise currently employ foreign workers?
     1. Yes   2. No

     30-1.   What is the major reason for hiring foreign workers?
     _____

     30-2.   How many foreign workers has your enterprise employed?
             Male _____   Female _____

31. Would your enterprise like to use foreign workers?
     1. Yes   2. No

VII. Enterprise Strategy (Redundancy, Retraining, and Retention)

32. Does your enterprise expect or plan to increase or reduce the number of employees in the next two years?
     1. Increase   2. Reduce   3. No change

     32-1.   If any change, what are the main reasons? (If more than one, list them in descending order in importance)
     _____   _____   _____   _____

33. Does your enterprise have retention strategies now?
     1. Yes   2. No

     33-1.   If yes, what kind of retention strategies do you have?
     _____   _____   _____

34. Does your enterprise offer any training schemes for the currently employed?
     1. Yes   2. No

     34-1.   If yes, what kind of training scheme do you have?
     _____   _____   _____

VIII. Labor Unions

35. Labor-management relations in your enterprise can be described as:

1	2	3	4	5
Cooperative		Neutral		Confrontational

36. To what extent do labor unions affect your enterprise strategy?

1	2	3	4	5
Considerably		Moderately		Negligibly

IX. Management Opinions

37. In the last two years, do you think the public sector including government was supportive of enterprise management in terms of:

	Very supportive		Neutral		Supportive
1. Marketing	1	2	3	4	5
2. Infrastructure provision	1	2	3	4	5
3. Industrial relation	1	2	3	4	5
4. Information and consultation	1	2	3	4	5
5. R&D support	1	2	3	4	5

38. What programs would your enterprise like provided by the public sector to facilitate enterprise development?

Notes

1. The questionnaire reproduced here only includes those core, common questions which have been used in the Hong Kong and Singapore surveys. Minor changes in the wordings of the questions and coding of answers are allowed to adjust to local circumstances.

2. This section reproduces the set of questions on contract work, part-time, and shift used in the Singapore survey. A different set of questions is used in the Hong Kong survey to probe employers' use of different forms of informal work.

Abbreviations

ARDS	Applied Research and Development Scheme
ASEAN	Association of Southeast Asian Nations
CCP	Chinese Communist Party
COWEC	Company Welfarism Through Employers' CPF Contributions Scheme
CPF	Central Provident Fund
DBS	Development Bank of Singapore
EDB	Economic Development Board
EEC	European Economic Community
ERB	Employees Retraining Board
FDI	Foreign Direct Investment
GATT	General Agreement on Tariffs and Trade
GDP	Gross Domestic Product
GLC	Government-Linked Company
HKPC	Hong Kong Productivity Council
IMF	International Monetary Fund
ITCC	Hong Kong Industrial Technology Centre Corporation
JIT	Just-in-Time System
LEFS	Local Enterprise Finance Scheme
MAS	Monetary Authority of Singapore
MFA	Multi-Fibre Arrangement
MNC	Multinational Corporation
MOL	Ministry of Labour
MTI	Ministry of Trade and Industry
NIC	Newly Industrializing Country
NIE	Newly Industrialized Economy
NTUC	National Trade Union Congress
NWC	National Wages Council
OEM	Original Equipment Manufacturing
PAP	People's Action Party
PRC	People's Republic of China
R&D	Research and Development
SATU	Singapore Air Transport Workers

SDF	Skills Development Fund
SESDAQ	Stock Exchange of Singapore Dealing and Automated Quotation System
SHB	Singapore Harbour Board
SIFS	Small Industry Finance Scheme
SME	Small and Medium Enterprise
TDC	Trade Development Council
TFP	Total Factor Productivity
UNCTC	United Nations Centre on Transnational Corporations
VITB	Vocational and Industrial Training Board

References

Amsden, Alice H. 1989. *Asia's Next Giant.* New York: Oxford University Press.

Arrighi, Giovanni. 1994. "The Rise of East Asia: World-system and Regional Aspects." Paper prepared for the conference "L'economia mondiale in transformazione." October 6-8, Rome.

Arrow, Kenneth. 1974. *The Limits of Organization.* New York: W.W. Norton & Company.

Bailey, T. 1993. "Organizational Innovation in the Apparel Industry." *Industrial Relations* 32: 30-48.

Balassa, B. 1988. "Lessons of East Asian Development: An Overview." *Economic Development and Cultural Change* 36: S273-90.

Barro, R. 1992. "Industrial Policy, a Tale of Two Cities." *The Wall Street Journal* April 1.

Bauer, J. 1992. "Industrial Restructuring in the NIEs: Prospects and Challenges." *Asian Survey* 32: 1012-25.

Berger, Peter L. 1986. *The Capitalist Revolution.* New York: Basic Books.

———. 1988. "An East Asian Development Model?" in Peter Berger, and Michael Hsiao, eds., *In Search of An East Asian Development Model.* Pp. 3-11. New Brunswick: Transaction Books.

Berger, Suzanne, and Michael J. Piore. 1980. *Dualism and Discontinuity in Industrial Societies.* Cambridge: Cambridge University Press.

Birnbaum, D. 1993. *Importing Garments Through Hong Kong.* Hong Kong: Third Horizon Press.

Breen, M.J. 1935. *Report of the Commission on the Causes and Effects of the Present Trade Depression in Hong Kong.* Hong Kong: Government Printer.

Bristow, Roger. 1984. *Land-use Planning in Hong Kong.* Hong Kong: Oxford University Press.

Bryant, R.C. 1989. "The Evolution of Singapore as a Financial Centre," in K.S. Sandhu, and P. Wheatley, eds., *Management of Success: The Moulding of Modern Singapore.* Pp. 337-72. Singapore: Institute of Southeast Asian Studies.

Buchanan, Ian. 1972. *Singapore in Southeast Asia: An Economic and Political Appraisal.* London: G. Bell and Sons Ltd.

Burton, Jonathan. 1992. "Writing on the Wall." *Far Eastern Economic Review* August 27: 59-60.

Business Times. July 11, 1986. S'pore Showing the Way in Disk Drive Production.

———. January 25, 1989. Seven Workers Lost for Every Eight Hired, MNCs Report High Turnover of Staff.

———. April 26, 1989. Asian NIEs Labour Costs Provide the Edge in World Trade: Report.

————. May 26, 1989. Conveyor System to Boost Garment Trade Productivity.

————. September 25, 1991. Govt Can Help Companies Go Regional.

————. October 15, 1991. BG Lee Urges Moderation in Wage Rises, Hiring of Foreign Workers.

————. December 13, 1991. Strategic Investments Abroad Mostly by Govt-linked Firms.

————. March 6, 1992. Manufacturers Relocating to Beat Rising Wage Costs.

————. March 24, 1992. A Stitch in Time.

————. November 29, 1992. S'pore Govt Unveils First Major Investment in China.

————. September 19, 1993. TDB Cuts Export Quotas of 10 Garment Firms for Flouting Rules.

————. June 2, 1994. Penang-Singapore Rivalry Sharpens.

Butters, J. 1939. *Report on the Labour and Labouring Conditions in Hong Kong*. Hong Kong: Noroha & Co.

Castells, M. 1992. "Four Asian Tigers with a Dragon Head: A Comparative Analysis of the State, Economy and Society in the Asian Pacific Rim," in R.P. Appelbaum, and J. Henderson, eds., *States and Development in the Asian Pacific Rim*. Pp. 33-70. Newbury Park: Sage.

Castells, M., L. Goh, and Y.W. Kwok. 1990. *The Shek Kip Mei Syndrome: Economic Development and Public Housing in Hong Kong and Singapore*. London: Pion.

Census and Statistics Department. 1982a. *Hong Kong 1981 Census, Main Report, Vol.1: Analysis*. Hong Kong: Government Printer.

————. 1982b. *Hong Kong 1981 Census, Main Report, Vol.2: Tables*. Hong Kong: Government Printer.

————. 1991. *Estimates of Gross Domestic Product: 1966 to 1990*. Hong Kong: Government Printer.

————. 1992. *Estimates of Gross Domestic Product: 1966 to 1991*. Hong Kong: Government Printer.

————. 1993a. *Estimates of Gross Domestic Product: 1966 to 1992*. Hong Kong: Government Printer.

————. 1993b. *Hong Kong Population Census: Main Report*. Hong Kong: Government Printer.

————. 1993c. "Structural Changes in Manufacturing Industries 1981-1991," in *Hong Kong Monthly Digest of Statistics* September. Pp. 113-23.

————. 1994. *Revised Estimates of Gross Domestic Product, 1961 to First Quarter of 1994*. Hong Kong: Government Printer.

————. 1995. "Trading Firms with Manufacturing-related Functions," in *Hong Kong Monthly Digest of Statistics* August. Pp. FA1-FA8.

————. Various years. *Annual Digest of Statistics*. Hong Kong: Government Printer.

Chan, K.W., et al. 1994. Women Workers under Industrial Restructuring in Hong Kong. Mimeograph.

Chang, E.R. 1969. *Report on the National Income Survey of Hong Kong*. Hong Kong: Government Printer.

Cheah, Hock Beng. 1988. "Labour in Transition: The Case of Singapore." *Labour and Industry* 1: 258-86.

Chen, E.K.Y., and Anna Ho. 1994. "Southern China Growth Triangle: An Overview," in M. Thant, M. Tang, and H. Kakazu, eds., *Growth Triangles in Asia*. Pp. 29-72. Hong Kong: Oxford University Press.

Chen, E.K.Y. and K.W. Li. 1991. "Industry Development and Industrial Policy in Hong Kong," in E.K.Y. Chen, M.K. Nyaw, and T.Y.C. Wong, eds., *Industrial and Trade Development in Hong Kong*. Pp. 3-47. Hong Kong: Centre of Asian Studies, University of Hong Kong.

Cheng, Siok Hwa. 1991. "Economic Change and Industrialization," in Ernest C.T. Chew, and Edwin Lee, eds., *A History of Singapore*. Pp. 182-215. Singapore: Oxford University Press.

Chew, Ernest C.T., and Edwin Lee, eds. 1991. *A History of Singapore*. Singapore: Oxford University Press.

Chew, Soon Beng. 1991. *Trade Unionism in Singapore*. Singapore: McGraw Hill.

Chia, L.S. 1989. "The Port of Singapore," in K.S. Sandhu, and P. Wheatley, eds., *Management of Success: The Moulding of Modern Singapore*. Pp. 314-36. Singapore: Institute of Southeast Asian Studies.

Chia, Kay Guan, and Kwei Cheong Wong. 1989. *Venture Capital in the Asia Pacific Region*. Singapore: Toppan Co.

Chia, Siow-yue. 1981. "Foreign Direct Investment in Manufacturing in Developing Countries: The Case of Singapore," in F.E.I. Hamilton, and G.J.R. Linge, eds., *Spatial Analysis, Industry and the Industrial Environment*. New York: Wiley & Sons.

――――. 1989. "The Character and Progress of Industrialisation," in K.S. Sandhu, and P. Wheatley, eds., *Management of Success: The Moulding of Modern Singapore*. Pp. 250-79. Singapore: Institute of Southeast Asian Studies.

Chiu, Stephen W.K. 1987. Strikes in Hong Kong: A Sociological Study. M.Phil. Thesis, University of Hong Kong.

――――. 1992. The State and the Financing of Industrialization in East Asia. Ph.D. Thesis, Princeton University.

――――. 1994a. "The Changing World Order and the East Asian Newly Industrialized Countries," in David Jacobson, ed., *Old Nations, New World: The Evolution of a New World Order*. Pp. 75-114. Boulder: Westview.

――――. 1994b. "The Politics of Laissez-faire: Hong Kong's Strategy of Industrialization in Historical Perspective." Hong Kong: Occasional Paper No. 40, Hong Kong Institute of Asia-Pacific Studies, The Chinese University of Hong Kong.

Chiu, Stephen W.K., and David Levin. 1993. "Labour under Industrial Restructuring in Hong Kong." Hong Kong: Occasional Paper No. 21, Hong Kong Institute of Asia-Pacific Studies, The Chinese University of Hong Kong.

Chiu, Stephen W.K., and Tai-lok Lui. 1995. "Hong Kong: Unorganized Industrialism," in Gordon Clark, and W.B. Kim, eds., *Asian NIEs and the Global Economy*. Pp. 85-112. Baltimore: Johns Hopkins University Press.

Chiu, T.N. 1973. *The Port of Hong Kong*. Hong Kong: Hong Kong University Press.

Choi, Y.P., H.S. Chung, and N. Marian. 1985. *The Multi-Fibre Arrangement in Theory and Practice*. London: Frances Pinter.

Choy, Kah Wai. 1985. A Review of the Government Assistance Scheme to Small Industry in Singapore. Unpublished academic excercise, School of Postgraduate Management Studies, National University of Singapore.

Chu, Y.W. 1988. Dependent Industrialization: The Case of the Hong Kong Garment Industry. M.Phil. Thesis, Sociology Department, University of Hong Kong.

Clark, David. 1971. "Labour Market and Industrial Relations," in Poh Seng You, and Chong Yah Lim, eds., *The Singapore Economy*. Pp. 307-27. Singapore: Eastern Universities Press.

Commissioner for Labour. Various years. *Annual Departmental Report*. Hong Kong: Government Printer.

Cumings, B. 1987. "The Origins and Development of the Northeast Asian Political Economy: Industrial Sectors, Product Cycles and Political Consequences," in F.C. Deyo, ed., *The Political Economy of the New East Asian Industrialism*. Pp. 182-202. Ithaca: Cornell University Press.

Dataquest. 1991. *Techno-economic and Market Research Study on Hong Kong's Electronics Industry 1988-1989*. Hong Kong: Government Printer.

David, Paul A. 1986. "Understanding the Economics of QWERTY: The Necessity of History," in William Parker, ed., *Economic History and the Modern Economist*. Pp. 30-49. Oxford: Blackwell.

———. 1994. "Why are Institutions the 'Carriers of History'?: Path Dependence and the Evolution of Conventions, Organizations and Institutions." *Structural Change and Economic Dynamics* 5: 205-20.

Davies, S.G. 1949. *Hong Kong in its Geographical Setting*. London: Collins.

Demas, W.G. 1965. *The Economics of Development in Small Countries with Special Reference to the Carribbean*. Montreal: McGill University Press.

Department of Statistics. 1983. *Economic & Social Statistics Singapore 1960-1982*. Singapore: Department of Statistics.

———. Various years. *Yearbook of Statistics Singapore*. Singapore: Department of Statistics.

Deyo, Fred. 1989. *Beneath the Miracle*. Berkeley: University of California Press.

Dicken, P. 1992. *Global Shift: Industrial Change in a Turbulent World*. 2nd edn. London: Harper and Row.

DiMaggio, Paul. 1994. "Culture and Economy," in Neil J. Smelser, and Richard Swedberg, eds., *The Handbook of Economic Sociology*. Pp. 27-57. Princeton: Princeton University Press.

Doshi, T. 1989. *Houston of Asia: The Singapore Petroleum Industry*. Singapore: Institute of Southeast Asian Studies.

Economic Development Board. 1985. *A Review of Singapore's Semiconductor Industry*. Singapore: Economic Development Board.

———. 1988. *Census of Industrial Production 1988*. Singapore: Economic Development Board.

———. 1990. *Survey of Business Expectations of Industrial Establishments*. Singapore: Economic Development Board.

———. 1991. *Census of Industrial Production 1991*. Singapore: Economic Development Board.

———. 1992. *Census of Industrial Production 1992*. Singapore: Economic Development Board.

Economist Intelligence Unit. 1962. *Industry in Hong Kong*. Hong Kong: South China Morning Post.

Electronics. 1992. "A Mentor for Product and Quality Development Projects." February: 114-22.

Electronic Components. 1993. "Bankrolling the Small Business." June: A22-28.

Endacott, G.B., and A. Hinton. 1968. *Fragrant Harbour — A Short History of Hong Kong*. Hong Kong: Oxford University Press.

England, Joe. 1989. *Industrial Relations and Law in Hong Kong*. 2nd edn. Hong Kong: Oxford University Press.

Evans, P.B., D. Rueschemeyer, and T. Skocpol. 1985. *Bringing the State Back In*. Cambridge: Cambridge University Press.

Federation of Hong Kong Industries. 1990. *Hong Kong's Offshore Investment*. Hong Kong: Industry and Research Division, Federation of Hong Kong Industries.

———. 1992. *Hong Kong's Industrial Investment in the Pearl River Delta*. Hong Kong: Industry and Research Division, Federation of Hong Kong Industries.

———. 1993. *Investment in China*. Hong Kong: Industry and Research Division, Federation of Hong Kong Industries.

Fields, Karl. 1995. *Enterprise and the State in Korea and Taiwan*. Ithaca: Cornell University Press.

Financial Secretary, Hong Kong. 1985. *Estimates for the Year Ending 31st March 1985 Volume 1: Expenditure*. Hong Kong: Government Printer.

Flexible Wage System Review Committee. 1993. *Report of the Flexible Wage System Review Committee*. Singapore: SNP Publishers.

Frank, A.G. 1982. "Asia's Exclusive Models." *Far Eastern Economic Review* June 25: 22-23.

Friedland, Roger, and A.F. Robertson, eds. 1990. *Beyond the Marketplace*. New York: Aldine de Gruyter.

Friedman, Milton, and R. Friedman. 1980. *Free to Choose*. Harmondsworth: Penguin Books.

Friedmann, John. 1986. "The World City Hypothesis." *Development and Change* 17: 69-83.

———. 1995. "Where We Stand: A Decade of World City Research," in Paul Knox, and Peter Taylor, eds., *World Cities in a World-system*. Pp. 21-47. Cambridge: Cambridge University Press.

Friedmann, John, and G. Wolff. 1982. "World City Formation: An Agenda for Research and Action." *International Journal of Urban and Regional Research* 6: 309-44.

Fröbel, F., J. Heinrichs, and O. Kreye. 1980. *The New International Division of Labour*. Cambridge: Cambridge University Press.

Fry, Maxwell. 1988. *Money, Interest and Banking in Economic Development*. Baltimore: Johns Hopkins University Press.

Fujita, Kuniko. 1991. "A World City and Flexible Specialization: Restructuring of the Tokyo Metropolis." *International Journal of Urban and Regional Research* 15: 269-84.

Gao, Sheldon C. 1992. An Analysis of the Hong Kong Stock Market. Ph.D. Thesis, Cornell University.

Gereffi, G. 1990. "Paths of Industrialisation: An Overview," in G. Gereffi, and D.L. Wyman, eds., *Manufacturing Miracles: Paths of Industrialisation in Latin America and East Asia*. Pp. 3-31. Princeton: Princeton University Press.

———. 1992. "New Realities of Industrial Development in East Asia and Latin America: Global, Regional and National Trends," in R.P. Appelbaum, and J. Henderson, eds., *States and Development in the Asian Pacific Rim*. Pp. 85-112. Newbury Park: Sage.

———. 1994. "The International Economy and Economic Development," in Neil J. Smelser, and Richard Swedberg, eds., *The Handbook of Economic Sociology*. Pp. 206-33. Princeton: Princeton University Press.

Gereffi, G., and D.L. Wyman, eds. 1990. *Manufacturing Miracles: Paths of Industrialisation in Latin America and East Asia*. Princeton: Princeton University Press.

Gerschenkron, A. 1966. *Economic Backwardness in Historical Perspective*. Cambridge, Mass.: Harvard University Press.

Ghadar, F., W.H. Davidson, and C.C. Feigenoff. 1987. *U.S. Industrial Competitiveness, the Case of the Textile and Apparel Industries*. Lexington, Mass.: Lexington Books.

Gilb, C.L. 1989. "Third World Cities: Their Role in the Global Economy," in R.V. Knight, and G. Gappert, eds., *Cities in a Global Society*. Pp. 96-107. Newbury Park: Sage.

Gilpin, Robert. 1987. *The Political Economy of International Relations*. Princeton: Princeton University Press.

Giordano Holdings Ltd. 1991. *Giordano Holdings Limited: New Issue*. Hong Kong: Giordano Holdings Ltd.

Goh, Keng Swee. 1977. *The Practice of Economic Growth*. Singapore: Federal Publications.

Goodstadt, L. 1969. "Profits in Pawn." *Far Eastern Economic Review* April 17: 224-26.

Government Information Service. Various years. *Hong Kong*. Hong Kong: Government Printer.

Government Printer, Hong Kong. 1932. *Historical and Statistical Abstracts of Hong Kong*. Hong Kong: Government Printer.

Granovetter, Mark, and Richard Swedberg, eds. 1992. *The Sociology of Economic Life*. Boulder: Westview Press.

Greenwood, J. 1990. "Hong Kong: The Changing Structure and Competitiveness of the Hong Kong Economy." *Asian Monetary Monitor* 14: 21-31.

Grimwade, Nigel. 1989. *International Trade*. London: Routledge.

Haggard, Stephan. 1990. *Pathways from the Periphery*. Ithaca: Cornell University Press.

Haggard, Stephan, Chung H. Lee, and Sylvia Maxfield, eds. 1993. *The Politics of Finance in Developing Countries*. Ithaca: Cornell University Press.

Hall, Peter. 1986. *Governing the Economy*. Cambridge: Polity Press.

Hamashita, Takeshi. 1991. "China's Silver Absorption Capacity and Tributary Trade Relations," in T. Hamashita, and H. Kawakatsu, eds., *Asian Trade Sphere and Japanese Industrialization 1500-1900*. Pp. 21-50. Tokyo: Libro Press.

Hambro, Edward. 1955. *The Problem of Chinese Refugees in Hong Kong*. Leyden: A.W. Sijthoff.

Hamilton, C. 1983. "Capitalist Industrialisation in East Asia's Four Little Tigers." *Journal of Contemporary Asia* 13: 35-73.

Hamilton, Gary G., and Nicole Woosley Biggart. 1988. "Market, Culture, and Authority: A Comparative Analysis of Management and Organization in the Far East." *American Journal of Sociology* 94 Supplement: 52-94.

Harrison, L.E. 1992. *Who Prospers: How Cultural Values Shape Economic and Political Success*. New York: Basic Books.

Harvey, D. 1989. *The Condition of Postmodernity*. Oxford: Blackwell.

Hayashi, Toshiaki, et al. 1990. *Singapore's Industrialization: Asia's Business Center*. Tokyo: Institute of Developing Economies. [In Japanese]

Henderson, J. 1989. *The Globalisation of High Technology Production*. London: Routledge.

Henderson, J., and R.P. Appelbaum. 1992. "Situating the State in the East Asian Development Process," in R.P. Appelbaum, and J. Henderson, eds., *States and Development in the Asian Pacific Rim*. Pp. 1-26. Newbury Park: Sage.

Hill, H. 1990. "Foreign Investment and East Asian Economic Development." *Asian Pacific Economic Literature* 4: 21-58.

Hill, H., and S. Suphachalasi. 1992. "The Myth of Export Pessimism (even) under the MFA: Evidence from Indonesia and Thailand." *Review of World Economics* 128: 310-29.

Hirono, Ryokichi. 1969. "Japanese Investment," in H. Hughes, and P.S. You, eds., *Foreign Investment and Industrialisation in Singapore*. Pp. 86-111. Canberra: Australian National University Press.

Ho, H.C.Y. 1979. *The Fiscal System of Hong Kong*. London: Croom Helm Ltd.

Ho, K.C. 1988. "From Port City to City States: Development, Technology and Spatial Consequences." Paper presented at the International Sociological Association International Conference on "Information, Technology, and the New Meaning of Space." May, Frankfurt.

Ho, K.C., and Alvin Y. So. Forthcoming. "Semi-Periphery and Borderland Integration: Singapore and Hong Kong Experience." *Political Geography*.

Ho, L.S., P.W. Liu, and K.C. Lam. 1991. "International Labour Migration: The Case of Hong Kong." Hong Kong: Occasional Paper No. 8, Hong Kong Institute of Asia-Pacific Studies, The Chinese University of Hong Kong.

Ho, Y.P. 1992. *Trade, Industrial Restructuring and Development in Hong Kong.* London: Macmillan.

Ho, Y.P., and Y.Y. Kueh. 1993. "Whither Hong Kong in an Open-door, Reforming Chinese Economy?" *The Pacific Review* 6: 333-51.

Hong Kong Business Annual. 1993. "Electronics: The Signs of Maturity." Pp. 58-63.

Hong Kong Productivity Centre. 1984. *Study on the Hong Kong Electronics Industry.* Hong Kong: Government Printer.

Hong Kong Times. January 17, 1992. All Hong Kong Workers' Representative Committee Passed the Establishment of Strike Fund. [In Chinese]

Hsiao, Michael. 1988. "An East Asian Development Model: Empirical Explorations," in Peter Berger, and Michael Hsiao, eds., *In Search of An East Asian Development Model.* Pp. 12-23. New Brunswick: Transaction Books.

Huff, W.G. 1994. *The Economic Growth of Singapore.* Cambridge: Cambridge University Press.

Hughes, H. 1988. "Preface," in H. Hughes, ed., *Achieving Industrialization in East Asia.* Pp. xv-xvi. Cambridge: Cambridge University Press.

Hymer, S. 1972. "The Multinational Corporation and the Law of Uneven Development," in J.N. Bhagwati, ed., *Economics and World Order from the 1970s to the 1990s.* Pp. 113-40. London: Macmillan.

Industrial Bank Committee. 1960. Report of the Industrial Bank Committee. Mimeograph.

Industry Department. 1989/1990/1991/1992a/1993/1994. *Hong Kong's Manufacturing Industries.* Hong Kong: Industry Department.

———. 1992b. *Report on Industrial Automation Study.* Hong Kong: Government Printer.

———. 1995. *Report on Techno-Economic and Market Research Study on Hong Kong's Electronics Industry 1993-1994, Volume 2: Phase 1 Study, Industry Analysis.* Hong Kong: Government Printer.

Ingham, G. 1984. *Capitalism Divided?* London: Macmillan.

Jao, Y.C. 1974. *Banking and Currency in Hong Kong.* London: Macmillan.

Johnson, C. 1982. *MITI and the Japanese Miracle.* Stanford: Stanford University Press.

———. 1987. "Political Institutions and Economic Performance: The Government-Business Relationship in Japan, South Korea and Taiwan," in F.C. Deyo, ed., *The Political Economy of the East Asian Industrialism.* Pp. 136-64. Ithaca: Cornell University Press.

Joint Associations Working Group. 1989. Report on Hong Kong's Labour Shortage. Mimeograph.

Kamil, Y., M. Pangestu, and C. Fredericks. 1991. "A Malaysian Perspective," in T.Y. Lee, ed., *Growth Triangle: The Johor-Singapore-Riau Experience.* Pp. 37-74. Singapore: Institute of Southeast Asian Studies and Insitute of Policy Studies.

Karp, Jonathan. 1994. "Alarm Bells." *Far Eastern Economic Review* July 28: 84.

Katzenstein, P.J. 1985. *Small States in World Markets.* Ithaca: Cornell University Press.

Keen, Peter G.W., and J. Michael Cummins. 1994. *Networks in Action: Business Choices and Telecommunications Decisions.* Belmont: Wadsworth.

Keenan, F. 1995. "The Latest Thing: Hong Kong Garment Makers Must Sell as Well as Sew." *Far Eastern Economic Review* June 8: 46-47.

Kitchen, Richard. 1986. *Finance for Developing Countries.* New York: John Wiley.

Koh, Douglas [comp.]. 1976. *Excerpts of Speeches by Lee Kuan Yew on Singapore 1959-1973.* Singapore-Malaysia Collection, National University of Singapore.

Kotkin, Joel. 1992. *Tribes: How Race, Religion and Identity Determine Success in the New Global Economy.* New York: Random House.

Krause, Lawrence B. 1985. "Introduction," in W. Galenson, ed., *Foreign Trade and Investment: Economic Development in the Newly Industrialising Asian Countries.* Pp. 3-41. Madision, Wisconsin: University of Wisconsin Press.

———. 1988. "Hong Kong and Singapore: Twins or Kissing Cousins?" *Economic Development and Cultural Change* 36 (supplement): 45-66.

Kurt Salmon Associates, Inc. 1987. Final Report on Techno-economic and Marketing Study on the Textiles and Clothing Industry for Hong Kong Government Industry Department. Mimeograph.

———. 1992. *Techno-economic and Market Research Study of Hong Kong's Textiles and Clothing Industries: 1991-1992.* Hong Kong: Government Printer.

Kwon, Jene. 1994. "The East Asia Challenge to Neoclassial Orthodoxy." *World Development* 22: 635-44.

Lai, O.K., et al. 1995. "Women Workers' Employment Issues in the Context of Industrial Restructuring." *Hong Kong Economic Monthly* 223: 36-40. [In Chinese]

Lau, Siu Lun. 1994. A Matter of Trust: The Relation Between the Banking and the Manufacturing Sectors. M.Phil. Thesis, The Chinese University of Hong Kong.

Lau, Teik Soon. 1991. "Singapore in South-East Asia," in Ernest Chew, and Edwin Lee, eds., *A History of Singapore.* Pp. 371-84. Singapore: Oxford University Press.

Lee, Edwin. 1989. "The Colonial Legacy," in K.S. Sandhu, and P. Wheatley, eds., *Management of Success: The Moulding of Modern Singapore.* Pp. 3-52. Singapore: Institute of Southeast Asian Studies.

Lee, S.A. 1973. *Industrialisation in Singapore.* New York: Longman.

Lee, Tsao Yuan. 1992. "Economic Restructuring Policies in the 1980s," in Linda Low, and Mun Heng Toh, eds., *Public Policies in Singapore.* Pp. 30-54. Singapore: Times Academic Press.

Leeming, Frank. 1975. "The Earlier Industrialization of Hong Kong." *Modern Asian Studies* 9: 337-42.

Leggett, Chris. 1988. "Industrial Relations and Enterprise Unionism in Singapore." *Labour and Industry* 1: 242-57.

Leung, W.T. 1986. "The New Towns Programme," in T.N. Chiu, and C.L. So, eds., *A Geography of Hong Kong.* 2nd edn. Pp. 251-78. Hong Kong: Oxford University Press.

Levin, David, and Stephen W.K. Chiu. 1993. "Dependent Capitalism, Colonial State and Marginal Unions: The Case of Hong Kong," in Stephen Frenkel, ed., *Organized Labor in the Asia-Pacific Region.* Pp. 187-222. Ithaca: ILR Press.

Lim, Chong-yah. 1984. *Economic Restructuring in Singapore*. Singapore: Federal Publishers.

Lim, Linda. 1978. "Women Workers in Multinational Corporations: The Case of the Electronics Industry in Malaysia and Singapore." Ann Arbor: Occasional Papers No. 9, Women's Studies Program, University of Michigan.

Lim, Linda, and E.F. Pang. 1982. "Technology Choice and Employment Creation: A Case Study of Three Multinational Enterprises in Singapore." Singapore: ERC Occasional Paper No. 4, Chopmen.

Lin, Tzong-biau, and Victor Mok. 1985. "Trade, Foreign Investment, and Development in Hong Kong," in Walter Galenson, ed., *Foreign Trade and Investment*. Pp. 219-58. Madison: University of Wisconsin Press.

Linge, G.J.R., and P.C. Rich. 1991. "The State and Industrial Change," in P.C. Rich, and G.J.R. Linge, eds., *The State and Management of Industrial Change*. Pp. 1-21. London: Routledge.

Lui, Tai-lok. 1994. *Waged Work at Home: The Social Organization of Industrial Outwork in Hong Kong*. Aldershot: Avebury.

Lui, Tai-lok, and Stephen Chiu. 1993. "Industrial Restructuring and Labour Market Adjustment under Positive Non-interventionism." *Environment and Planning A* 25: 63-79.

———. 1994. "A Tale of Two Industries: The Restructuring of Hong Kong's Garment-making and Electronics Industries." *Environment and Planning A* 26: 53-70.

———. 1996. "Interpreting Industrial Restructuring in Hong Kong: State, Markets and Institutions," in J. Lele, and K. Ofori-Yeboah, eds., *Unravelling the Asian Miracle*. Pp. 40-65. Aldershot: Darmouth Publishing Company.

Lui, Tai-lok, and Thomas W.P. Wong. 1994. "Chinese Entrepreneurship in Context." Hong Kong: Occasional Paper No. 38, Hong Kong Institute of Asia-Pacific Studies, The Chinese University of Hong Kong.

Mahbubani, Kishore. 1994. "The United States: 'Go East, Young Man.'" *The Washington Quarterly* 17: 5-23.

Martin, W.G. 1990. "Introduction: The Challenge of the Semiperiphery," in W.G. Martin, ed., *Semiperipheral States in the World Economy*. Pp. 3-41. Newbury Park: Sage.

Massey, D. 1984. *Spatial Divisions of Labour*. London: Macmillan.

McHugh, F. 1994. "Designer Duds." *Sunday Morning Post Magazine* October 30: 15-17.

Mills, Lennox. 1942. "Hong Kong," in Lennox Mills, ed., *British Rule in Eastern Asia*. Pp. 373-513. Hong Kong: Oxford University Press.

Ming Pao Daily News. October 5, 1991. HKPC Arrange for Development in Palmtop Computer. [In Chinese]

———. January 12, 1992. Unions of Different Political Stands Going Their Own Ways. [In Chinese]

———. June 7, 1995. Retraining Scheme Has No Practical Effect. [In Chinese]

Ministry of Labour. 1992. *21 Years of the National Wages Council (1972-1992)*. Singapore: SNP Publishers.

Ministry of National Development. 1983. *1982 Land and Building Use*. Singapore: Ministry of National Development.

Ministry of Trade and Industry. 1986. *Economic Survey of Singapore 1985*. Singapore: Department of Statistics.

————. 1993. *Economic Survey of Singapore 1992*. Singapore: SNP Publishers.

————. 1994. *Economic Survey of Singapore 1993*. Singapore: Singapore National Printer.

Mirza, H. 1986. *Multinationals and the Growth of Singapore Economy*. London: Croom Helm Ltd.

Mody, A., and D. Wheeler. 1990. *Automation and World Competition*. New York: St. Martin's Press.

Morrison, C.E. 1985. *Japan, the United States and a Changing Southeast Asia*. New York: University Press of America.

Murray, R. 1989. "Fordism and Post-Fordism," in S. Hall, and M. Jacques, eds., *New Times*. Pp. 38-53. London: Lawrence & Wishart.

Ng, Sek-hong. 1982. "Labour Administration and 'Voluntarism': The Hong Kong Case." *Journal of Industrial Relations* 24: 266-81.

Ng, S.H., F.T. Chan, and K.K. Wong. 1989. *A Report on Labour Supply Shortage*. Hong Kong: Hong Kong Economic Research Centre.

Ng, S.H., Tai-lok Lui, and F.T. Chan. 1987. *Report on the Survey on the Conditions of Work for Female Workers in Tsuen Wan*. Hong Kong: Government Printer.

Ngo, H.Y. 1994. Economic Development and Labour Market Conditions in Hong Kong. Mimeograph. [In Chinese]

North, Douglass C. 1990. *Institutions, Institutional Change and Economic Performance*. Cambridge: Cambridge University Press.

O'Connor, Kevin. 1995. "Change in the Pattern of Airline Services and City Development," in J. Brotchie, M. Batty, E. Blakely, P. Hall, and P. Newton, eds., *Cities in Competition: Productive and Sustainable Cities for the 21st Century*. Pp. 88-104. Melbourne: Longman.

Onis, Z. 1991. "The Logic of the Developmental State." *Comparative Politics* 24: 109-27.

Owen, Nicholas. 1971. "Economic Policy," in Keith Hopkins, ed., *Hong Kong: The Industrial Colony*. Pp. 141-206. Hong Kong: Oxford University Press.

Pang, E.F. 1988. "The Distinctive Features of Two City-States' Development: Hong Kong and Singapore," in Peter Berger, and Michael Hsiao, eds., *In Search of An East Asian Development Model*. Pp. 220-38. New Brunswick: Transaction Books.

Park, S.O. 1996. "Seoul, Korea: City and Suburbs," in Gordon Clark, and W.B. Kim, eds., *The Asian NIEs in the Global Economy*. Pp. 143-67. Baltimore: Johns Hopkins University Press.

Patrick, H., and Y.C. Park, eds. 1994. *The Financial Development of Japan, Korea and Taiwan*. New York: Oxford University Press.

Polanyi, Karl. 1957. "The Economy as Instituted Process," in Karl Polanyi, Conrad Arensberg, and Harry Pearson, eds., *Trade and Market in the Early Empires*. Pp. 243-70. Glencoe: The Free Press.

Pye, L.W. 1988. "The New Asian Capitalism: A Political Portrait," in Peter Berger, and Michael Hsiao, eds., *In Search of An East Asian Development Model*. Pp. 81-98. New Brunswick: Transaction Books.

Rating and Valuation Department. 1991. *Property Review: 1991*. Hong Kong: Government Printer.

Richter, H.V. 1966. "Indonesia's Share in the Entrepôt Trade of the States of Malaya Prior to Confrontation." *Malayan Economic Review* 11: 28-45.

Riedel, J. 1988., "Economic Development in East Asia: Doing What Comes Naturally?" in H. Hughes, ed., *Achieving Industrialisation in East Asia*. Pp. 1-38. Cambridge: Cambridge University Press.

Rodan, Gary. 1989. *The Political Economy of Singapore's Industrialization*. London: Macmillan.

Salih, K., M.L. Young, and R. Rasiah. 1988. "The Changing Face of the Electronics Industry in the Periphery: The Case of Malaysia." *International Journal of Urban and Regional Research* 12: 375-403.

Sassen, Saskia. 1991. *The Global City*. Princeton: Princeton University Press.

Saul, S.B. 1982. "The Economic Development of Small Nations: The Experience of North West Europe in the Nineteenth Century," in C.P. Kindleberger, and G. Tella, eds., *Economics in the Long View, Vol. 2*. Pp. 111-31. London: Macmillan.

Saw, Swee Hock. 1984. *The Labour Force of Singapore*. Singapore: Census Monograph No. 3, Department of Statistics.

———. 1991. "Population Growth and Control," in Ernest Chew, and Edwin Lee, eds., *A History of Singapore*. Pp. 219-41. Singapore: Oxford University Press.

Schiffer, J. 1991. "State Policy and Economic Growth: A Note on the Hong Kong Model." *International Journal of Urban and Regional Research* 15: 180-96.

Selden, Mark. n.d. China, Japan and the Regional Political Economy of East Asia, 1945-1995. Mimeograph.

Sit, V.F.S. 1991. "Hong Kong's Industrial Out-processing in the Pearl River Delta of China," in Edward K.Y. Chen, et al., eds., *Industrial and Trade Development in Hong Kong*. Pp. 559-77. Hong Kong: Centre of Asian Studies, University of Hong Kong.

Sit, V.F.S., and S.L. Wong. 1989. *Small and Medium Industries in an Export-oriented Economy: The Case of Hong Kong*. Hong Kong: Centre of Asian Studies, University of Hong Kong.

Sit, V.F.S., et al. 1979. *Small Scale Industry in a Laissez-faire Economy*. Hong Kong: Centre of Asian Studies, University of Hong Kong.

Skeldon, Ronald. 1986. "Hong Kong and its Hinterland: A Case of International Rural-to-urban Migration?" *Asian Geographer* 5: 1-24.

———. 1995. "Labour Market Changes and Foreign Worker Policy in Hong Kong." Paper presented at the Conference on "Migration and the Labour Market in Asia in the Year 2000" organized by the Government of Japan, the OECD and the Japan Institute of Labour. January 19-20, Tokyo.

Smart, J., and A. Smart. 1991. "Personal Relations and Divergent Economies: A Case Study of Hong Kong Investment in South China." *International Journal of Urban and Regional Research* 15: 216-33.

SME Committee. 1989. *SME Master Plan 1989*. Singapore: Economic Development Board.

Smelser, Neil J., and Richard Swedberg, eds. 1994. *The Handbook of Economic Sociology*. Princeton: Princeton University Press.

Smith, Carl. 1971. "The Emergence of a Chinese Elite in Hong Kong." *Journal of Hong Kong Branch of the Royal Asiatic Society* 11: 74-115.

So, Alvin Y., and Stephen W.K. Chiu. 1995a. *East Asia and the World Economy*. Thousand Oaks: Sage.

————. 1995b. "The Three Paths of Development in East Asia: Origins and Transformation." Paper presented at the 1995 American Sociological Association Annual Meeting. August 19-23, Washington, DC.

Stock Exchange of Hong Kong. 1987. *Companies Handbook*. Hong Kong: Stock Exchange of Hong Kong.

————. 1994. *Stock Exchange Fact Book 1993*. Hong Kong: Stock Exchange of Hong Kong.

Stock Exchange of Singapore Journal. 1994. Volume 11(September).

Straits Times. April 20, 1970. Textilemen Now Have New Problems.

————. October 28, 1978. Loans and the Varying Views of a Banker and Industrialists.

————. June 28, 1979. SNEF Chief: It's a Bombshell.

————. July 2, 1979. The NWC Hike and the Angry Bosses.

————. June 1, 1980. Need to Continue Phasing Out Labour Intensive Industry.

————. July 11, 1980a. NWC and the Multinationals.

————. July 11, 1980b. Wages Up But Attitude Down.

————. May 23, 1984. Backdooring Garment Maker Lose Export Quotas to US.

————. September 10, 1985. Hitachi Plans $22.5 million Expansion.

————. April 4, 1987. The High-noon Challenge.

————. September 1, 1987. Garment Firms Concerned Over Quota Review Plan.

————. December 19, 1987. Electronics Firms Hit by Higher S'pore $.

————. November 18, 1988. Electronics Industry may be Slowing Down: BG Lee.

————. October 20, 1990. Sony to Procure in S'pore Up to 60% of Parts Needed Globally.

————. August 2, 1991. BG Lee Spells Out EBD's New Priorities.

————. February 17, 1992. Four Firms Barred from Bidding for Textile Quotas.

————. February 10, 1993. 3 MNCs 'to Set Up Wafer Fabrication Plants Here'.

Sutu, H., et al. 1973. A Study of Government Financial Assistance to Small Industries, with Special Reference to Hong Kong. Unpublished paper, The Lingnan Institute of Business Administration, The Chinese University of Hong Kong.

Swedberg, Richard, ed. 1993. *Explorations in Economic Sociology*. New York: Russell Sage Foundation.

Szczepanik, Edward. 1958. *The Economic Growth of Hong Kong*. London: Oxford University Press.

Tai, H.C. 1989. "The Oriental Alternative: An Hypothesis on Culture and Economy," in H.C. Tai, ed., *Confucianism and Economic Development*. Pp. 6-37. Washington, DC: Washington Institute Press.

Tan, Hui-Boon. 1969. *A Study of Commercial Banking Practices in Singapore*. Singapore: Economics Section, Economic Development Division, Ministry of Finance.

Tan, Tiam-hon, ed. 1994. *Corporate Handbook: The Definitive Guide to Singapore Listed Companies*. Singapore: Thomson Information.

Taylor, Michael. 1991. "Into the Hinterland." *Far Eastern Economic Review* June 27: 36-37.

Tham, L. 1992. Packing Up, Going North. Unpublished academic exercise, Department of Sociology, National University of Singapore.

The Advisory Committee on Diversification. 1979. *Report on the Advisory Committee on Diversification*. Hong Kong: Government Printer.

The Hong Kong Junior Chamber of Commerce. 1955. *This is Hong Kong, 1955: An Economic Report*. Hong Kong: Hong Kong Junior Chamber of Commerce.

Todd, D. 1990. *The World Electronics Industry*. London: Routledge.

Toh, P.K. 1970. *The Oil Search in Southeast Asia*. Singapore: Ministry of Finance.

Trade Development Council. 1991. *Survey on Hong Kong Domestic Exports, Re-exports and Triangular Trade*. Hong Kong: Trade Development Council.

Tradespur. 1992. "Solid Electronics Support Services." March: 1-2.

Tsang, Steve. 1988. *Democracy Shelved: Great Britain, China and Attempts at Constitutional Reform*. Hong Kong: Oxford University Press.

Turnbull, C.M. 1969. "Constitutional Development 1819-1968," in Jin Bee Oi, and Hai Ding Chiang, eds., *Modern Singapore*. Singapore: University of Singapore Press.

Turner, H.A., et al. 1980. *The Last Colony: But Whose?* Cambridge: Cambridge University Press.

United Nations Centre on Transnational Corporations [UNCTC]. 1986. *Transnational Corporations in the International Semiconductor Industry*. New York: United Nations.

————. 1987. *Transnational Corporations and the Electronics Industries of ASEAN Economies*. New York: United Nations.

Van Liemt, G. 1992 "Introduction," in G. Van Liemt, ed., *Industry on the Move: Causes and Consequences of International Relocation in the Manufacturing Industry*. Pp. 3-24. Geneva: International Labor Office.

Wade, R. 1985. "East Asian Financial Systems as a Challenge to Economics." *California Management Review* 27: 106-27.

————. 1988. "The Role of Government in Overcoming Market Failure: Taiwan, Republic of Korea and Japan," in H. Hughes, ed., *Achieving Industrialization in East Asia*. Pp. 129-63. Cambridge: Cambridge University Press.

————. 1990. "Industrial Policy in East Asia: Does It Lead or Follow the Market?" in G. Gereffi, and D.L. Wyman, eds., *Manufacturing Miracles: Paths of Industrialisation in Latin America and East Asia*. Pp. 231-66. Princeton: Princeton University Press.

Walton, J. 1992. "Making the Theoretical Case," in C.C. Ragin, and H.S. Becker, eds., *What is a Case?* Pp. 121-37. New York: Cambridge University Press.

Ward, Donna. 1993. "Visions of Grandeur." *Hong Kong Business* September: 42-45.

Ward, M. 1991. "Fashioning the Future: Fashion, Clothing, and the Manufacturing of Post-Fordist Culture." *Cultural Studies* 5: 61-76.

Weber, Max. 1978. *Economy and Society*. Berkeley: University of California Press.

Wheelwright, E.L. 1965. *Industrialization in Malaysia*. Melbourne: Melbourne University Press.

Wigglesworth, J.M. 1971. "The Development of New Towns," in D.J. Dwyer, ed., *Asian Urbanization: A Hong Kong Casebook*. Pp. 48-69. Hong Kong: Hong Kong University Press.

Wong, Lin-Ken. 1978. "Singapore: Its Growth as an Entrepôt Port, 1819-1941." *Journal of Southeast Asian Studies* 9: 50-84.

―――. 1991. "Commercial Growth Before the Second World War," in Ernest Chew, and Edwin Lee, eds., *A History of Singapore*. Pp. 41-65. Singapore: Oxford University Press.

Wong, S.L. 1988. "The Applicability of Asian Family Values to Other Sociocultural Settings," in Peter Berger, and Michael Hsiao, eds., *In Search of An East Asian Development Model*. Pp. 134-54. New Brunswick: Transaction Books.

World Bank. 1993. *The East Asian Mircale: Economic Growth and Public Policy*. New York: Oxford University Press.

Yen, Ching-hwang. 1986. *A Social History of the Chinese in Singapore and Malaysia*. Singapore: Oxford University Press.

Yeo, Kim Wah, and Albert Lau. 1991. "From Colonialism to Independence, 1945-1965," in Ernest Chew, and Edwin Lee, eds., *A History of Singapore*. Pp. 117-54. Singapore: Oxford University Press.

Yoshihara, Kunio. 1976. *Foreign Investment and Domestic Response*. Singapore: Eastern Universities Press.

Young, Alwyn. 1992. A Tale of Two Cities: Factor Accumulation and Technical Change in Hong Kong and Singapore. Mimeograph.

Zysman, J. 1983. *Government, Markets and Growth*. Ithaca: Cornell University Press.

About the Book and Authors

This is the first serious comparative study of two dynamic Asian city-states that are emerging as key regional—indeed global—cities. Providing both historical comparisons and analyses of contemporary issues, the authors consider the patterns, strategies, and consequences of industrial restructuring. They build their analysis around the interrelationships of four institutional spheres: the global economy, the state, the financial system, and the labor market. This leads to a unique emphasis on the distinctiveness of individual newly industrialized countries (NICs), as opposed to much of the literature in the field, which tends to group these Asian dragons together as a single, undifferentiated case.

The book addresses three basic sets of questions tied to industrial restructuring in Hong Kong and Singapore: First, what are the basic patterns of restructuring in the two economies? What corporate strategies have manufacturers used to restructure their operations? Are Hong Kong and Singapore diverging or utilizing the same restructuring strategies? Second, how should the process of restructuring in the two economies and the concomitant similarities or divergencies be explained? Third, what are the consequences of the restructuring process for the two economies? How are these processes shaped by the shared histories of Hong Kong and Singapore as colonial port cities, their current status as NICs "squeezed" between industrialized western societies and the Third World, and their role as important regional cities in East and Southeast Asia?

Stephen W.K. Chiu and **Tai-lok Lui** are lecturers in the Department of Sociology at The Chinese University of Hong Kong. **K. C. Ho** is a senior lecturer in the Department of Sociology at the National University of Singapore.

Index